Tsar of Freedom

TSAR
OF
FREEDOM

THE LIFE AND REIGN
OF ALEXANDER II

BY

STEPHEN GRAHAM

ARCHON BOOKS
1968

Library of Congress Catalog Card Number: 68-15345
Printed in the United States of America

CONTENTS

ILLUSTRATIONS

PREFACE

THE age of Alexander II in Russia corresponds in some respects to that of Victoria in England, an age of developing industrialism, of liberalism and the progressive guarding of the rights of individuals, an age of pacifism marred by wars. It was an age of very remarkable national self-expression. The Victorian age was made glorious by its poets, thinkers, novelists; its Tennyson and Browning, Carlyle, Dickens and Thackeray. The Alexandrian age produced Dostoievsky, Turgenief, Tolstoy and many other fine writers, poets and thinkers. The development of Russia under the Romanofs then reached its zenith, and Britain under the present dynasty entered a golden age.

But there is a great difference between Russia and Great Britain. The one had ripened slowly through the centuries; the other burst into sudden flower and gave fruit within the process of a few decades. Russia had no age of Shakespeare and Elizabeth, no brilliant eighteenth century. In the nineteenth century she rose suddenly from barbarism to culture.

In the Victorian age, success was accompanied by rapturous loyalty to the throne and an uncommon solidarity of the nation. But in Russia, the gain in self-expression, though increasing national pride, let loose destructive forces the chief of which, Nihilism, developed into the more positive but also destructive Marxism.

The natural starting-point for a biography of Alexander II would be an account of the Crimean War which was in progress when he came to the throne. But in a study of this kind much depends on the beginning. The struggle for the liberation of the serfs, which began before the Crimean War and was achieved after it, is a more significant matter than the war itself. Twenty-three millions, about one third of the total number of the Tsar's subjects, were in serfdom at the accession of Alexander II, some enjoying a partial freedom on the payment of a yearly ransom to their owners, others sunk in villeinage upon the soil, and the remainder personal slaves. The liberation of this enormous proportion of the population from bondage was of necessity a new starting-point in Russian national development.

The emancipation made necessary many other liberal reforms, such as local self-government, trial by jury, popular education and the relaxation of the censorship upon journalism. These reforms together caused the nation to be aware of itself as a democracy, and out of the new democratic self-consciousness came the extravagant exuberance of the Slavophiles and the destructive fanaticism of the Nihilists.

The Crimean War had made emancipation more urgent, but the significance of that war is secondary, though important also—for the war cast seeds into the future and bore a new harvest in the Turkish campaign of 1877. And in turn, the Turkish war of 1877 threw seeds into the future and bore other wars, culminating in the catastrophe of 1914–18.

There are therefore two strands of vital interest in the life of Alexander II, one the domestic problem, Russia developing as a nation; the other the international problem, Russia's ambition in conflict with the ambitions of the West.

Alexander came to the throne in March, 1855, the Treaty of Paris was signed in 1856. As a power in Europe, the influence of Russia was immediately diminished, but except in inability to obtain financial assistance, she did not greatly suffer. Her prestige was built up afresh by Gorchakof and the Tsar in league with Prussia. The victories of Prussia over Austria and France in 1866 and 1870, respectively, by weakening other European powers, raised the status of Russia. In her international relationships, the ill effects of the defeat in the Crimea were completely effaced. The "Eastern Question," as it was called, had remained in abeyance, and during the first fifteen years of his reign, no one could have said that Alexander intended following in his father's footsteps and making a "bid for Constantinople." Except for the crushing of the Polish mutiny in 1863, and the representations of the Western Powers, the real history of the period is a domestic one and the vital matters of a biography must be those relating to the reforms.

But Nicholas I, besides bequeathing to his son a nation in bondage and the problem of making a peaceful revolution to conform with the requirements of the dawning industrial age, bequeathed this Eastern Question which, sooner or later, was bound to be given to Alexander II to answer.

The Treaty of Paris may be said to have perpetuated the Eastern Question. It made Europe responsible for Turkey. It should be observed that before the Crimean War Russia had a free hand in dealing with the Turks. The peace of Vienna in 1815, by which the Napoleonic conflict was settled, made no provision for the future of Turkey, which was practically excluded from the family of the Christian nations. But by the peace of Paris in 1856, the European Governments made Turkey the fulcrum of the balance of power.

Turkey was declared independent, but their Majesties, that is, Queen Victoria, the Emperor Napoleon III, and the Emperor Franz Joseph, "engage, each on his own part, to respect the independence and the territorial integrity of the Ottoman Empire: guarantee in common the strict observance of that engagement: and will, in consequence, consider any act tending to its violation as a question of general interest."

Certain parts of the Turkish Empire—Serbia, Wallachia, and Moldavia—had, after many struggles with the Turks, wrested certain local privileges and liberties guaranteed in the past by Russia in various treaties with the Porte—the Treaty of Kainardji in 1744, of Jassy in 1792, of Bukharest in 1812, of Ackerman in 1825, and of Adrianople in 1829. Russia had been the recognized protector of the vassal states. By the twenty-second article of the Treaty of Paris, the European Powers collectively took over the mandate of Russia and assumed the responsibility of checking the Moslem whenever the Christian races were persecuted. The right of Russia to interfere in the Balkans was explicitly denied. But the weakness of the new arrangement lay in the fact that England, France and Austria were not akin to the Slav population of the Balkans. Also it could be seldom to the commercial and political interests of the Western Powers to interfere. It was especially not to the interests of England and France, who lent money to the Sultans and were anxious that the interest on loans should continue to be paid. This substitution of European for Russian authority in curbing the barbarity of the Turks was essential to the whole of the Treaty of Paris.

In order to safeguard this new arrangement, the famous Black Sea clauses were introduced into the treaty. The French, before leaving Sebastopol, destroyed all the fortifications and port works. That was characteristic. Russia was debarred from becoming a naval power on the waters of the Black Sea. The Black Sea was "formally and in perpetuity interdicted to the flag of war." No armed vessels were permitted even for the protection of Russian ports or for boats attacked by pirates. The Turks were allowed to make the Bosphorus a naval arsenal and a place where the fleets of her enemies could assemble to intimidate Russia if ever she showed herself disposed to act in defiance of the treaty.

It is now generally conceded that the Black Sea clauses were unnecessary and imprudent. It was not to be expected that Russia would consent to remain helpless on a sea where she possessed nearly a thousand miles of coast line. In 1870 Russia profited by the downfall of Napoleon III at the hands of Prussia to denounce the Black Sea clauses.

The Eastern Question was opened again. For the subject races in the Turkish Empire had much to complain of and they did not obtain redress of grievances. England, France and Austria were too much occupied by Western politics to exercise their protectorate of the rights and liberties of the Slavs. The Slavs again looked to Russia who, having become strong enough to denounce the Black Sea clauses, might be strong enough to resume the championship of their interests as well.

In Russia the new democracy which had arisen with

the emancipation of the serfs, popular education and the birth of journalism, was impatient of the pretensions of autocracy and was eager to say *its* word on the Eastern Question.

The two factions in Russia were both extreme in view. The cautious Tsar stood between. One faction, called Slavophile or nationalist, was utterly defiant of the West. It believed that Russia should act on her own responsibility, occupy the Balkan Peninsula and make a settlement on her own terms. The other faction, the revolutionary extremists, welcomed the prospect of a war without caring about the causes: for a war would undermine the tsardom, frustrate the good effects of all the liberal reforms of the reign, and make a revolution possible.

In the war or rather in the post-war situation, the two strands of interests met. The resultant was the Nihilist terror of 1879–81, the assassination of the liberal Tsar, and, to glance beyond these pages, the reaction under Alexander III.

The revolutionaries were suppressed by Alexander III. There was peace in the Balkans. But again in the reign of Nicholas II, the Eastern Question had to be faced. The presumption of the revolutionaries in 1881 was justified in 1917, when a war on behalf of Serbia resulted in the destruction of tsardom and the inauguration of a Communist regime.

The reign of Alexander II is particularly significant in that in it may be descried most of the underlying causes of the war of 1914–18 and the Russian revolution of 1917.

TSAR OF FREEDOM

I.

THE EMANCIPATION OF THE SERFS

IN one of the long conversations between Ivan and Alyosha in *The Brothers Karamazof* there is a harrowing story of a child slave who was thrown to the hounds to tear to bits for having dared to throw a stone at one of them. "And long live the liberator of the people!" exclaimed Ivan Karamazof, referring to the reigning monarch Alexander II, who set the slaves of Russia free.

Prior to 1861, Russia was a slave state, and the curious position of the serfs in the old Russia has been suggested to Western readers by the novel of Nicholas Gogol entitled *Dead Souls*. Serfs were called "souls." A certain Tchichikof goes from estate to estate throughout Russia buying up the serfs who have died since the last census was taken. In truth the slaves are dead, but they are still on the register of the living, and Tchichikof's fraudulent plan is to mortgage them to the state bank and amass a fortune wherewith he will buy himself live souls.

Gogol's novel appeared in 1842 during the reign of the predecessor of Alexander II, the Tsar Nicholas I. It created a great stir in Russia, violent criticism which so depressed the author that he lost faith in himself as a writer, destroyed the sequel he had written, and in fact contributed no more to Russian imaginative literature.

Russians asked: "Is the state of the landed gentry and their serfs as bad as this?" They did not doubt but that it was, but the truth was more distasteful to some than sheer error could have been. Nevertheless the book was not banned, even under the vigilant censorious regime of Nicholas I. That was due to the fact that Gogol was to some extent a privileged person. He had already dared to write a play which threw a baleful light on the corruption and incompetence prevalent in provincial administration. This satirical comedy, *Revisor*, was produced on the stage in St. Petersburg in 1836, and the Emperor himself had applauded it. The Tsar Nicholas I, father of Alexander II, was well aware of the need for social reform, and at least in the first half of his reign set himself seriously to make some change, especially in the status of the serf. He is commonly called a "reactionary" which is merely a term of abuse, since up to the time of Nicholas I Russia had not yet enjoyed, except under the auspices of Peter the Great, any particularly liberal or progressive rule. The Tsar Nicholas I had not the intellectual capacity necessary for grappling with the very difficult problem of serfdom. He was by preference a military ruler and lacked both suppleness and sympathy; he could not get round obstacles, he did not feel in his bones the tragic state of Russia. And there were always standing near him courtiers ready to whisper that what had been had stood the test of time, and that the surest way out of difficulties lay in loyalty to the ancient traditions of Russia.

Slave trading within the British dominions had been abolished by the Act of 1807, and the example of Great Britain had been followed by the other European States. It may be said that with the dawning of the nineteenth century the conscience of civilized man became intolerant of servitude. The universal abolition of slavery did not depend for its realization upon the good will, sense, power or ability of certain individuals. It was assured by the will of mankind as a whole and was inevitable. In mid-century it lingered on in Russia, and in America where the Southern states still "kicked against the pricks"; but these countries lagged, that was all, and slavery was bound to go in both of them.

In Russia the number of serfs has been estimated at thirty millions; some writers have even put the figure at forty millions, but that is an exaggeration. According to statistics furnished by the Russian Ministry of the Interior, there were upwards of twenty-three millions. Doubtless in this counting some were overlooked. About one third of the whole Russian population was enslaved. Russia, against her will and despite her idleness, was moving to become a modern commercial state, but a third part of her population was human chattels and could be bought and sold almost like ordinary merchandise. The western wind which was blowing, which would eventually blow revolution in Russia, blew steadily against the institution of slavery. It had been blowing noticeably throughout the reign of Nicholas I: it blew a hurricane at the accession of Alexander II and in the peace which followed the conclusion of the Crimean War.

There was an actual but not a legal distinction between village serfs and household serfs. Village serfs were real estate; household serfs were in fact personal property. The former were peasants, laborers or rural craftsmen; the latter were servants. Estates were reck-

oned not so much by the dessiatine, by the acre, as by
the number of serfs, thus "a property of 5,000 souls"
rather than "a property of so many acres." In legal
theory, though not in practice, "souls" could not be
sold apart from land. Serfs meant estate. As regards the
political position of serfs and slaves there had been,
since the time of Peter the Great, very little difference.

The origins of slavery in Russia were (1) indebted-
ness in which a man's freedom was mortgaged to a
creditor; (2) default in the payment of taxes and feudal dues; (3) forfeiture of freedom after conviction of
crime; (4) prisoners of war. But despite this analysis
it would be truer to say that the greater part of the
rural masses lapsed into slavery owing to passivity and
ready subservience to masters.

The serfs either worked on the land in the direct
service of their owners, or they commuted for a money
payment, called *obrok*. In the nineteenth century the
obrok system had become widespread and many landowners lived merely on the revenue derived directly
from their serfs. Industrialism was developing; factories were increasing in number. *Obrok* serfs worked
in the factories and on the railroads and had some small
margin left over for living when they had paid the dues
to their owners. Some of these *obrok* slaves became rich,
paying annual dues to their masters amounting to many
thousands of roubles. Some bought their freedom for
very large sums. Some of them founded large and successful businesses. Indeed the great cotton industry of
Russia was largely founded by serfs.*

But the owners' power was almost absolute. A land-

* D. S. Mirsky in *Russia, a Social History* remarks, "there grew up
a *bourgeoisie* of more or less rich serfs."

lord could not sentence a slave to death, but he had the power to banish him to Siberia. He could punish him in all sorts of ways, and the most popular was the brutal mode of flogging. There was naturally much abuse of power, but the majority of serf-owners were indolent and easy going. There was less flagrant cruelty than in the Southern states of America. The scandal of slavery in the middle of the nineteenth century in Russia was not one of cruelty and barbarity, but of the anachronism of the system. Moreover, it was becoming clear that free "cheap" labor would be more profitable than slave labor in the growing industrial state.

Nicholas I has been likened to Peter the Great, with whom, however, he had scarcely anything in common. All the world was following the industrial leadership of Great Britain, and Russia under Nicholas was caught up in the movement. In 1825 in England the first passenger train, the *Experiment*, started running between Darlington and Stockton. The next twenty years witnessed the great "railway mania" in England and Scotland. But the first quaint locomotives were puffing not only in Great Britain, but in all parts of the civilized world.

In 1835 was begun, and in 1838 completed, the first tiny railway in Russia, sixteen miles of track laid from St. Petersburg to Pavlovsk, the Tsarskoe-Selo railway, made primarily for the personal use of the Emperor in travelling to Tsarskoe Selo. In 1843, the Tsar Nicholas made that famous gesture of an autocrat in ruling a straight line on the map of Russia to show how he wished the railroad to be laid from St. Petersburg to Moscow. There was naturally a vast amount of talk of railways in Russia before they came into being. Every time a carriage with horses got stuck in the mud, people exclaimed: "How different it will be when we have trains!" The Tsar counted the days it took him to go to Moscow and said he looked forward to going to Moscow to dinner and getting back to the capital the same day. The farmers said: "When we have trains, we will be able to get our produce to market before it rots." They claimed that the railroad would solve all the grave economic problems of the age. The militarists said: "With railways we shall double or treble the effectiveness of our armies."

But it took eight years and cost one hundred million roubles to build the first great line, from St. Petersburg to Moscow. Even with the employment of slave labor it cost a hundred millions. Plans were made to connect St. Petersburg with Warsaw, the third city of the Empire, and to carry the iron way from the Polish capital to the Austrian frontier. But there was discouragement in higher circles. Russia had very few engineers, no special knowledge. The foreign aid sought was mostly incompetent. And had Nicholas been a Peter, he would not have allowed the graft which made the construction so costly. The Tsar procrastinated and was engaged in the Crimean War before he could make any great use of railways for military transport. It was only in 1857 that a concession was granted for the construction of a railroad from Moscow to the Crimea. Four main lines were sanctioned that year, the most important from a commercial point of view being that from Moscow to Nizhny Novgorod.

Railway trains began to course through the slave-bound state, bringing more rapid exchange of news and opinions, certainly a symbol of the new era dawning in Russia, as in England and elsewhere.

The virgin forests proved the chief obstruction to railway progress, but otherwise the great Russian plain presented few difficulties for the surveyor and the engineer.

The Russians have proved to be great railwaymen, but the flatness of the territory has helped them, and where confronted with real difficulties, as in the Caucasus, they have left gaps in their system, unbridged till this day. The Tsar saw in the railway a means of rapid transport for troops. But he was also alive to the commercial value of the new facility of transit. His first interest in life was the army; his second was commerce. He kept aloof from his nobility, whom he regarded with suspicion, and made contact with the new rising class of rich industrialists. He was the first tsar to visit the great fair of Nizhny Novgorod. To him commercial men were as good Russians as men of any other class. And among the most energetic business men starting the new commercial Russia were many slaves.

We have the anomaly that some of the first capitalists in Russia were serfs, serfs who owned serfs. Hakthausen declares that one of the chief manufacturers of silk was a serf even to the date of emancipation. The founders of the cotton industry at Ivanovo were mostly serfs, and some of them were employing more than a thousand workmen. Savva, a weaver belonging to a landowner called Rumin, was the progenitor of the Morozof millionaires. A certain cotton manufacturer, Garelin, a serf, owned the whole village of Spasskoe and its population. At the same time there was a strong development in home industry, and thousands of serf craftsmen were able to sell their handicraft and pay *obrok* to their masters, thus avoiding villeinage on the land. It is sometimes said in error that Count Tolstoy liberated his slaves before the date of general emancipation. In truth the greater part of them were out on *obrok*.

It will thus be seen that a new growth was rising from the human swamp of serfdom, like a forest rising through a decayed undergrowth.

The Russian slave-owners began to perceive that they could not go on forever living on the labor and profit of their human chattels. To do them justice, at least one half of their number was liberal in political tendency and wished the emperor would do something to regulate the position, making the serfs at least free in legal theory, if still serving their interests and bringing them revenue. And the new industrial manufacturer class was convinced that emancipation would be more profitable for Russia as a whole than a continuance of the bondage.

In 1816, 1817 and 1819, under Alexander I, a beginning was made, and the serfs were released in the Baltic provinces, but on such restricted terms that freedom was not much better than slavery, and the agricultural laborers of what is now Esthonia and Latvia became bitterly disaffected. More generous plans for the abolition of slavery throughout Russia began to be formulated at this early date, but they aroused contention and were not approved. Mordvinof wished to establish a tariff for liberty. The freedom of a child up to the age of ten was to be purchasable for a hundred roubles. A working man or woman between the ages of thirty and forty could ransom himself for two thousand roubles. Beyond the age of forty the price was scaled down according to capacity. The virtue of this plan was thought to lie in the fact that it placed a premium on industriousness and personal ambition. The serf must win his freedom. Count Alexei Arakcheyef put forward a scheme, probably the Emperor's own, promulgated in the name of his favorite. His plan was to assign five million roubles annually for the purchase of serfs from the landowners. No constraint was to be placed upon the masters to sell their slaves to the Government, but it would be made profitable for them to do so. It does not appear that it was the Tsar's intention to grant such purchased serfs complete liberty at once, but to hold them in durance on the *obrok* system till they had paid the indemnity of freedom.

The one outstanding statesman of capacity during the reign of Alexander I was undoubtedly Count Michael Speransky, who wished to constitutionalize the tsardom by creating a duma. His liberal influence was felt during his lifetime and until long after his death. Both Alexander I and Nicholas I who succeeded were convinced by the opinion of Speransky that the emancipation of the slaves was a political necessity. But the difficulty was not so much in seeing the necessity for emancipation as in compassing it without impoverishing the treasury and without ruining the nobility or inflaming a revolt. Some earlier tsar would no doubt have been able to free the slaves by ukase without compensation to anyone, but these were not the days of Ivan the Terrible, nor even of the great tyrannical Peter. The nobility had wrested privilege and security from the tsars; they were no longer terrorized by the sovereign. Nicholas I was a despot, but in the history of the tsars only a petty despot. The outset of his reign was marked by the insurrection of a number of aristocrats imbued with Western ideas, the rebellion of the *Dekabristi*. The leaders were hanged and over a hundred of their followers were sent to penal servitude in Siberia. It seemed that a terrible tsar had once more ascended the throne of Russia. But in truth the force of terror had spent itself. Nobles caught in open revolt could be summarily punished, but it was not possible for the Tsar and his minions to prosecute a general destruction of suspected persons. The creed of absolutism remained but it was to some extent impotent. Nicholas I was an autocrat who did not wish to delegate authority, but he was unable to enforce completely this authority which he kept jealously in his own hands. It is true that the number of secret police had been greatly increased and that implied an increase in suspicion. Time was when the barest suspicion might cost a man his life. Suspicion was dispersed by executions. But in the reign of Nicholas, after the *Dekabristi* had been dealt with, there were no executions of important personages and banishments were comparatively infrequent. It was possible for a noble to be opposed to the Tsar's will and still live in freedom. So, behind the lip service of the courtiers, there grew up a formidable opposition.

Nicholas I dallied with the problem of emancipating the serfs. Privately persuaded that emancipation was inevitable, he proceeded secretly, almost stealthily, as if a rash move in that direction might cost him his life. He wished first of all to forbid the sale of serfs without land attached. He was in favor of estates being reckoned in acreage, not in number of serfs. He wished to make it a law that in the case of the mortgaging of an estate, the banks should take as security land but not serfs. But he failed to make even these first elementary provisions. In 1842, shortly after the publication of *Dead Souls*, he proclaimed to the slaves a sort of liberty within their bondage. He was half-hearted about it, but had the slave-owners as a whole taken him at his word it must have resulted in emancipation during his reign. Only one of them tried to implement the Tsar's will, Vorontsof, but no official would coöperate with him. He was snubbed for his pains.

Nicholas I was in any case preoccupied with wars and foreign policy. A war with Persia in 1826 was followed by a war with Turkey. In 1830 the Poles revolted against Russia and mobilized an army of 80,000 men against the Tsar. In the course of a year's hostilities the Polish patriots were crushed and the measure of autonomy which they had previously enjoyed was taken from them. The Tsar visited England in 1844, his object being to insure England's neutrality or coöperation in case he should decide to make a bid for Constantinople. He first called the Sultan the "sick man of Europe" and he mooted the idea of the eventual partition of Turkey. He was well received by Queen Victoria, who admired his appearance, thought highly of his character, but considered him rather stupid. It is not probable that he was capable of influencing British foreign policy or of foreseeing the turn it might take in certain eventualities. He believed that the influence of Cobden and Bright must preclude England's going to war with him should he make another onslaught upon Turkey. In his closing years he made that bid for Constantinople which resulted in the unfortunate Crimean War.

Alexander, his eldest son, the heir to the throne, was born in 1818. His mother was the Princess Charlotte (renamed Alexandra Fedorovna), daughter of Frederick William III of Prussia. As his grandmother was also a German, Sophia of Württemberg, and his great-grandmother was Catherine II, it will be realized that there was a strong strain of German blood in his veins. A German rather than a Slav outlook prevailed at court. The first tutor engaged for the child was a German and a Lutheran. The military tradition of Berlin had invaded St. Petersburg, and the Tsar Nicholas designed the young Alexander to be a soldier and an army builder.

From the age of nineteen until he died, Nicholas I was never seen publicly in civilian attire. He wore his uniform all the while. He was a man of buttons. When he received his portrait, painted by a German artist, he counted the number of buttons in the picture and finding they were one short, had the work of art returned. He lived in a swirl of men in uniforms decorated with orders. He was in his favorite element at a parade and had the eye of a martinet sergeant major for the slightest disorder in dress. He forced the Russian *moujik* to perform elaborate mechanical movements of drill. In his private apartments he had large toy soldiers to keep him company when the live ones were out of sight. The Tsarevitch Alexander grew to adolescence with a father who was always the commander in chief. Soldiers in uniform were the child's nursery wall paper. Nevertheless the young Alexander grew to be indifferent to military parade. He had a surfeit of it in his early years and, besides that, he had a tender soul open to romantic influences. There was not in him the making of a soldier tsar. He had sympathy for the unfortunate and a desire to understand and forgive enemies. "And how would you have punished the *Dekabristi*, Sasha?" Nicholas is supposed to have asked him when he was fourteen years old. "I should have pardoned them," the boy replied.

The heir to the throne was fortunate in his tutors, the chief of whom were Karl Moerder, the German, and Vasilly Zhukovsky, court reader and poet. Moerder was more than merely a good soldier with an approved good character and a capacity for teaching. He had conscience; he was interested in men as men, and not merely as soldiers or subjects of the Tsar. When he drove with the child on long journeys across provincial Russia, as for instance when he took him to the coronation at Warsaw, he was full of reflections upon the sad state of the peasantry under the yoke of slavery. The distress was alike where the land was good and where the land was poor. It was said that the serfs had become idle, but in truth there was little incentive to work, and a peasantry cannot be flogged to good husbandry. One of the things which struck the Prince and his mentor was the almost complete absence of market gardens. Probably Moerder's plea was that Alexander's father, the Tsar, wished above everything to set the slaves free and would do so when he had overcome all opposition. Moerder had a Protestant conscience and approached his God direct in personal prayer. He talked religion and duty to his charge. Alexander must first of all live to please God. Moerder taught him that life itself was a school and that God was the headmaster, a teaching which is German and disciplinary. But the intimate side of court life was German rather than Russian. Alexander did not grow up to be more than conventionally religious. He believed that religion was doing good and submitting humbly to the will of God. But he had been born on an Easter Day—he believed in resurrection, in new life.

Vasilly Zhukovsky, the principal other tutor, was a good German scholar and owed his position at court to his facility in that language, his habit of writing patriotic verse and sending it to court, and his ability to please as a courtier. He was a true poet and has his place in Russian letters, a contemporary of Pushkin, a predecessor of Turgenief and Dostoievsky. But he was a curious choice for tutor to the heir. He was the illegitimate son of a certain Afanasy Bunin and a sixteen-year-old Turkish girl, Fatima, a spoil of war. The portraits of him which exist show a heavy Turkish type of man. He was brought up in the Bunin household, a good boy who showed an uncommon aptitude at school. He was sent to Moscow and had a university career. He studied well, and he wrote and published verse. In 1802 his translation of Gray's *Elegy* into Russian verse attracted considerable attention. We find him versifying and teaching for the next ten years, and then he volunteered to serve in the army against Napoleon. His flare of patriotic fervor then became transmuted to devotion to the Emperor, Alexander I. He was bidden to court and read German or translated Russian books orally into German for the old Empress Sophia (Maria Fedorovna), the widow of the Emperor Paul, and Marie Louise of Baden (Elizaveta Fedo-

The Young Alexander

rovna), the wife of Alexander I. He began a life in palaces which caused other literary men in Russia to look askance at him as at a court lick-spittle. The fat, heavy poet in his tight uniform, and the everlasting simper on his countenance, were not exactly pleasing to writers shut out from palaces. But Zhukovsky was not a snob. He was a Turk who could eat toads and thrive on them. He was an easy-going, good-natured loyalist. He had an oriental gift for exaggerated compliments. But he was incapable of tyranny and disliked it. He said he would have pardoned the *Dekabristi*, and it was probably from him that the young Alexander took a like opinion. He was a sentimental idealist who in a burial place of serfs could quote Gray's *Elegy:*

> Perchance in this neglected spot is laid
> Some heart once pregnant with celestial fire

and shed tears. He had amassed a small fortune. He had slaves of his own, but he was ardently in favor of emancipation and set his own bondsmen free long before Alexander II came to the throne.

He was forty-four years of age when Alexander, aged nine, was intrusted to him. The boy was more attached to Moerder who remained associated with Zhukovsky another seven years. Alexander sometimes wept when he was separated from Moerder. He wrote him habitually as "dear precious Karl Karlovitch" and signed himself "with eternal devotion." But Zhukovsky had the stronger influence. And Zhukovsky was nearer to the mother with whom he shared a great enthusiasm for the German romantic writers. The Empress, Alexandra Fedorovna, had seven children and her family interest was naturally divided, but though little has been recorded of her influence on the development of the character of her first-born, it must have been considerable. Alexander learned German equally with Russian, from the cradle, and when he came to travel in Germany was as much at home in that country as in his own.

Zhukovsky placed history first, as the most educative of all studies. What he said about the study of history was almost identical with what Thomas Carlyle wrote at a later date in England. Possibly both derived the view from the same German sources. It was history with much moralizing, much reference to the judgment of God and "man's duty here below." As far as Russian history is concerned, Alexander and his tutor were fortunate in having at their disposal the works of Karamzin, who had written the first clear authoritative history of Russia. Karamzin, who died about the time when Zhukovsky was asked to formulate a plan for the education of Alexander, was an apologist for autocracy and had been *persona grata* with Alexander I—he died in a palace, but he was a religious man, possessed of a high moral sense of the responsibility of rulers, not in truth towards those they ruled, but towards God, which may be interpreted to mean the same thing.

Alexander II was the first tsar who in childhood had had the history of his country placed before him in an adequate scholarly presentation. Much in his wise and liberal rule may be ascribed to the influence of Karamzin, interpreted by Zhukovsky, who saw a moral in every event and a visitation of Providence in every catastrophe.

And when Alexander had done his lessons well, money was given him to place in a money-box and that money was saved for good actions, "for God himself when he sent his Son among us, sent him in the likeness of love." Even the money-box had its tract. But Zhukovsky did more than moralize. He associated precept with example, and out of his own savings he bought slaves from their masters and set them free.

Compiled from the archives, the two large volumes descriptive of the education of Alexander* taken together must be pretty well as long as the Holy Bible. Alexander's brain was packed with smatterings of all known sciences, but the first place should probably be given to history and languages. He obtained a real grasp of European history and the tendencies since the French Revolution, and he became a fine linguist. It is curious that the despotic Nicholas, so limited in his sympathies, nevertheless provided that his son and heir should be broad-minded, liberal and European.

In 1837, Zhukovsky in consultation with another tutor, Arsenief, planned an extensive itinerary for a tour of the Tsarevitch in Russia and Siberia. The second phase of his education began—travel. It was before the era of railways: he must travel in a carriage or by boat. The horses were driven at a gallop from post-station to post-station. Police agents and other officials tried to keep the roads clear of people. Peasants were told to remain in their houses until the carriages had passed. At the towns the real population was almost hidden by the wall of uniforms of officials. But nevertheless the object of the Prince's travels could not be

* *Years of Education of His Imperial Highness, the Heir, Alexander Nikolaievitch.*

entirely defeated by the precautions of the imperial
bureaucracy. And Alexander had Zhukovsky at his
elbow, pointing out to him what the poet professor
thought significant or worthy of notice as the suite
whirled along. The tour combined the visiting of places
of historical interest with the social educational purpose of seeing Russia. The visit to western Siberia
(Tiumen and Tobolsk) was considered daring, but it
was hardly a visit to the main region of punishment
which was far beyond Tobolsk. The tutor could point
out places which had history, but of course could not
tell of the history which was to come. On May 30,
1837, they were in Ekaterinburg near the Siberian border, but Alexander would have looked at that town
with more interest could he have known that within
eighty-odd years his grandson and family would be
murdered there and the tsars would come to an end.

What did begin to be whispered was that if the serfs
were not liberated, the time would assuredly come
when they would take matters into their own hands
and liberate themselves, and that that might mean
revolution. The danger of revolution in Russia was,
even at this early date, a real consideration with the
house of Romanof.

The Russian-Siberian tour was followed by a European one. It was a startling change to pass from the
filth and disorder of "mother Russia" to the cleanli-
ness and order of Germany, and it is not surprising that
the susceptible adolescent fell in love with a German
princess. He was his mother's child, seeking in the
young feminine what he was already familiar with in
his own mother. At Darmstadt he chose his wife, electing thereby to cross the already feeble strain of Ro-

manofs with another German. The beautiful Wilhelmina Marie of Hesse was not chosen for him, nor indeed was she at once approved. Alexander found her for himself. In 1841 he married her, and she became known in Russia as Maria Alexandrovna. In course of time she bore him six sons and two daughters. Her second son became Alexander III; her grandson was Nicholas II.

At the time of his engagement to Wilhelmina, Alexander was reputed to be one of the most handsome princes in Europe, but the fame of good looks was due to the pardonable exaggerations made by Russian travellers in Europe. He was not more than ordinarily good looking. He looked much better in civilian attire than in a military uniform. He was over medium height, but stout for his years. His countenance bore a receptive expression: there was nothing there either daring or aggressive. To some his face must have seemed babyish. He looked more of a north German than a Slav, but there was no Prussian severity in his demeanor. He was modest and gracious, ready to listen to others, not eager to advance his own opinions. "If he ever comes to the throne," wrote De Custine in 1839, "he will obtain obedience through the constraint of a gracious character rather than by terror."

He was not an original character, and he was not perverse. He was used to having someone at his elbow to tell him what was good or wise, and he readily assimilated good advice. He had tact or was merely disinclined to quarrel. While he failed to share his father's military enthusiasm, he meekly fulfilled arduous duties on the parade ground and in the field. He had sympathy for the victims of his father's tyranny, but seldom interceded for anyone. He seemed colorless and did not promise to be a great tsar. What won him most favor was the mildness and graciousness of his disposition.

There were thousandfold gifts to the poor on the occasion of Alexander's marriage to the beautiful Wilhelmina. The Tsar took great pleasure in his heir's choice of a bride. He was liberal and magnificent in action. All the imprisoned debtors in the land were taken out of jail and told that the Tsar had paid their debts. Many thousands of prisoners were set free and unhappy exiles in Siberia told that they might return to the bosom of their families in Russia. Alexander, finding his father in this relenting mood, had asked him for a full and complete amnesty for all prisoners.* But the Tsar would not pardon dangerous political enemies, nor indeed any convicted of a capital crime. The most he would do for these was to lighten the sentences.

Zhukovsky had said that if a ruler would be loved by his people, he must show first that he loved them, and it was possibly at his suggestion that Alexander had asked for an unlimited clemency. Tsar Nicholas went his own way, but he never resented the idealistic training of his heir. He made Zhukovsky a privy counsellor. He was indeed well pleased with the training of Alexander and approved him. From the date of the marriage he accorded Alexander an authority almost equal to his own. By the imperial ukase of April 28, 1841, Alexander was made a member of the Council of Empire, where actually and officially he replaced the Emperor Nicholas. The British Ambassador, Lord

* Lacroix, B., *Histoire de la vie de Nicolas I, CCLXXIV.*

Clanricarde, returning to England in May, remarked that Russia seemed to have two emperors.

The following year appeared *Dead Souls*, satirizing the position of the slave-owners, and that year also was promulgated the only comprehensive measure dealing with emancipation. That measure had no effect, because only one serf-owner dared to try to put it into effect on his estates, and from that date, 1842, onward in the reign of Nicholas I, the cause of liberation languished.

Nicholas regarded himself as the champion of absolutism and the divine right of rulers. He was possessed of an undying hatred of democracy and therefore of all reforms which might lend themselves to democratize his power. Emancipation in some form might be ultimately inevitable, but he was bound to doubt the effects of it upon the popular mind. A voice in government is essential to freedom. A slave first desires to be made free, but having freedom, his desires do not cease. He wishes to become part of the will and conscience of the nation.

Queen Victoria wrote of Nicholas after his visit to England in June, 1844:

The Tsar Nicholas is stern and severe—with fixed principles of duty which *nothing* on earth will make him change; very *clever* I do *not* think him, and his mind is an uncivilised one: his education has been neglected; politics and military concerns are the only things he takes great interest in; the arts and all softer occupations he is insensible to, but he is sincere, I am certain, *sincere* even in his most despotic acts, from a sense that that *is* the *only* way to govern; he is not, I am sure, aware of the dreadful cases of individual misery which he so often causes, for I can see, by various instances, that he is kept in utter ignorance of many things which his people carry out in most corrupt ways, while he thinks that he is extremely just, and I am sure much never reaches his ears, and how can it? He is, I should say, too frank, for he talks so openly before people, which he should not do, and with difficulty restrains himself. His anxiety to be believed is very great, and I must say his personal promises I *am inclined* to believe; then his feelings are very strong, he *feels* kindness deeply . . . He is *not* happy, and that melancholy which is visible in the countenance made me sad at times: the sternness of the eyes goes very much off when you know him, and changes according to his being put out or not. He is bald now, but in his Chevalier Garde uniform he is *magnificent* still, and very striking.

The Queen's characterization was shrewd. Her judgment erred in one respect: Nicholas had some interest in the arts, especially in the ballet and drama. A gala performance of the ballet *Flora and Zephyr* was one of the chief features of the wedding festivities of Alexander and Wilhelmina. Nicholas was also a patron of the theatre and was not deaf to Zhukovsky's verse. But the Queen saw in him the strong, stern man, was sorry for him because he had a great burden of power and responsibility on his shoulders, more than any one man ought to have, and yet admired him because he took that burden as a glory and as a divine right. And a greater mind than that of Victoria admired him. Thomas Carlyle found him admirable in that he was drilling "an immense semi-barbarous, half-world from Finland to Kamchatka into subordination and civilization," and not saying too much about it.

But Nicholas I was vain without being a boaster. Silence can cover an immense vanity. He believed he was a great man, a great soldier, a champion of right, a controller of history. And in 1844 he had two fixed ideas, at that time unexpressed: one was to stop the progress of democracy, the other to raise the Russian eagle over the minarets of Constantinople. The first fixed idea found resounding expression in the year of European revolutions, 1848: the second resulted in the Crimean War.

The year 1848 was one of the most remarkable in the history of the nineteenth century. A violent revolutionary storm swept the whole of Europe. How explain it? "The wind bloweth where it listeth and no man knows whence it cometh or whither it goeth." It was a wind blowing against thrones and the unlimited power of individuals. Its rise could be explained by the dawning consciousness of the new proletariat brought into being at the birth of the machine age. But doubtless that explanation is not entirely adequate. There was a "blow, blow, blow the man down" ferment in France and it blew away Louis Philippe. There was revolution in Vienna, and the Austrian Emperor Ferdinand was driven out and took refuge at Innsbruck. Hungary revolted under the leadership of Kossuth. In Berlin the revolutionary mob brought the absolute monarch Frederick William of Prussia to his knees. The revolutionary movement was the most widespread in modern history. In England certainly, there was little disturbance, only a resurgence of the Chartist movement which came to nothing. But it was distinctly felt in Russia, where revolutionary enthusiasm infected a group to which the young Dostoievsky belonged, a group clamorous for the emancipation of the serfs. It was in the following year that Dostoievsky was arrested and sentenced to four years' penal servitude in Siberia.

When Nicholas I obtained the news of the establishment of a new republic in France, he was greatly agitated. It was the last ball of the season in St. Petersburg and the Tsar interrupted it, striding into the midst of the dance, holding in one hand the document he had received. The hall of the Winter Palace was stiff with the uniforms of Guards' officers. It is only a legend, but the Tsar is supposed to have broken silence with the words: "Saddle your horses, gentlemen, a rep. lic has been proclaimed in France!"

The music and quadrilles in the Winter Palace ceased abruptly, and then whispers of war and immediate military preparation were heard. It is said that the Tsar's nervousness and perturbation showed plainly that with the advance of years he was feeling the strain of lonely autocracy. He showed for the first time the lack of balance in judgment which led him ultimately into that desperate conflict known as the Crimean War. Nicholas was a man of great physical reserve, an indefatigable monarch who worked deep into the night, trying to cope single-handed with the administration of personal government. He had many enemies and had cause to be eternally vigilant. It is not surprising that in 1848 he obtained at once an exaggerated notion of the danger to himself inherent in the revolutionary storm in western Europe. Late into the night after he received from Paris the news of the revolution, he worked with his state secretary, Baron Korf, concocting messages and taking measures. He issued a *ukase* to his Minister of War, Prince Chernyshof, which was published the following day. The terms of this *ukase* indicate his state of mind:

In western Europe there have happened events which show a criminal tendency to overthrow legitimate rulers. The pacts and conventions which unite Russia with her neighbors make it our sacred duty to take the necessary measures and place part of our army in the field in readiness for war, so that should circumstances exact it, we should be in a position to oppose a strong barrier to stem the destructive torrent of anarchy.

Some days later in concluding a long and somewhat noisy manifesto to the Russian people, he said:

. . . To-day, revolutionary audacity, recognizing no limits, dares even to menace the Russia whose destiny God has committed to our hands.

But following the example set us by our predecessors, faithful to our Orthodox creed, and after having called Almighty God to our assistance, we shall stand firm against our enemies, from whatever quarter they may assail us. We shall defend the honor of the name of Russia and the inviolability of our frontiers. We are persuaded that each Russian, each of our Russian subjects, will rally to our ancient cry, *For the Faith, Our Tsar and Country.* To-day, as ever in the past, that will point us the way to victory. And then, full of pious gratitude, as to-day we are full of holy confidence in God, we will say together— *God is with us! Bethink ye, ye nations and submit, for God is with us!*

And the Tsar was not content to thunder with words merely. He sent an army into Hungary to help the Austrian Emperor to suppress the insurgent Magyar patriots. He did not make any other military intervention, but his firm stand drew attention to tsardom from all the radicals and revolutionary sympathizers of western Europe. From his attitude in 1848 began the ceaseless propaganda against the tsardom and Russian national institutions which did not cease till the culminating revolution of 1917.

In 1848 Alexander, aged thirty, was not, like his father, devoted to military affairs and foreign politics. We find him championing the cause of the serfs and asking for their liberation. He believed that the holding of slaves was contrary to the teaching of the Bible, and he had told his father so when he was a mere child. It is not likely that he had departed from that simple judgment when in later years he saw the iniquities of serfdom for himself. In 1847 he had himself appointed to a commission inquiring into the barbarous treatment of serfs on Russian estates. Serf-owners were liable to be punished by imprisonment or partial sequestration of their estates, if excessive cruelty could be proved against them. But there was little redress because serfs were not allowed to plead in court. The only hope for ill-treated bondsmen lay in the investigation by such commissions as that on which the Tsarevitch had appointed himself. It was the duty of officials to keep unpleasant facts from the cognizance of the heir to the throne, but the scandal of slavery had grown so large that no band of officials could hide it. In Alexander's travels through Russia he had seen much, but during the sitting of the commission he saw much more and was utterly shocked by the discoveries he made. As a result he addressed a memorial to his father, imploring him to liberate the serfs and showing how, in his opinion, it could be done. Nicholas replied that while emancipation was certainly desirable, it would most likely result in a Russian revolution. Events in Europe seemed to confirm the Tsar's opinion, and the plan was shelved. Alexander is said to have declared that nevertheless he would himself free Russia, because he could not contemplate becoming the emperor of a nation of serfs.

Alexander was of course free of tutors and mentors,

an independent man now, judging affairs of state on his own responsibility, and without inspiration except from his wife and mother, both of whom were good women, sentimental, idealistic. Zhukovsky ceased to exert a personal influence beyond that which endured from his training of the Tsarevitch. In his old age, the poet had married; he was still a court figure, but his way of life had changed. He travelled much in Germany and was dismayed by the revolutionary manifestations which he witnessed in 1848. He was a fervent believer in Nicholas I as a champion of right—by which he meant a champion of Christendom. The Tsar had raised his standard against freethinkers and infidels. Bethink ye, ye nations! Zhukovsky was even hoping for another war on the Turks, and there is a letter of his extant addressed to Alexander's brother, Constantine, written in 1850, in which the poet expressed his belief that it was the Tsar's mission to capture the Holy Sepulchre in Jerusalem and take over the holy sites of the East. Zhukovsky lent his countenance to the mirage of Saint Sophia, and we have the first hint that after the revolutionary storm had passed, the Tsar Nicholas and his people would address themselves to the capital folly of a bid for Constantinople.

There were in Russia at the time several currents of political opinion, one of which was for the necessity of domestic reform and the growing urgency of the serf problem. But that did not inflame imagination. The poor we have always with us and for that reason the poor can wait. But the Tsar's tirades against the freethinkers of France and the West had stirred what may be vulgarly styled religious jingoism. The Tsar Nicholas did not move against the Turks without a strong

and clamorous national backing. The animosity against
the second Republic of France did not die down when
Louis Napoleon gained the suffrage of the French, nor
when in 1852 he became the Emperor Napoleon III. At
the same time the Tsar made grave mistakes in foreign
policy. He ignored Lord Palmerston's friendly over-
tures in 1848 and he allowed two great maritime powers, England and France, to combine to frustrate his
Eastern policy. The main object of Napoleon III's policy was to strengthen his position as Emperor by re-
gaining for France what had been lost by Bonaparte in
1815. He must recover lost empire and he required
prestige. He did not intend to allow Russia and England to carve up Turkey and its dominion. When it
came to distributing the territory of the Sultan, it was
his secret hope that France would obtain a lion's share.
As regards the question of prestige, Nicholas did not
improve matters by hesitating to recognize Napoleon's
title of Emperor.

In the middle of the nineteenth century might was
right and even virtuous and God-fearing Germany
helped herself to Schleswig-Holstein at the expense of
feeble Denmark. The Tsar alienated the Prussians by
failing to condone the war on Denmark, and one must
not blame him for trying to thwart tyranny, but blame
him for lack of tact. He could ill afford to lose the support of Frederick William.

Nicholas, cocksure that he was the greatest power in
Europe, irritable and tactless, came to the conclusion
that he could deal with the Turkish Question unaided,
and repel any interference from any other power in
Europe.

There is no doubt that the health of the Tsar broke

down between 1845 and 1850. In 1849 the English physicians, Dr. Granville and Sir Henry Holland, reported that he was visibly suffering from cerebral excitement. He suffered from severe gout and erysipelas. In 1852 he went to Ems for a cure, and the Germans observed that he had become absent-minded, and talked to himself as he walked. He had called the Sultan of Turkey the "sick man of Europe" while he was, in effect, himself the sick man of Europe. The peace of Europe depended upon the decision of an unbalanced and sick monarch of almost unlimited powers. The millions of Russians, and among them over twenty millions were slaves, were at the mercy of that same man.

Had the Tsarevitch Alexander been less passive, it is possible that he would have exercised a great influence for peace. There was considerable rivalry, not to say ill feeling, between Alexander and his bellicose younger brother Constantine. Constantine as a young man had the characteristic challenging spirit of a second son. He would have liked to have been the heir to the throne and could not be reconciled to the fact that prior birth would give the succession to the milksop, Alexander. On one occasion Constantine had even had the audacity to place his elder brother under arrest—by mistake of course, but the unpleasant jest had been deliberately contrived.

The Grand Duke Constantine was all for war, for military and naval adventure. The Tsarevitch Alexander, could he have had his way, was for peace and social reform, but he was the Tsar's son, rendering implicit obedience to his father, and if his father went to war he was ready to do his part in the campaign.

The chief prelate of the Russian Orthodox Church,

the Metropolitan Philaret, was also of the war party. He was possessed of that crusading spirit which imagines that it is pleasing to Christ to fight for His Sepulchre. He was also imbued with a less excusable feeling, a bitter animosity against the Latin Church. And France had stirred up strife by persuading the Turks to hand the keys of the shrine of Bethlehem in Palestine to the Roman Catholics. Louis Napoleon, Napoleon III, needed Catholic votes in France and was willing to do Holy Church this service, and he could hardly have imagined that one lucifer could set Christendom on fire. The Russian Church as a whole, its bishops, monks and priests, the Russian pilgrims, the Russian religious masses, in short, Holy Russia, talked of war, war for the Sepulchre, for Bethlehem, for the cathedral of St. Sophia in Constantinople.

Prince Menshikof was the Tsar's envoy to the Porte. To his way of thinking, to parley with the Turks was waste of time. Better to strike them first and talk with them afterwards. Menshikof must be regarded as belonging also to the war party.

The Tsar Nicholas insisted on regarding Turkey as dead, ready for dismemberment and distribution. He embarked upon a war with the corpse and then found to his dismay the diplomats of France and England propping it up, and then behind the diplomats, ships and armies—invincible armanents ranged against him.

On January 27, 1854, England and France declared war on Russia. Turkey, supposed dead, had offered a very stout resistance before the allies came on the scene. The Russians had already evacuated the Danube provinces and in a sense the war was at an end when France and England decided to invade the Crimea.

In September the armies landed unmolested in the Crimea and in the same month defeated Menshikof on the heights of the Alma and marched upon Sebastopol. The Tsar's conceit that he had the best army in Europe was shattered, and he began pathetically to rely on "generals January and February," not on fire, but on frost. The equipment of his forces was out of date and many soldiers carried flintlocks. His artillery, while quick to change positions under command, could not hit targets. His officers were most incompetent. Only one great soldier emerged on the Russian side, the heroic defender of Sebastopol, General Todleben.

Menshikof counter-attacked with fury in October, bringing enormous masses of men into the field. There ensued the great confused conflict of Inkerman. The sheer force and fury of the Russians almost won the day. But the tenacity of the British, opportunely aided by the French, proved sufficient to withstand the great odds. Menshikof retreated, and Nicholas had to acknowledge another terrible defeat.

The war continued through the winter of 1854–55, and the rigors of January and February, though they worked havoc in the allied armies, did not destroy them. But the Russians defending were more redoubtable than the Russians attacking. The success of France and England was held up by Todleben, and the gaze of all Europe was directed to the spectacle of the siege of Sebastopol.

The Tsar Nicholas might have taken heart from Todleben's heroism, but his humiliation by invasion and defeat, his sense of utter failure as soldier and Tsar, proved too much for his mind. On March 2, 1855, he died. It was said at the time that he died of an

apoplectic seizure following influenza. In a heavy per-
spiration caused by taking a drug, he went out in the
bitter February air in St. Petersburg, to a military inspection. His physician remonstrated: "It will mean
your death."

"And what of it?" the Tsar replied. "And if I die
for my country's sake?"

Modern historical assumption is that Tsar Nicholas I
committed suicide.

The gossip of St. Petersburg society at the time was
that the Tsar had hastened his end by taking poison.
He died on the simple little single bed in his study in
the Winter Palace, far from the region where his subjects were falling in the war he had kindled.

It is clear that he was glad to leave the throne to
Alexander who was already beloved by the Russian
masses and was held in good repute abroad, even in
England, where at the time every calumny was heaped
on the head of Nicholas. In England, even deeds committed by Ivan the Terrible in the sixteenth century
were ascribed to Nicholas I. The English conscience demanded that the enemy sovereign should have a very
bad character. But even the calumniators of tsardom
looked with relief to the accession of the idealistic Alexander. The Tsarevitch had not been engaged in the
Crimean conflict. He was Military Governor of St. Petersburg. When it appeared likely that Austria might
join forces with France and England, he was made
commander of an army of defence posted along the
Polish-Austrian frontier. But the Austrians did not
fight, and this army never came under fire. In December, 1854, Alexander returned to St. Petersburg where
his mother was seriously ill. It may be imagined that

The Coronation of Alexander II
Procession to the Uspensky Cathedral

Alexander had no personal inclination for active campaigning nor any great enthusiasm for the cause of the war. But he had no choice in the matter. The person of the heir to the throne must never be endangered.

There was a demonstration of national sentiment upon the death of Nicholas; the Russian nation did not blame him for getting them into a bad war. It seemed that the Tsar had died a martyr to duty. His death was another triumph for the hateful enemy. Alexander, now Emperor Alexander II, was ready to negotiate for peace, but the nation clamored for revenge. The dead of Alma and Inkerman must be revenged! The foreigners must be driven from Russian soil before there could be talk of peace. Alexander received many petitions, prayers that he would not conclude peace until justice had been done to the enemy. The Church was as urgent for the continuance of the war as was the nobility. Had Alexander made peace in 1855 he would have been in real danger of assassination.

The Tsarina was supposed to be eager for peace, and her carriage on one occasion was followed by demonstrators, a howling mob calling for a continuance of the war and for revenge on Russian enemies. Public opinion was too strong for the Tsar: he was obliged to allow the war to run its course.

That course was not favorable to Russia—in September, 1855, Sebastopol fell. Its defence was more glorious than any victory of the war, but nevertheless its fall made the English and French masters of the Crimea.

In the new Tsar's estimation peace could wait, but the emancipation of the serfs could not. The great nobles were in favor of an energetic prosecution of the war, but they were also for the most part suspicious of Alexander's desire to free the slaves. The Tsar had to count on serious opposition from many landowners. What made the problem thorny for Nicholas I still made it thorny for Alexander II. He found he could not make freedom by a stroke of the pen, by imperial order. There were too many opposing interests in Russia. But he gave his opinion plainly, "If we do not liberate the slaves, self-liberation will set in from below." He had a committee engaged to thresh out the problem, and from the first he urged this committee to action.

I wish and demand of our committee general conclusions, how to approach this business, not making all sorts of excuses to postpone a plan of legislation until the Day of Judgment. . . . I hope that after all the palaver you are actually going to make a move to do something.

He told the committee plainly that it was not part of a circumlocution office, and that he would not brook the dilatoriness which had served in his father's reign. The minutes of that committee as preserved in the archives are all scored with the Emperor's urgent and impatient remarks.

Meanwhile the Crimean War came to an end. It lasted a year after the death of Nicholas I. The armies were reduced; the military slaves returned to the villages and the estates, or to factory and workshop, bringing the sense of the defeat of their masters to give courage to all malcontents. But the discontent was allayed by the common belief that the new Tsar Alexander was about to grant freedom, and not only freedom, but land. "God made the land for the people." The dangerous doctrine was even then abroad: the owners would have to give up not only their slaves but their land as well. A serf considered himself plus the land he could cultivate an indivisible unit. Freeing him meant putting him freely in possession of land.

To give the land meant to ruin the nobility, and to give freedom without land meant to ruin the peasantry. The state treasury, impoverished by the vast expenses of war, could not afford to indemnify either party. There lay the problem. Could the serfs be made to pay for their freedom? Could the serf-owners be granted loans on the security of their estates? Would not twenty-two million slaves suddenly set free combine to take matters into their own hands?

The position of most large landowners was this. They lived in St. Petersburg or some other great city. They did not farm their estates. They had stewards who administered their property and collected their revenue. They had numbers of serfs out on the *obrok* system, paying a handsome annual tribute for their partial freedom, a tribute which the landowners' agents strove incessantly to increase. It was their slaves rather than their land which brought them income.

In case of emancipation they felt they must let their land to the free peasants at a high rent to preserve their incomes.

The affairs, even of the most liberal of the nobles, were complicated by the *obrok* system.

Such was the position of Prince Gagarin, who was considered an authority on the serf problems, and of Count Kiselief, to whom Nicholas I had at one time intrusted the drawing up of a measure of emancipation.

A gallant young officer, just back from the heroic defence of Sebastopol, idealistic, patriotic, Count Tolstoy might have liberated his serfs in anticipation of the imperial decree, but it was as difficult for him to make his slaves free as it was for the others.

In April, 1856, Tolstoy wrote in his "Diary": "My relation to my serfs is beginning to trouble me much, I feel the need of learning, learning, learning." That is, of learning how emancipation could be effected. His estate, meaning his serfs and land, was mortgaged to a bank for twenty thousand roubles. His serfs were mostly out on the *obrok* system. Out of what they paid for the privilege of working for themselves, a sum representing the interest on the mortgage was paid, and what was left over became income for Tolstoy.

Tolstoy saw Kavelin, a liberal-minded professor who was studying the problem. Kavelin took him to see Levshin, assistant to the Minister of the Interior. He had a draft of a workable plan in his pocket. But the Ministry had a glut of plans from landowners, and it is not likely that Levshin paid much attention to Tolstoy's scheme. Still there seemed no reason why he should not put his plan into practice for himself.

He called his serfs together and offered them their freedom. It was freedom on the hire-purchase system. Each family should receive twelve acres of land. They must pay twenty roubles a year for thirty years on this twelve acres; four roubles a year would go to pay off the mortgage, and the remaining money to complete the purchase. But the serfs refused the offer, feeling sure that something much better would come later, by the Tsar's command—freedom and land without rent or payment.

On June 4, 1856, Tolstoy noted in his "Diary":

"Went to the peasants. They don't want their freedom."

It was not until November, 1857, that the imperial committee was able to present a statement which could form the basis of a rescript on the subject of emancipation. Nominally, this rescript was addressed to the northwestern provinces, but actually it was to the governors of all the provinces of Russia. But it was, after all, little more than a re-statement of the stillborn emancipation law of 1842.

The landowners were to remain owners of all their land, but the serfs had the right to purchase land from them on payment spread over a number of years. Landowners were to retain their magisterial jurisdiction over the "free" workers on their estates.

The Kiselief law of 1842 definitely tied the agricultural worker to the land cultivated. The rescript of 1857 was silent on the point whether the freed serfs had the right to remove to other districts and seek to sell their labor where they could get more for it. There was a placid assumption that the free men would not use their freedom. Moreover, where slaves were out on the *obrok* system it was assumed that they would redeem the capital value of the annual payments they had been in the habit of making. And actual personal liberation would not be a legal fact until complete monetary redemption had been accomplished.

Committees of nobles, in every province, were set up with a view to realizing the new plan. The Tsar's manifest opinion was that the slave-owners as a whole must be won over to the reform. He must have their coöperation. In the reign of Nicholas I, the Tsar had been in one camp and most of the nobility in another. There was a passive mutual hostility. Alexander held out a hand and asked the nobility to work with him. They responded.

The committees commenced their proceedings with banquets, with toasts in honor of Alexander II, and speeches in honor of the Russian nobility, with balls at which thundered the music of serf-orchestras—showing that the approach to peasant reform was not the heavy blow for the serf-owners which it sometimes appeared to them to be later, as a *fait-accompli.**

Of the 1337 members of the provincial committees not one ventured to declare a belief in leaving things as they were. Suddenly all doubt seemed to have been dissipated by the Tsar's command and there was even great rejoicing, and exaggerated optimism, as if these gentry were preparing the millennium. For the first time in Moscow the nobility and the manufacturer fraternized, drinking the Tsar's health together, standing before the portrait of Alexander and singing "God Save the Tsar" to the face of the sovereign. Actually free labor was going to be much more profitable to the manufacturer than to the landowner, and he saw it. No one anticipated the emancipation with more excitement than the industrial employer.

Alexander II did much to sustain the enthusiasm for reform by travelling about the country and thus keeping personal contact with the committees. His leadership had changed influential opposition into influential support. It seemed that if it depended on these committees he would be able to grant a larger measure of freedom than he had foreshadowed in his rescript of

* Pokrovsky, M. N., *History of Russia in the Nineteenth Century,* Vol. III.

1857. That is not to say that there was no opposition whatever. There were what would be called in our day "die-hards." In Russia they were called *Krepostniki*. Some of these were just the old dyed-in-the-wool flogging gentry, too stupid or brutal to change with the times. But there were others of cool judgment who, unmoved by the verbiage of the reformers, realized that for them the emancipation of the slaves was bound to mean a serious impoverishment. They demanded in recompense capital wherewith to reëquip their farms and change over from primitive to modern agriculture. Then they would produce more, and with the service of the new railways, they could send their products to good markets, and make up their income to the previous figure.

It was pointed out to them that in the year of the argument, 1858, land unencumbered by serfs could be sold for a better price than land and serfs together. It therefore followed that whether capital was available or no, land freed from serfs was more valuable than land with serfs. But that was not true of estates where many serfs were out on *obrok*, and paid their owners heavy dues.

In the early months of 1859 the provincial committees finished their work and concluded their deliberations by signing each its own agreed project of liberation. In the presence of wonder-working ikons and dignitaries of the Church, with banquets and oratory, they concluded much as they had begun, in a spirit of exaggerated self-congratulation.

Russians have a dual nature. "Scratch a Russian and you find a Tartar," is the saying. It is not quite so simple. The Slav in the Russian is in fact greater than the oriental in him. Treat a Russian generously and he will outdo you in generosity. Appeal to his idealistic side and he will go much further than you will in idealism. But begin to chaffer with him over money or try to drive a bargain and the Slav will disappear. In place of the prodigal exuberant believer who wants to kiss you on both cheeks in his excitement, you find a cold, hard, mean and even tricky personality whose only desire seems to be to do you down for his own advantage.

Alexander, in instituting the provincial committees, had appealed to the Slav and he obtained a Slav answer. It was going to be different when an Executive Committee, a committee of committees, was established in St. Petersburg to draft the actual terms of the bargain with the serfs and frame a national agreed decree which the Tsar would sign. In the provincial capitals the landowners were characteristically Slav: at St. Petersburg most of them seemed to be Tartars. Then it appeared that the almost unique idea of most of the representatives was to rob the men and women they were freeing, take more from them in freedom than they had done in bondage, and fix them in bonds of service more intolerable than they had borne before. And this recalcitrancy was aided and abetted by the bureaucracy. Obstruction became fashionable, and the Tsar unpopular in his own court.

Even his eldest son, the heir to the throne, Nicholas, aged fifteen, told him that "Emancipation will never bring anything but misfortune to the country."

The first committee for dealing with the emancipation problem had been convoked again. Besides that there was an editing committee, *Redaktsionny Komitet*, which, although allotted a secondary rôle, actually did most of the work and framed the terms of the decree. It seemed almost to usurp the function of the new committee of committees from the provincial capitals which came into being late in 1859. There would appear to have been a certain awkwardness in having various distinct committees sitting at St. Petersburg. Autocracy was fumbling with Government by consent. The result was such a conflict of opinion as would have taken a Solomon to resolve.

Alexander in person attended the meetings of the committees at various times and, encountering opposition, set himself to wear it down by sheer physical endurance, sometimes sitting with the nobles and bureaucrats for seven hours at a stretch.

In the rural depths of Russia expectations ran high, but were not marked by rioting or agitation. Just after the Crimean War and demobilization there had been evidence of the birth of a violent agrarian movement. But the occupations of peace laid a calming hand on the returned soldiers. Moreover, there was great faith in the Tsar. Some of the landowners were enemies of the peasants, but what did that matter, they had the Emperor as friend. Tolstoy in 1856 wrote: "If within six months the serfs are not freed there will be a conflagration. Everything is ready for it; treasonable hands are not lacking to light the fire of tumult and then the fire will spread everywhere." But he was entirely mistaken. By 1859 there was serene peace on the estates. Indeed, the new sense of security did something to harden the hearts of the serf-owners and cause them to try to drive a harder bargain.

Some of the recalcitrant landowners tried to blackmail the Government by hinting that if the serfs were liberated some sort of constitutional regime would become necessary in Russia. Making twenty-three million men free was a revolution. It changed Russia from a feudal state to a young democracy. But Alexander was not alarmed, being ready to consider ultimately a constitution of some kind, if that was the political requirement of Russia. The suggestion that constitutional government might become necessary was hardly put forward in good faith—but there was logic in it. There is logic to be found in change, for one change leads to another.

Count Jacob Rostovstsef, General-Adjutant, and at one time a chief of staff of Nicholas I, was nominated by Alexander President of the Editing Committee. Nicholas Miliutin, assistant of Lanskoy, was the moving spirit of that committee, but he found it very difficult to agree to work under Count Rostovstsef, who he thought would be likely to try to frustrate every good intention of reform. Rostovstsef had been associated with the repressive rule of Nicholas I and had served the Tsar with a dog-like devotion. By reputation he was far from being a liberal and he had a sarcastic tongue and a facility for petty witticisms which caused his opponents to have an exaggerated notion of his unpleasantness. He was a man who generally had the right word at his command when addressing his sovereign, and Miliutin no doubt thought he had deceived Alexander II by flattery and obtained the position of president of the committee by intrigue. To the nobles he was equally obnoxious because he was an upstart, not of noble origin, and because at the outset of the reign of Nicholas I he had caused the ruin of many nobles, denouncing them as participants in the *Dekabrist* conspiracy. But Alexander chose Rostovstsef because he saw in him an obedient servant always ready to do what the Tsar told him to do. And he was supposed to have no particular convictions regarding emancipation.

Miliutin, on the other hand, was a convinced emancipationist. He was more earnest than most others at the time; his enemies called him a communist. He was actually an enlightened materialist, wishing to free the peasants so as to improve their lot. The industrial and machine age had arrived and he wanted the masses to have more food, more comfort, less toil and higher wages. "I wish to raise the oppressed masses of Russia and place them on their feet," said he. His type in modern Western politics would be Lloyd George, the early Lloyd George of Land Reform years. Yet Rostovstsef nicknamed him the nymph Egeria. He was earnest and pathetic where Rostovstsef was cynical and time serving. He wrote to his uncle, Count Nicholas Kiselief: "It is sad to reflect how this mysterious and difficult business is being conducted. The nobility, avaricious, unprepared, undeveloped, has everything in its hands. I cannot imagine what will come of it in the face of the brutal opposition of the highest dignitaries, the intrigue and lack of conscience. One cannot but be astonished at the rare firmness of the Tsar who alone checks reaction and sets his face against passive resistance."

The first positive result of the deliberations of the committees may be said to be the recognition of the village community, the mir, as a permanent institution. The dealings of the landowners would be with the mir, the village commune, rather than with their slaves personally or individually. And the authority of the mir

over the peasants would replace the authority of the
squire. The mir would be responsible for freedom dues
and taxes, for sending conscripts, for allotting peasants
for labor on estates, etc. That the peasants would
thereby obtain a measure of self-government and learn
to think collectively like socialists was in general overlooked.

The Ministry of the Interior was persuaded to accept the transfer of authority to the mir, but the question who or what should control the mir, a head man
or a committee of nobles or the police, caused infinite
wrangling. Serf-owners, if the serfs were to be freed,
must part with their rights. Some of them were so perverse as to wish to retain the right to flog the peasants
who worked on their estates and they saw with chagrin
the prospect of the rights to flog being transferred
from themselves to the police. There were impassioned
speeches on the subject of flogging. Peter the Great had
flogged the Russian people out of apathy. Some seemed
still to believe that Russia owed her greatness to corporal punishment. But Miliutin and Lanskoy led the
new liberal opposition. No free man should be flogged
without conviction and then only by the police. Some
members of the committee wished to abolish corporal
punishment altogether, but they were overruled. The
only compromise they could obtain at the time was
that women, and educated serfs, be made immune from
the rod and the lash.

The deliberations of the committee might have ended
in mere words and good intentions, but for the Tsar's
will for reform. The reformers, especially Miliutin,
feared that at the last moment Alexander II might go
back on their efforts and side with the selfish and avari-

cious. The memoranda addressed to the Tsar in August, 1859, by Lanskoy, the Minister of the Interior, but actually written by Miliutin, are supposed to have had considerable influence in holding Alexander to reform.

In the second of these Lanskoy wrote in July: "One thing is dangerous, and that is that the people lose faith in the word of the sovereign. The peasants know of the Tsar's wish for the betterment of their lot and they await fulfilment with exemplary patience and submissiveness. But God knows what will happen if the peasantry in freedom find themselves again under the heel of the nobility."

The Tsar agreed. He took inspiration from Lanskoy and Miliutin, and his answer to them was: "I place all my hope for the resolution of this vital question in God, and in those who, like you, serve me in faith and truth, and in whose thoughts the fatherland and its sovereign are one."

All the autumn of 1859 and the winter of 1859–60, there continued a bitter struggle between Miliutin and the serf-owners. The nobles sent Alexander wordy petitions and protests which the Tsar annotated with such remarks as: "Rubbish," "Immeasurable impertinence," "Sophistry," "So that's what you fellows think!"

Count Rostovstsef died in February, 1860. It is thought that the nervous strain of facing both ways in the serf question hastened his end. He had not escaped violent attacks by the nobles and had even been denounced to the Emperor as a revolutionary. It seemed amusing to Alexander II that the time-serving Count Jacob should be denounced. But criticism may have played on the nerves of this fat man, who was not sufficiently fit physically to withstand the storm raging about him. His place as President of the Editing Committee was sought by Lanskoy, the Minister of Interior. But the Tsar did not wish to make the committee purely departmental and he appointed Count V. N. Panin, the Minister of Justice. Panin was not in sympathy with the reform movement, but it seems to have been the Tsar's policy to make those opposed to peasant freedom achieve it.

The debate reported verbatim would show the nobles and landowners to have been extremely shabby. They bickered over the amounts of the redemption money to be paid, over the minimum amount of land they could grant to the village commune. Had it not been that Alexander II eventually commanded them to come to agreement, nothing would have been decided upon.

In February, 1860, Alexander, in anticipation of granting general freedom, had liberated the Crown serfs. It took yet another year before it was possible to proclaim emancipation for all. The date of the great liberation was 1861, the nineteenth of February, old style, the third of March, new style.

The total number of serfs in European Russia on January 1, 1861, according to statistics supplied by the Ministry of the Interior, was 22,558,748. Of these 21,-976,232 were the personal property of the landowners; 541,962 belonged to the proprietors of factories and workshops, and 40,554 belonged to various other establishments. The total population was given as 60,143,-478. The proportion of serfs to free men was 37.51 per cent.

In Siberia there were only 4,338 serfs, and in the

Caucasus and Caspian regions there were half a million, a grand total of just over twenty-three millions.

It was placed upon the serfs to buy the land they lived on, and the terms were not generous. For rich wheat-producing land—"black earth,"—they were to pay in gross 342 million roubles, while the market value was only 284 millions, a difference of 58 million roubles. For inferior land they were to pay in gross 342 millions, but the actual value was only 180 millions, a difference of 162 million roubles.*

The system of paying off redemption was so complicated that no peasant could at once grasp what he had to do. It seemed strange to be pronounced free and yet to have to continue to work two days a week for masters to pay for the land, and to go on paying *obrok*. The peasants in general believed that it was a fraud and that the Tsar's will was being overborne by others. Presently the Tsar would step forth and proclaim complete unconditional freedom!

There was manifestly no immediate prospect of a betterment of the economic position of those who had been slaves. But the main fact of emancipation remained. From the day of the manifesto, March 3, 1861, no man or woman in Russia could be sold. Human property ceased. The landowners had no power to interfere with marriages or to forbid them, or to dispose of peasant laborers' property. Those who had been slaves obtained equal rights of citizenship with others and obtained the protection of the law, the right of education, the justification of ambition.

The Government covered the whole of the financial

* Lositsky, *Redemption Operations.*

transaction of redemption by the issue of long-dated interest-bearing treasury certificates. The slave-owner parting with property in the shape of land or serfs received financial certificates to the value of the said land or serfs. Thereby the redeemed slave became in debt to the Government for his freedom, not to his late owner. In effect the Government paid the owners and hoped to indemnify itself from the freed slaves. The amount paid out to landowners in the shape of financial certificates was very large. Many of the owners sold the certificates for what they would fetch in hard cash, and finding themselves in possession of capital, lived on it prodigally, in St. Petersburg, Paris and elsewhere. Money talked.

The day of the promulgation of the manifesto was the first day of Lent. It was deliberately chosen that the tidings of freedom should be given at the beginning of the great fast. At that time at least Lent was rigorously observed by the people. It was impossible to celebrate freedom with feasting and dances. The clergy announced the freedom quietly in the churches. It was not desired that the serfs should get an exaggerated notion of their change of position. It was feared that the hotheads and revolutionary propagandists might rouse the masses to widespread disorder and that freedom might be interpreted as freedom to loot estates and drive landowners from their homes. The Tsar's manifesto was printed and distributed and read aloud. But it was received in complete humility.

On many estates where the owner called his serfs together to tell them the good news, the bondsmen and bondwomen heard him kneeling. They understood only one fact, that whereas they had been bound they had become free. It took them a long while to grasp that they would have to pay heavily for their freedom, and not one scrap of the wide land of Russia was to be had without paying for it. When some who could read tried to interpret the terms of the deal to the others they were flogged for their pains.. One Russian writer remarked, "Never were the peasants flogged so violently as in the time immediately following the publication of the manifesto of emancipation."*

The masters gave their parting blow.

That most of the landowners had been selfish and many were brutal cannot be denied. Possibly it was against the will of Russia as a whole that she moved towards freedom, came out of the dark age of feudalism into the dawn light of democracy. But there is no necessity to stigmatize the Russian opposition. Liberation was achieved without civil war. On the day on which freedom was made known to the Russian slaves, Abraham Lincoln in America took the oath as President. In the following month the Stars and Stripes were hauled down from Fort Sumter, and the bitter war of North and South began, the issue being fundamentally whether the negro slaves should be freed. In a sense Russia was ahead of the enlightened Americans, and freedom was achieved in the face of a less violent opposition.

The chief difference between the American and Russian problem was that in America the slaves were of African and savage origin whereas in Russia they were mostly Russian. The serfs were one with their master in race, and potentially the equals of those who held them in bondage.

* Pokrovsky, *Peasant Reform.*

America, when the Civil War was over, granted the slaves freedom on much more generous terms than Russia had done. Russia granted a bare freedom in which the lot of the freed man did not at once seem much improved. Some revolutionaries, not all of them, called the world to witness that Alexander II had given the serfs a shabby deal. But as a demagogue has said: "The only cure for freedom is more freedom." Freedom is like life itself, a condition of growth. It is true that masses of redeemed serfs remained for decades in a state of abject poverty and economic thraldom. But it is also true that others found a way to prosperity. While some ex-owners gambled away the redemption money in Paris and Monte Carlo, some redeemed serfs made money, lent money, built up little fortunes. The story told in Chekhof's *Cherry Orchard* was not uncommon in life. Some improvident family of landowners returns from Paris to the old estate and finds it in the clutches of a hard, matter-of-fact Lopatkhin, the son of a serf. The peasant enters into possession: the jaded gamblers move out. Who could have thought in March, 1861, that within sixty years all the broad lands of Russia would be in the hands of ex-serfs and proletarians, and that there would not be gentry in possession anywhere? It is enough to prompt the reflection that Alexander II had been wrong. But that is not so. He moved with the times. He could not help signing the abdication of the landowners any more than in 1917 his grandson could help signing the abdication of the throne.

II.

THE RETURN OF DOSTOIEVSKY

SOME significance attaches to the fact that the years of the reign of Alexander II correspond to the years of the literary activity of Fedor Dostoievsky. Prior to his sentence to penal servitude in Siberia Dostoievsky had written only *Poor Folk* (1846) and *The Double* (1847). The first work had been hailed by the critic Belinsky as one of great talent; the second was too fantastic and was almost ignored. Dostoievsky was neither in fame nor in achievement a great writer when he was banished to Siberia. He returned to blossom into the national life of Russia in Alexander's liberal reign, which saw all his triumphs and covered all the fruitful years of his life; for Alexander II died in March, 1881, and Dostoievsky in the preceding February.

The period of Alexander's reign was that of the greatest self-expression of Russia. Before Alexander we have only Pushkin, killed in a duel in 1837; Lermontof, killed in another duel in 1841; Gogol and Zhukovsky, who both died in 1852. We may add the poet Nekrasof; the historian Karamsin; the dramatist Ostrovsky and the critic Belinsky. Russia had no voice in literature before the nineteenth century. She had had no Elizabethan age of poetry, no brilliant eighteenth century of prose and verse as in France and England. Russia had been inarticulate. But with Alexander II came the great masters of the Russian word, never excelled or equalled—Dostoievsky, Turgenief, Tolstoy.

The repressive regime of Nicholas I had been unfavorable to literature, but it is not clear that it stopped any writer of talent. Gogol was allowed free play. Zhukovsky was a court favorite. Dostoievsky was banished to Siberia, but exile, instead of killing him, developed his powers and brought him closer to the life of the poor and the unfortunate. The last years of the reign of Nicholas I have been called the "Censor's Reign of Terror," but the terror was visited more upon journalists and polemical students than on artists. The period 1848–55 was a dead time, a time of enforced silence. The only important work published during these years was Turgenief's *Sportsman's Sketches* (1852). It was the time of Nekrasof's pessimism and his "Who Can Be Happy in Russia?"

But with Alexander II the inspiration of letters, or at least of the idealistic Zhukovsky, began to rule. At once the influence of Alexander's education and training began to be felt. When peace had been concluded with England and France in 1856 and the army demobilized, the Tsar promised a four years' immunity from recruiting. He stopped the insensate mechanical drilling which had been a feature of his father's military rule, and he put the standing army into more comfortable uniforms.

At Alexander's wedding there had been a partial amnesty for prisoners. His father had not gone as far as Alexander had wished in that respect. At his coronation he consummated his earlier desires and made what was practically a jail clearance in Russia. He granted pardons at last to the exiled *Dekabristi*, as many of them as remained alive. On the Emperor's birthday in April, 1857, when he was looking about for more prisoners to release, it was found that there was nobody confined in the fortress of St. Peter and St. Paul.

The work for the liberation of the slaves had been proceeding all the while under the leadership of the Tsar. The will of Alexander was for liberty, therefore his ministers and gentry must work for liberty even against their convictions or personal faith. All Russia became conscious of a new spring. The silence of winter was past and the new season became alive with voices.

The censorship remained but it was relaxed. Numbers of periodicals were published—the Slavophile *Russkaya Beseda* in 1856, and then *Molva*, *Parus*, *Den*. Revolutionary sheets published abroad found their way into Russia and were not confiscated. Herzen, the Russian revolutionary exile living in England was responsible for a paper which had a very great influence. *Kolokol* (The Bell) had, of course, been banned in Russia, but it found its way over the frontier, and few were afraid to be seen reading it in St. Petersburg. It is said that Alexander himself read it and to a great extent approved its liberal program. The three principal demands of *The Bell* were: the emancipation of the serfs, abolition of corporal punishment, and the curtailment of the censorship. Herzen was also a champion of the oppressed Poles. He was a man who lived on wrongs, could not see the positive side of Russian national life and thus continued to paint the country black for foreign eyes. Even after the achievement of Alexander's reform he remained an unsympathetic revolutionary.

Most newspapers and reviews in Russia at the time

were of a liberal complexion. The *Sovremennik*, the *Russkoye Slovo*, *Russkiya Vedomosti*, *Russky Vestnik*, were all bursting with new ideas and arguments.

A Russian commentator says:

> The whole significance of the new journalistic movement of the sixties was bound up in the break with the past. It was brought about by the inevitable conflict between the representatives of separate progressive groups and particularly by the conflict between the people of the forties and the democrats of the sixties.

The new literature was a literature of discovery, of the revelation of new types. Turgenief picked Rudin, the plausible, talkative, impotent intellectual, who has no real will or life-force behind his clever sayings. Rudin was a type. When the novel was published in 1855 Russians looked about them and saw many Rudins. But Goncharof went one better than Turgenief in his famous novel *Oblomof*, published in 1858. Oblomof was the archetype of Russian indolence and will-lessness, exaggerated to the point where the reader is tempted to say that no such man exists or ever existed, but devastating as a portrait, because it caught and synthesized the traits of innumerable Russians. It created a greater shock than the portraits of the landowners in Gogol's *Dead Souls*. It did the great service of holding the mirror in front of the Russian and bidding him look into it. It had its moral reaction. It stirred up the young to be energetic and realistic, made possible the emergence of a new type, the questioning, restless, matter-of-fact Bazarof, portrayed in Turgenief's *Fathers and Sons* in 1862.

Dostoievsky, when he had served his term, did not enter upon complete freedom but was drafted into the

Seventh Siberian Regiment. Although it was the time of the Crimean War he saw no active service. In January, 1856, he was made a corporal and remained with his regiment at Semipalatinsk, performing parade duties, but also writing. He did not rebel against the soldier's life, though he found it hard. Nor was he bitter against authority. Doubtless he was still in favor of the liberation of the serfs but he had abjured his other Western political ideals, the socialism, the progressivism which had caught up Petrashevsky and his other comrades of 1848. When one of his friends remarked that his punishment had been unjust, he replied, "No, just! The people would also have condemned me had they had to judge my crime. I felt that fact when I was in penal servitude. And you know, perhaps the Almighty had to send me to Siberia . . . to teach me something . . ."

Dostoievsky was more than loyal to Alexander II. In a letter that he wrote at Semipalatinsk he referred to him as "our Angel Tsar."

In March, 1859, he obtained his discharge from the army, with freedom to live in any part of the Russian Empire except Moscow and St. Petersburg. In the same year he published *The Uncle's Dream* in the *Russkoye Slovo*. In September, 1859, he was back in Russia proper and took up residence in a provincial city— Tver—yearning, however, for permission to go to St. Petersburg. He was already in rivalry with Turgenief and intent on earning a greater success than he, and really on displacing him in the popular mind.

In 1860 Turgenief and Herzen were leaders of thought and literature. One was a literary artist, the other a pamphleteer and agitator. But both were possessed by the notion that the West was better than the East, that Russia was an object of criticism rather than an inspiration of art. Dostoievsky had come back from Siberia with the belief that the Russian people itself had wisdom and could be a supreme teacher, and that Russia must develop along her own lines. Her destiny would not depend on Europe but Europe's destiny might depend on her. In the realm of ideas the creed of Dostoievsky was distinctly counter-revolutionary.

When the life of Dostoievsky comes to be written adequately it must be a record of spiritual values, and must divorce itself from the story of his debts and his struggle to pay bills. If his life meant anything it was a spiritual life. When he came from Siberia he found the already famous Turgenief possessing 2,000 inherited serfs and a pen, while he possessed nothing but a pen. Dostoievsky as a prisoner had not been allowed to write. But he had grown spiritually all the while he was in banishment and in a sense he was a much richer man than Turgenief when he reëntered the world of literature. But that is not to say that he could at once make a contribution to Russian literature. He had to find his bearings in the new Russia of Alexander. The critics had not entirely forgotten him or his first book, *Poor Folk*, but he was nevertheless comparatively unknown. It is remarkable that the first novel which he wrote after banishment was that extremely light comedy entitled *The Uncle's Dream*. It contains no message of any kind and it would be difficult to guess that it had been written by a man inspired by suffering, just freed from servitude in Siberia.

Dostoievsky as a young writer had been greatly under the influence of Gogol. Nekrasof had indeed

Fedor Dostoievsky

called him a new Gogol and Belinsky had rejoined: "New Gogols grow up overnight like mushrooms." *Poor Folk* was very much in the manner of Gogol's famous story *The Cloak*. *The Uncle's Dream* had the humor of Gogol without the tragic seriousness. The new Dostoievsky with his messianic message to Russia announced himself first in the Notes from *The House of the Dead*, a powerful book on his Siberian experience. He meditated writing a great national novel. He wrote to a friend of such a novel which he had planned while doing time in Siberia. This novel evidently was *Crime and Punishment*. He would also make his contribution to portraits of types, revealing Russia to herself, and giving Russians someone more startling than Oblomof or Rudin to consider, Raskolnikof, the young man who believed his own destiny to be worth so much that he was justified in murdering an old woman to help it forward. Raskolnikof must confess and expiate his crime by suffering, by going patiently to Siberia. The assumption of Western materialism was that all suffering was evil and must be eliminated. The elimination of human suffering was the significance of progress. But Dostoievsky answered with the counter-cry that only out of suffering and self-sacrifice can good come to a man or a nation.

At the date of the emancipation of the serfs Tolstoy was thirty-two years of age, an extremely active landowner, well-known but not famous. Great things were expected of him but he had not at that time shown the high moral earnestness and artistic talent which ultimately brought him a vast following of disciples and admirers in every country in the world. He had merely written a number of short stories and in 1855 he published his *Sebastopol*, which first attracted national attention to his literary gifts. Then, at once Tolstoy was regarded with expectancy. Young Russia craved literature and gave the utmost encouragement to writers. There is an exceedingly interesting letter from the critic Druzhinin, written in 1860, reproaching Tolstoy with not following up his initial success. He wrote:

Every writer has his moments of doubt and self-dissatisfaction, and however strong and legitimate this feeling may be, no one on that account has yet ceased his connection with literature; everyone goes on writing to the end. . . . On all of us lies a responsibility rooted in the immense importance of literature to Russian society. An Englishman or an American may laugh at the fact that in Russia not merely men of thirty, but grey-haired owners of 2,000 serfs sweat over stories of a hundred pages, which appear in the magazines, are devoured by everybody, and arouse discussions in society for a whole day. However much artistic quality may have to do with this result, you cannot explain it merely by Art. What in other lands is a matter of idle talk and careless dilettantism, with us is quite another affair. Among us things have taken such shape that a story—the most frivolous and insignificant form of literature—becomes one of two things: either it is rubbish, or else it is the voice of a leader sounding throughout the Empire. . . . By some strange instinct the Russian public has chosen from among the crowd of writers four or five bell-men whom it values as leaders, refusing to listen to any qualifications or deductions. You—partly by talent, partly by the practical qualities of your soul, and partly owing simply to a concurrence of fortunate circumstances—have stepped into this favourable relation with the public. On that account you must not go away and hide, but must work, even to the exhaustion of your strength and powers. . . . If you tear yourself off from the circle of writers and become inactive, you will be dull, and will deprive yourself of an important rôle in society.*

* Maude, Aylmer, *The Life of Tolstoy*, Vol. I.

Although Tolstoy had been moved by the conditions of the Russian serfs, it is not clear that he was much excited when the actual emancipation took place. On March 3, 1861, he was in London, confabulating with Herzen, but he did not stay for the dinner which Herzen gave to celebrate that event. On the same day he left London to return leisurely to Russia. It took him a month to get back to his estate, but 1861 was the first year of a new era in Russia and he must have been aware of it.

Actually it would seem that the success of Turgenief spurred Tolstoy to rivalry much as it was spurring Dostoievsky. The honor of expressing awakening Russia to herself was very covetable. Turgenief had established himself and held the pride of place. He was an older man and much more accomplished than his competitors. One might doubt the authenticity of his inspiration, but one could not doubt the supremacy of his style. His novels were works of art, most easy to read, most difficult for anyone but Turgenief to write. Their brevity, their limpid simplicity, were the despair of rivals. It was easier to deny that these novels were Russian, to deny their merit entirely, than to criticize them.

Tolstoy and Turgenief were intimate friends—at least they addressed one another in their letters as "Dearest"—but Tolstoy was not a whole-hearted admirer of Turgenief. He found *On the Eve* full of banalities and he wilfully fell asleep reading *Fathers and Sons*. The facile success of the great novelist irritated him, but the only way to overcome this irritation, which was becoming chronic, was to write something better, announce himself to Russia as a great man. In 1863 he began to write *War and Peace*.

How profound was his animosity against his successful friend Turgenief may be judged by the fact that over some petty disagreement at table he actually challenged him to a duel—not as a gesture, but with pistols, hoping to kill. It is strange to reflect that yet another of Russia's great writers might have died in a duel. But the significance of that challenge did not lie in a quarrel of two men. It was the rebellious young Tolstoy feeling in his bones that he was greater than Turgenief, but frustrated in soul by Turgenief's success. Luckily the challenge was not accepted. If Tolstoy wished satisfaction he must achieve it in the literary field.

In 1861 Tolstoy was no revolutionary. When the news came of the emancipation of the serfs, Herzen in London felt that nevertheless he could not drink to the health of the Emperor Alexander II. But Tolstoy at a banquet at Tula in the summer of 1861 felt he could gladly drink to the health of the Tsar-Liberator.

And he is reported to have said to a neighbor at table, "I drink this toast with particular pleasure. No others are needed, for in reality we owe the emancipation to the Emperor alone."

The rise of the three, Turgenief, Dostoievsky and Tolstoy, gave increasing stature to the reign of Alexander II, as the emancipation of the serfs and other reforms gave it breadth. Russia was becoming yearly more spacious. In this spaciousness there were poets singing like Afanasy Fet. There was also music, and fine art. Glinka had died in 1857, but the young Peter Tchaikovsky, a clerk in the Department of Justice in 1859, already believed that he would win fame equal to Glinka's, transferred to the Conservatoire in St.

Petersburg and emerged as an original musical composer within the sixties. In fine art Verestchagin appeared, followed closely by Ilya Repin. Russia also had a new historian of note, Serge Solovyof, who during the years 1851 to 1879 turned out volume after volume of his authoritative history of Russia.

III.

FAMILY LIFE

THE lack of sympathy which seemed to exist between Alexander and his brother the Grand Duke Constantine disappeared when Alexander became Tsar. A family loyalty supervened, and Constantine turned into one of the most energetic workers in the cause of emancipation. Loyalty became a marked feature of the Grand Duke Constantine. His military vainglory may have been merely loyalty to his military father. Nicholas I, with no sense of humor, had given the child Constantine the rank of general at the age of four, and he was soon afterwards proclaimed an admiral of the fleet. Eventually he became grand admiral. As a soldier he was sent with the Russian army in 1849 to help Austria against the insurgent Hungarians and was supposed to have distinguished himself as grand dukes must. But even that mild campaign damped his martial spirit. He was, in truth, no soldier, and the failure of Russian arms in the Crimea finally convinced him that he was a man of peace. His interest in ships was, however, unfeigned, and he did a service to Russian commerce by bringing a fleet of steamboats on to the Black Sea in 1856, and starting the Black Sea Steamship & Trading Company.

With his brother Alexander on the throne, Constantine became a progressive, and the right-hand man of the Tsar in fighting the opposition to the emancipation of the serfs. He was not only a convinced liberationist but associated himself warmly with the whole liberal humanitarian movement of the sixties, worked to stop torture and corporal punishment in jails and in the army, and to lift the blight of censorship from journalism and literature. He said that his experience of army life had convinced him that corporal punishment for soldiers was not of the slightest value in enforcing discipline.

The vigor of Constantine's reform enthusiasm gave a strong moral and physical support to the Tsar, who thereby avoided the opprobrium of being thought an eccentric monarch moving alone against established tradition and the mass of conservative opinion of old Russia.

When freedom for the serfs had been won, Alexander was sincerely happy and excited. In the senate he publicly thanked his brother Constantine for his assistance and kissed him several times.

In truth there were not many exalted persons in favor of freedom. Both the Empress and the Dowager Empress doubted that emancipation would be good for Russia. But one personage in the German entourage of Alexander stands out as a strong sympathizer, the Grand Duchess Helen (of Württemberg), widow of the Grand Duke Michael Pavlovitch, a woman of encyclopædic knowledge and wide interests. She was a centre of artistic and cultural interests, but besides that engaged in the hobby of sifting out the Russians at court and recommending those of real talent and capacity to the Emperor. The Grand Duchess Helen was the patroness of Nicholas Miliutin, and effectively shielded him during the time when his progressive leadership of the reform committee drew upon him the resentment of the reactionaries. She was herself an enthusiastic worker for the emancipation of the serfs and showed her enthusiasm practically by liberating the serfs on her estate at Karlovka in anticipation of the decree.

The Empress Wilhelmina of Hesse-Darmstadt (Maria Alexandrovna) bore to Alexander her seven children before 1860, and her interests must have been more in her family than in external happenings. But the Empress contributed to the reform movement by espousing the cause of the education of women, and having secondary schools for girls established in every city in Russia.

In 1843 the Empress had given birth to a son and heir, the Grand Duke Nicholas Alexandrovitch. As a token of gratitude the Tsar gave a large sum of money to pay off debts, and released a number of debtors from prison. That seems to have been his favorite way of expressing thanks. But Alexander II, though father of his people, was not in any way remarkable as father of a family. He did not take as much care over the upbringing of Nicholas as his father had done for him. He did not procure another Zhukovsky to train the heir to the throne. The education of the prince was confused and ill balanced: he was crammed with dry learning, while physical development suffered. The Tsar expressed his opinion that Nicholas was *trop efféminé* and then gave instructions that something be done to make his son more manly. The new exercises were probably overdone. In 1860 Nicholas fell from a horse in a riding school at Tsarskoe Selo and fractured his spine. Ten years later he died in great agony of cerebral spinal tuberculosis and the Tsar acknowledged "a dreadful blow from the Almighty."

Still, Nicholas had not been an only son. The second son, Alexander Alexandrovitch, destined to be Alexander III, became, upon the death of his elder brother, heir to the throne.

One of the principal influences molding the character of the new heir was that of Constantine Pobiedonostsef, who held a chair of civil law at Moscow University. Pobiedonostsef was far from being a liberal; he was a ruthless authoritarian of considerable intellectual capacity, a man bound to impress his character on others. He taught Alexander Alexandrovitch, gained his confidence, became his friend. The intimacy begun in the adolescence of the heir was not cut short when the Grand Duke became Alexander III and Pobiedonostsef's influence in Russian politics lasted right through to the fateful reign of Nicholas II.

In the years immediately succeeding the Crimean War the Court was not kept up on such a lavish scale as under Nicholas I. Russia was impoverished by the war, and great demands on her finances were bound up in the reforms which the Emperor had at heart. At the same time both he and the Empress were liberal almsgivers and believed they should not live in ostentation while there were so many poor in the land.

The Tsar's family commonly spent the summer at Hapsal on the Gulf of Finland—Alexander liked the Finns. The life there was simplicity itself, walking with the children, sea bathing, riding, shooting wild duck. The Tsar had more pleasure in shooting than in almost any other diversion.

In 1857 the Tsar and Tsarina visited Germany. There were fêtes in honor of the Tsar in Berlin. There was a meeting of the Tsar Alexander II and the Emperor Napoleon III at the court of the King of Würt-temberg. The Tsar did not conduct himself as a great potentate as his father Nicholas had done in Germany. He was content to have a pony carriage without escort meet him at Stuttgart station.

Napoleon III, since peace had been made between France and Russia, ardently sought friendship if not alliance with his ex-enemy. He was a very showy figure at the court of Württemberg and Alexander distrusted him. In his heart Alexander found it difficult to forgive the European powers which had fought his father.

In November, 1860, Alexander's mother died, a kindly old lady who had been an invalid for many years. Like all the German consorts of the later tsars she was a good and pious woman, and although she was a daughter of Frederick William III, it cannot be said that she brought the harsh Prussian military spirit into court life. On the contrary she brought a certain gentleness and a love of God interpreted as love of one's fellow beings. Bismarck describes the old lady as he saw her in the year before her death:

In her amiable naturalness of manner she has, I think, something really motherly, and I can speak out to her as though I had known her from a child. To-day she talked for a long time and on many subjects with me. Dressed in black, she lay on a couch, on a balcony looking out on green trees, knitting a red and white woollen shawl with long needles, and I could have listened to her deep voice and true-hearted laughter and scolding for hours. I had come for a couple of hours, and in evening dress; but when at last she said that she did not want to say good-bye to me yet, but that probably I had a lot to do, I assured her, "Not the slightest," and she replied, "Then stay here [at Peterhof] and see me off to-morrow."

The idealistic Alexander owed much of his kindli-

ness to his mother. It is common to ascribe the unpleasant characteristics of the later Romanofs to their German blood, and their virtues to their Russian blood.
Probably the reverse is true.

Alexander was at Warsaw at the time his mother
became suddenly very ill, and he hastened back to
Tsarskoe Selo to her bedside. She died four days later
and there was deep mourning at the capital. The Tsar
Alexander, the Grand Duke Constantine, the Grand
Duke Nicholas, followed the bier on foot with hundreds of others from Tsarskoe Selo seven miles to the
church of the fortress of St. Peter and St. Paul, where
their mother was buried.

It was a critical time in the life of the Tsar. He was
forty-two years of age. He had lost his mother. His
wife, having given birth to her seventh child, Paul, was
unlikely to have more children. The Tsar began to be
restless and seek some further new feminine relaxation.
It is not altogether surprising that at an early date he
fell passionately in love for the second time in his life.
His union with Wilhelmina of Hesse-Darmstadt had
been a love-match, not an arranged marriage. It had
been happy, but did not prove adequate. With the
years Alexander tired somewhat of the Empress, possibly because she had a will of her own and asserted it
often, but more probably because she had ceased to be
the attractive creature she was when he found her. She
had become very pious. Despite her Protestant birth,
Wilhelmina of Hesse-Darmstadt had become most ardently Orthodox. It has been a peculiarity of German
princesses marrying into the Romanof family to become more Russian than the Russians in matters of religion. When she was betrothed to Alexander, Wilhel-

mina eagerly adopted the Russian Church, partly to insure her popularity in Russia but also to be in no way divided from Alexander, whom she adored. After marriage the Orthodox Church completely captured her imagination and she fell readily under the influence of her father-confessor, Bashanof. Alexander followed the way of Martha rather than the way of Mary. His religion was good works; he was no mystic. And he was tolerant; he did not rebuke his wife for her exaggerated piety. But in church observances and obedience to a confessor something was stolen away from the spiritual marriage portion of these two. Moreover, the Tsaritsa's beauty faded early. She soon became sickly and was often confined to her apartments for weeks owing to the "weakness" of her nerves. In conversation with the Emperor she became sugary, sentimental, plaintive, subservient. She ceased to have that ordinary daily inspiration which a husband needs if he is to remain in a state of complete and happy union with his wife.

And then affairs of state, the wearing struggle of obtaining the emancipation of the serfs, the inhuman daily labor of administration, told on Alexander's health. Most commentators agree as to the worn expression which appeared on his features soon after he became Tsar. Von Moltke wrote of him:

> He has not the statuesque beauty or the marble rigidity of his father, but is an extremely handsome, majestic man. He appeared worn, and I could perceive that events had impressed a gravity upon his noble features which contrasts strongly with the kind expression of his large eyes.

At Stuttgart he was described as "weary, out of humor, out of spirits, out of health." In 1860 he was for a while prostrate with asthma. We have a man who in adolescence was brought up to lean on others, mothered by the court women, mothered by his tutor and friend, Zhukovsky. He was rigidly obedient to his father—which meant obedient to authority, leaning on authority. But in mature years suddenly he must cease to lean, that all others might lean on him. He was a solid beefy man who had been spoon-fed with poetry. The poetry, though it had gone into him, did not come out of him. His speeches were plain. The acme of his expressed wisdom was a sort of German conscientiousness and decency, an appeal to common sense, a hope that his subjects would do their duty even as he with God's aid was striving to do his. He was the type which used to be known as a "good German." He would have coped better with orderly German subjects than with the anarchic, quarrelsome, undisciplined Russians. Alexander succeeded as a reformer in Russia, but the struggle was almost too much for him. The interior tension was nearly unbearable. Something must be found to make life easier, in short a new love, an inspiration in life, a secret and reserved tsardom of the heart where he could take strength to fight his battles in the world.

Alexander II was particularly susceptible to feminine charm. If he saw a beautiful young woman he became easily obsessed by passion. He was not a flirt, nor could he reasonably be called immoral. He was no cynic. He became suddenly but genuinely *épris*. It had happened several times. When he was nineteen he lost his heart to the daughter of a Polish general and thought no one else in the world would do for him but her. There was some difficulty in parting him from her. But there as on other occasions he was mistaken; the infatuation departed as quickly as it had come. In the same way he had been thunderstruck by love in the little court of Hesse-Darmstadt. He found Wilhelmina, not exactly a match for the heir to the throne of Russia, but nevertheless accepted because he wanted her so much. But after his marriage he still had eyes for other women—if they were young and beautiful. He made sentimental attachments—they did not amount to affairs. The chief of these was to Princess Alexandra Dolgoruky, a maid of twenty summers, beautiful, dashing, intelligent, nicknamed at court *La Grande Mademoiselle*. She shared the Tsar's sympathy for political reform, his thought for the betterment of Russia, but probably not his bed. She married General Albedinsky. The general was an old man, the Tsar made him Governor of Warsaw; he may have been a complaisant husband but of that there is no evidence. Alexander II found another Dolgoruky, Princess Catherine, who awakened a passion which endured for the rest of the sovereign's life. He had noticed her as a child when she was just ten years old. Her father had got into pecuniary embarrassment and the Tsar helped him and made himself responsible for the education of the children. Princess Catherine was sent to the Smolny Institute, and Alexander frequently visited the school and had conversation with her. The girl fascinated him, even then. There was that relationship which sometimes obtains between a middle-aged man and a little girl. He saw the fairy in her, the ikon face of St. Barbara, the inimitable grace of movement, the early morning light in the child's eyes, a certain crystal simplicity; and the big Alexander, with his side whiskers and bushy brows, his large kind eyes, his majesty of tsardom, could not but have an obsessive effect on this little Princess Catherine. The Emperor of seventy millions of Russians chose to spend hours talking with her, telling her his plans, playfully asking her advice.

Years passed. When Princess Catherine was seventeen years old Alexander began making love to her. She fell in love with him, and completely displaced the Empress in the Tsar's heart. He was soon telling Catherine that he regarded her as his wife before God, and that upon the first opportunity he would marry her.

An Ivan or a Peter would have at once banished the true Empress to a convent and have adopted the young *protégé* as Tsarina, but the times were changed. Autocrats were not the autocrats of their wives any longer. Alexander must wait for his wife to die, and if she died, it was not at all clear that the Senate would allow the sovereign to marry a Russian. The unfortunate custom held that tsars must marry into the royal houses of Europe.

The Empress must have known that Alexander had no further use for her as a wife. But she bore the humiliation with restraint. She found compensation in extra piety, preoccupation with miracles and divine manifestations within the Orthodox Church. There were no scenes, no appeals; only a coldness in which Wilhelmina of Hesse still worshipped her hero husband without, however, understanding his life.

The rift in domestic happiness was the more unfortunate because psychologically it divided the family into two camps. When father and mother are not in a complete union of love and mutual understanding the children commonly grow up to criticize the father and to form themselves upon a different model. At court there were many who whispered against Alexander II, especially after the liberation of the serfs, many who said that his liberal policy was wrongheaded and would bring ruin upon Russia. We have seen that the heir Nicholas, effeminate as he was, nevertheless stood up to his father and told him his political reforms were wrong. And when Nicholas died and the Grand Duke Alexander Alexandrovitch became heir to the throne, the Tsar had already grown completely cold to the mother. Alexander Alexandrovitch was a much more virile youth, cold-blooded, heavy-footed, rather stupid. His education had been somewhat neglected. He was tutored by Pobiedonostsef, who was unable to teach him anything and only succeeded in implanting prejudices. He was given the fiancée of his dead brother to wife, the Princess Dagmar of Denmark, and the person chosen to teach Dagmar was the Tsaritsa's father-confessor, Bashanof. One side of the court was becoming violently Orthodox. The atmosphere was one in which a spirit of reaction to the Tsar's liberalism could grow apace. Alexander Alexandrovitch, the heir, had in him the makings of a reactionary tsar, who, when he came to the throne, might undo much of the good work done by his father for the Russian serfs and for the Russian people. Alexander II did little to win the confidence of the youth who was going to be Alexander III.

IV.

THE POLISH MUTINY

THE position of eastern Poland, incorporated in the Russian Empire against its will, was unfortunate. Brotherhood of race is no guarantee of mutual sympathy and though the phrase "brother Slavs" sounds well, it does not preclude war and mutual hate. There has never been much brotherly feeling between Poles and Russians. Actually there is not very much in common between these nations. Poland, being ardently Catholic, could never be at peace in an empire of which the emperor was not a Catholic, and experience shows that Catholic nations are never submissive to a monarchy which owes allegiance to a different state religion.

Poland was crushed by her immediate neighbors, Prussia, Austria and Russia, and divided up between them in the eighteenth century. The Polish patriots took their revenge by fighting for Napoleon Bonaparte against the nations which had despoiled them. Bonaparte in return gave them an illusory aid which faded into ruin after the French retreat from Moscow. The history of Polish nationalism during the fifty years following upon the fall of Bonaparte is a record of despair—or rather of fanatical despairing efforts to rise out of death and destruction into new life.

Russian Poland was allowed a parliament by Alexander I, a measure of autonomy, the Polish constitution of 1815. The Tsar was Emperor of Russia, but also

King of Poland. Roman Catholicism was recognized as the state religion. Poland retained its army, a very considerable force, raised chiefly for the support of Bonaparte—to some extent raised by him. For Bonaparte recruited gladly from Poland. By the constitution of 1815 the Poles, under Russian control, obtained a measure of liberty, considerable immunity from interference for their press, schools, national language and courts. That is not to say that they were in any sense contented, though their lot as a Russian protectorate was much better than that of their compatriots in Prussia and Austria.

In 1830 Polish nationalism flared into insurrection. With the aid of the Polish army, the insurgent patriots attempted a *coup d'état*. The army was built up to a strength of 80,000 men and possessed 160 guns. The Russians mustered a force of 114,000 against the rebels. The Poles imagined vainly that Europe would rise to their support. They had clamorous sympathizers in most Western states. But no help was forthcoming. The army of Tsar Nicholas I vanquished the rebels, and Poland was deprived of the measure of liberty granted by Alexander I, and became merely a province of Russia. The Poles became subject to a repressive imperial rule. The universities of Warsaw and Vilna were closed. The army was disbanded as a national army and the individual soldiers distributed among Russian regiments. The Russian language invaded the schools and the courts. Russianization set in.

The wrongs of the Poles mooted abroad seemed an indictment of the absolute rule of the Tsar and made many enemies of tsardom in France, in England and

America. Every English schoolboy knew Campbell's famous line of poetry:

And Freedom shrieked when Kosciuszko fell.

The Poles were commonly regarded in the West as an unhappy, tragic nation. During the violent propaganda period of the Crimean War the alleged enormities of Russian rule in Poland were exploited by the enemies of Russia.

At once after the Crimean War the Indian Mutiny took place and England suppressed it as Nicholas I suppressed the Polish Mutiny. If the right of one race to rule another be admitted Russia had as much right to quell a mutiny in Poland as Great Britain had to quell a mutiny in India.

After 1830 Nicholas I had ruled Poland with a rod of iron. Alexander II, as was natural in a ruler educated in an atmosphere of Panslavism, strove to conciliate the overridden "brother Slavs." He granted a general amnesty to Polish prisoners, a dispensation of mercy which he had vainly urged upon his father Nicholas. At the same time Alexander made use of the famous words which caused much irritation: *"Point de rêveries!"* said he to the Poles. They would be granted a more liberal regime but they must give up dreaming of independence.

Alexander was crowned King of Poland at Warsaw, thus raising the status of the conquered province from the political serfdom into which it had fallen. On the day after his coronation the amnesty was proclaimed. About 9,000 exiles were restored from Siberia to their native land.

It may be thought that these liberated Polish patriots had done most of their dreaming in prison and penal servitude. Returning to their beloved Poland they were set on action. They trickled back in scores and hundreds between the years 1857 and 1860, and at once entered into the new movement for national independence.

Alexander went further: he restored to Poland all that Nicholas I had taken away, except the right to have a Polish national army and to convoke a diet. The Catholic bishoprics were restored. An Academy of Medicine was established in Warsaw and became the intellectual rallying ground of Polish youth. A representative agricultural society was also inaugurated by the Tsar, ostensibly to develop agriculture, but actually to take in hand the thorny problem of allotting land from the masters' estates to the Polish peasants and thus raising them out of serfdom. In 1860 the Tsar established municipalities to be elected by the Polish householders, and Russian officials were replaced by Polish officials in all subordinate posts throughout Poland.

Prince Michael Gorchakof, formerly Commander in Chief in the Crimea, had been appointed Governor-General of Poland in 1856. He was a capable soldier, he had taken part in the reduction of Warsaw in the insurrection of 1830–31, he had been commandant of Sebastopol throughout the famous siege. But it is doubtful whether his military type of mind suited him for civil administration. He found it difficult to cope with the complicated revolutionary activity of Warsaw. It was, however, his belief that Russia would be best served by allying itself with whatever loyal and positive elements could be found within the Polish nobility. But the hope of coöperation by the nobility was compromised by the project of regulating the position of the Polish peasants. The Polish serfs were supposed to have been liberated. They had been set free by Napoleon Bonaparte, but the French Emperor's decree remained a dead letter because the serfs thus "freed" had not been granted land. They were obliged to continue working for their old masters, and as conditions of service were not improved they had not emerged from bondage. The Polish estates were much more encumbered by peasant dependents than the estates in Russia, because the *obrok* system was not working in Poland. The serfs, being supposed free, could not be called upon to pay a handsome percentage on their earnings to the lord and master. Over the border in Russia, in 1861, after emancipation, the position of the peasants was manifestly better than that of the quasi-serfs in Poland.

The Polish landowners were willing to admit that the system of peonage on their estates could not continue indefinitely after the Russian serfs had been liberated. But if the status of their present bondsmen and bondwomen was to be changed they preferred to make the change themselves, on terms more profitable to themselves than the terms envisaged by the Russians. There was a greater hostility between peasants and gentlemen in Poland than there was in Russia. Liberating the Polish peasants meant liberating a revolutionary force whose will would not be so much against Russian overlordship as against their ex-masters. To the extent that they understood the position, the Polish peasants were more sympathetic to the Russian Tsar than to any purely Polish government. The agricultural laborers formed the one section of the Polish population favorable to Russia but they did not count for much as a political force.

The cities seethed with militant nationalism. In the first years of increasing freedom this did not express itself in overt acts of resistance to the Russian authorities. But there was partial, unorganized, sporadic boycott. The churches were hung with crape which it was said would not be removed till Poland had become an independent kingdom. Shopkeepers refused to serve customers who spoke to them in Russian. Polish ladies foreswore dancing and went into mourning as if they were just widowed. There were all manner of noisy parades and demonstrations. The spectacle of Garibaldi, leading his Italians in the fight for Italian independence, did much to inspire the forward movement in Poland. It seemed that if the Italians could throw off oppressors Poland could do so also. But Poland had no Garibaldi to lead it. Any sober judge of the situation could have seen that the mutinous spirit of the Poles, if developed into action, must result in catastrophe, and leave Poland in a more helpless condition of thraldom than in the years which immediately succeeded the rebellion of 1830.

Nevertheless it must be admitted that sobriety is seldom associated with patriotism. And Poland is a land of poetry and rhetoric rather than of prosaic common sense. It was aware of itself in the verses of the poet Mickiewicz and a hundred other poets. The Christianity of the Gospel and the Church was not enough. The Poles interpreted Christianity in terms of nationalism. The country of Poland, partitioned by the powers, was the raiment of Christ divided up among the Roman soldiers: "They parted my raiment among them and for my vesture they did cast lots."

In an exaggerated way, which has no counterpart in truth, they identified Poland among the nations as Christ among men—the sacrificial lamb. Poland had been a very wild lamb, possessed of some shockingly bad habits. Being crucified does not mean sanctification, and had Barabbas been crucified instead of Christ there is no reason to suppose that there could have been a religion of Barabbas.

Doubtless there were some Polish patriots who regarded the Christian interpretation of their movement with some cynicism. Not all the Poles of 1860 were Christians. Some were freethinkers. There was a Red movement as well as a White. There were Poles who thought of resurrecting the old kingdom of Poland with an elective monarch, perhaps Prince Napoleon, the son of Napoleon III; but there were other patriots who were republicans. The nobility and gentry wished the restoration of that old Poland in which they had been masters; but the students of the medical schools and the returned clubmen and café loungers from Paris wished liberty, equality and a measure of fraternity. The latter were naturally much more ready for the complete emancipation of the Polish serfs than the former. Still, as far as Russia was concerned, there was only one party in Poland, its elements merged in one shouting, parading, demonstrating nation.

In June, 1860, took place the first of the great national demonstrations in Warsaw. It was the occasion of the funeral of the widow of General Sovinski. Sovinski had died fighting the Russians in the rebellion of 1830–31. He died actually at the storming of Warsaw.

The Poles had learned a new hymn—"God Save Poland"—and they chanted it through the streets. The hymn was not seditious but the singing of it was calculated to provoke sedition. Under the liberal administration of Alexander II and his Viceroy Gorchakof it was impossible to forbid processions or the singing of hymns. But such a demonstration as took place at the funeral of Madame Sovinski was dangerous because the volatile Poles inflamed their own passions by their marching and chanting.

"God Save Poland" invaded the churches and interrupted the liturgy. It was sung by massed congregations. It invaded the restaurants and the clubs and was sung by men who raised their glasses to the resurrection of Poland. It became the anthem sung by all, standing; when it was performed in the streets passers-by must uncover their heads. Demonstration followed demonstration in the Warsaw streets. It was easy to find pretexts for new parades, for the singing of the revengeful hymn of patriotic faith.

The Russians did not interfere with this street parading until March 10, 1861, when a monster procession whose object was to sway the Agricultural Society came forth with banners and crucifixes. To the great surprise of the Poles, Gorchakof lost his patience and sent a squadron of mounted *gendarmerie* to disperse the demonstrators. Many arrests were made and many people were injured.

Those of the Polish nobility holding administrative positions demanded the release of the people who had been arrested, and being refused, they resigned. Gorchakof had no option of exercising clemency; the Tsar himself had made a change of front. Alexander was emphatic that order must be preserved and that the Poles must not be allowed to get out of hand.

The firebrands of the revolution required some evidence of Russian brutality; first to make their own movement more virile—swords win revolutions, not songs—and second, that they might have propaganda with which to encourage their sympathizers abroad. The serfs had been released in Russia proper. It was necessary to blanket that great act of liberation and hide the fact that the Polish landowners did not wish to grant their peasant laborers freedom and land.

Fanatical individuals are commonly silent under suffering, but fanatical mobs or nations shriek at the slightest chastisement. The hullabaloo over the charge of the mounted police was out of all proportion to the suffering inflicted. "They rode roughshod over innocent women and children," etc. "Strike us, would you!" The instigators of revolt bade the Russians come on. "Do it again, if you dare!" We see the birth of *provocation* as a political force. The patriots were resolved that they would make the Russians strike them again, that they might have the right to protest more loudly.

Two days later they came forth in a spirit of bravado, threatening to seize Warsaw if not prevented by force. They got what they wanted. They were met by rifle fire; five of the agitators were killed and many were wounded. The significance of the Russian resort to force was exaggerated hysterically by all "lovers of Polish freedom." Thus, Alexander Herzen—"Before the crucifixion of women, the volleys fired at people singing hymns and prayers, all distinctions are erased, all questions are voiceless." Prince Gorchakof allowed the Poles to stage a national funeral for the five who

had been killed. Naturally there was a most imposing
funeral procession. One of the interesting features was
that many Jews followed the coffins. Jewish rabbis
were to be seen following Catholic priests. The purely
Polish movement and the Jewish revolutionary movement united in sympathy.

> Then first appeared an idea destined to play an important
> rôle, the idea of brotherhood with the Jews, one of the charac-
> teristic moments of that moral revolution which heralded revo-
> lution with weapons in hand.*

The Agricultural Society became a political body
and it framed a petition to the Tsar asserting Poland's
national rights and demanding a redress of grievances.
The petition was handed to Prince Michael Gorchakof
who forwarded it to Alexander II. It was received fa-
vorably and the Tsar granted the right of electing provincial and local assemblies, soviets. A Polish noble,
the Marquis Wielopolski, was appointed to a position
which was virtually that of premier, but nevertheless
subordinate to the authority of Gorchakof and the
Tsar. Gorchakof said that he had found in him the
"homme d'état par excellence." But the appointment
did not appease the Poles. What rankled was the Russian military and police control. As long as these existed it was difficult to raise an armed force, impossible
to equip and drill an army of liberation.

On May 29, 1861, Wielopolski issued the order
placing the Polish serfs upon the *obrok* system, giving
to each a money value instead of a land value and as-
sessing the cost of individual redemption. But the Marquis and his Polish cabinet were incapable of quieting

* Lensky, Z., *The Polish Rising of 1863.*

the patriotic and revolutionary enthusiasm of the students and the townspeople, even had they wished sincerely to do so. Patriotic fervor had now merged in a demand for the union of Poland and Lithuania as an independent kingdom, a cry obnoxious to the Russians because they considered Lithuania an integral part of Russia. "I did not partition Poland," said Alexander in annoyance, "but you would have me partition Russia for your sake."

On May 30 Prince Gorchakof died. The turmoil of Poland had proved too great a tax upon the health of the old soldier. Warsaw was no field of glory for him. His body was taken to Sebastopol—his express wish— and buried there. He was succeeded as viceroy by General Sukhozanet, who after a few months gave way to Count Lambert. Wielopolski resigned at the end of October. The patriotic leaders began the secret organization of an armed rising. The Tsar sent for Wielopolski in order to learn directly from his own lips what was the cause of all the trouble and what could be done to remedy it. The result of the conversation between the Marquis and the Tsar was that Alexander asked his brother Constantine to take over the post of viceroy. The Grand Duke Constantine Nikolaievitch therefore returned to the Polish capital, taking Wielopolski with him. Wielopolski resumed the position which he had previously held. This was in June, 1862. The day they arrived in Warsaw three men attempted to assassinate them. They were arrested and executed.

The Grand Duke Constantine appealed to all to cooperate with him to restore peace and happiness to Poland, but that was too late in the day. The Reds were engaged in terrorism, and now the Whites, though far from sharing the political convictions of the Reds, condoned the acts they should have condemned. Count Andrew Zamoiski, the leader of the Polish nobility, replied to the Grand Duke that now Poles could not be deterred by executions, imprisonments, banishments, and that nothing would stop the movement till the Poles had a government of their own to be loyal to. Constantine had Zamoiski railroaded abroad, and several of his supporting nobles were banished to the interior of Russia.

Then an endeavor was made to round up all the more fiery leaders of the Polish youth movement and recruit them into the Russian army. That was a clumsy way of trying to stem the patriotic tide. Lord Napier, the British Ambassador in St. Petersburg, who reported the matter to Earl Russell, characterized it in strong terms:

> In fact it was a design to make a clean sweep of the revolutionary youth of Poland, to shut up the most dangerous and energetic spirits in the restraints of the Russian army. It was simply a plan to kidnap the opposition, and carry it off to Siberia or the Caucasus. . . . It seemed to my humble judgment to be the single considerable error committed in Poland since the nomination of Marquis Wielopolski; yet it had the approval of that statesman and the sanction of the Grand Duke Constantine.

Few of the young men thus conscripted gave themselves up voluntarily. Some skulked in the cities; the greater part took refuge in the forests. Nevertheless on the night of January 14, 1863, the police and military in Warsaw rounded up about two thousand of the men who had been listed. This dealt a serious blow at the revolutionary movement in the Polish capital, but while it decreased the chances of an armed rising in Warsaw, it had the unfortunate effect of goading on the patriots. Desperate and impotent rage caused a speeding up of the preparations for rebellion. These preparations were in the hands of a "Central Committee," a Red organization allied to revolutionary bodies in western Europe. It had its agents and rich sympathizers in France and England and was busily employed in buying arms abroad. A consignment of three thousand rifles was confiscated by the Prussian Customs authorities as it was in act of being smuggled across the frontier to Poland.

The Grand Duke Constantine, despite this conscriptive effort, pursued a conciliatory policy which was highly unpopular in Russia even among liberals. It may be said that he was a failure as viceroy, but he would have been equally a failure if he had had recourse to sterner measures. It was necessary for the Poles to try conclusions with their masters and there could be no settled peace of any kind till the strength of the patriotic movement had been put to the test of physical violence.

On January 16, 1863, the Central Committee informed its members that the insurrection had begun. That was not enough. The members demanded action, so the night of January 22 was fixed for a general rising against the Russian authority: that was to be a new night of St. Bartholomew.

That night bridges on the St. Petersburg–Warsaw Railway were blown up and telegraph wires cut. These unwarranted precautions were taken, as if at a blow the Russian garrisons would be rendered helpless.

Actually nothing took place in Warsaw or the big

cities. The more dangerous outbreak was provincial. Some fifteen bands of armed revolutionaries attacked small military posts of the Russians. They emerged from the woods, led by the wanted conscripts who had been in hiding. The rising was completely unsuccessful. It was guerrilla warfare with only one objective—the killing of Russians. The latter proved quite capable of reducing these undisciplined bands of patriotic youths. The nation as a whole did not follow the lead of the Central Committee, although it was always ready to shout for the national flag. It allowed the enthusiasts to fight the battles and take the losses.*

The Central Committee fatuously changed its name to Provisional National Government of Poland. The Bartholomew night had been a failure, but the Committee still hoped that the whole population would be caught up in the movement. The rising was not utterly crushed at once. There were thousands of devoted patriots ready to carry it on and harass the Russians. So they forced the liberal Alexander II to act like a tyrant in Poland. There could be no further question of conciliation or compromise. If the Russians wished to remain in Poland they had no choice of action: the mutiny must be put down with utter ruthlessness.

In the light of subsequent history it may be considered that the Russians would have done better to let the Poles have their way and resurrect an independent kingdom. A bitter, hostile Poland proved to be a weakness to the Russian Empire. If the Russians proved incapable of living on good terms with Poles they proved

* "The movement appears at present to be confined to the town-people, backed by the clergy, the peasant population holding aloof." Dispatch by British Consul at Warsaw.

even more incapable of grappling with the Jews, of whom there were a very great number in Poland. Poland became a breeding ground for revolutionaries, and the exaggerated ill fame which tsardom obtained in England and America was largely due to the ceaseless propaganda of the implacable foes it had made.

But the circumstances of one era should not be superimposed on the history of another. In 1863 that *might is right* was hardly questioned. "Those might take who had the power and let them keep who can." Prussia required Schleswig-Holstein, and she took it from Denmark. Poland had been divided up and was held by militant states. Had Russia relinquished her share of Polish territory there was no guarantee that it would not have been rapidly overrun by Austria and Prussia.

Prussia regarded the Polish outbreak with great hostility. She at once concluded a pact of mutual service with Russia and allowed Russian troops the right to cross her frontier to round up armed bands of Polish revolutionaries taking refuge in German Poland. Perhaps Russia did not stand in need of sympathy and assistance from Prussia, but she had them.

On the other hand both France and England showed sympathy for Poland. In England the efforts of Alexander II to conciliate Poland and restore her liberty were not regarded as generosity but as a belated effort of justice. In France the revolutionary element sympathized with brother revolutionaries, but the Emperor Napoleon III was at first indisposed to quarrel with the Tsar in the matter. He made a suggestion that the Grand Duke Constantine be made King of Poland, but that suggestion Alexander ignored as an impertinence. England saw in the Polish question an opportunity of

cooling the friendly relationship between France and
Russia which had come into being since the Crimean
War. Franco-Russian amenities were regarded with the
utmost suspicion. Napoleon III was in a quandary. He
wished friendship with Alexander, had even proposed
alliance, but he also required the continued suffrage
and support of the French people. And he must weigh
in the balance the dynastic traditions; for Napoleon
Bonaparte had been a supporter of the Poles. There
was also in the Polish dispute a possibility of embroiling the Western Powers with Russia, which was very
attractive to him. He had rather attack Prussia than
Russia. But probably what really decided him to
threaten Russia was the flame of popular sentiment in
France.

The revolutionary republican complexion of the Polish rising appealed to the sympathies of the French as
a whole. Not a few Frenchmen proved their sympathy
by going to Poland to fight for the insurgents. The same
could hardly be said for British sympathy, which confined itself to words and "representations."

Among the Powers, Great Britain took the most active part in championing the right of Poland, endeavoring to line up the allies of the Crimean conflict
against Russia once more. It was assumed that, having
lost one war against England and France, Russia could
be intimidated by a similar combination. Very soon
after Alexander II came to the throne, Lord Palmerston endeavored to obtain a promise from the Tsar that
Polish national institutions would be restored. The
Russian Foreign Office replied that it was the intention
of the Tsar to make that restoration, but England was
warned that if pressure was exerted from without it

was probable that the Tsar would postpone his action. Palmerston decided to let well enough alone. No public demand was made on Russia and the Tsar at his coronation in Warsaw began his work of conciliation by the granting of a complete amnesty to Polish political exiles.

By the Treaty of Vienna in 1815 the Grand Duchy of Warsaw was erected into a kingdom of Poland, to be inseparably attached to the Empire of Russia, on condition that a parliament and national institutions were upheld.

It had been the contention of Nicholas I that by entering upon the armed rebellion of 1830–31, the Poles had forfeited the right to national institutions. Could Russia hold Poland inseparably attached if the Poles retained the power to have their own army and fight at will for their complete independence? The same argument was applied with added force when the rising of 1863 took place.

But with that impulsive liberal, Earl Russell, at the British Foreign Office, there was no desire to understand the difficulties of the Russian position. Russell not only plied St. Petersburg with the most urgent representations; he sounded Paris and Vienna with a view to joint intervention. He was successful in preventing Austria joining Prussia in the pact of mutual assistance against the Poles, though in fact the Emperor Franz Joseph, in possession of Polish Galicia, could not view with sympathy any resurgence of Polish nationalism. England, France and Austria called Russia's attention to the terms of the Treaty of Vienna, but the participation of Austria in the joint note was a weakness rather than an addition of strength.

Napoleon III suggested a Congress of the representatives of the Powers at Paris. But the *pour-parlers* and earnest dispatches were entirely without effect upon Russia's policy and action. Revolt had started in Poland; Russia went her way stubbornly and patiently, stamping it out. As a precaution against eventualities she mobilized half a million men.

In Russia Alexander II's firmness was applauded. Even the critics of his reform policy and of the emancipation of the serfs rallied to his support, especially the nobility which pronounced itself ready to make any sacrifice to preserve the integrity of the Empire. On the occasion of the Tsar's birthday, the twenty-ninth of April, 1863, he received a national deputation which came to congratulate him and present an address. Alexander II answered them:

I thank you, gentlemen, for your kind wishes and especially for your patriotic expression with regard to the Polish disturbance, and the claims of our enemies . . . your address, as well as those I am daily receiving from all parts and all classes of my Empire, has been a great comfort to me in the midst of my cares. I am proud of the sentiments. They constitute our force. While they exist and while we pray the Almighty to support us He will not forsake us, and the unity of the Russian Empire will be unassailable. Our friends hope to find us divided at home but they will be disappointed. At the very idea of dangers appearing on the Russian horizon, all classes rallied round the throne and showed a confidence in me, which is more acceptable than anything else. As yet I hope there will be no general war, but should it be destined for us, I am convinced that with the Divine aid we can defend the frontiers of the Empire and the provinces inseparably united with it. . . .

I thank you once more for your feelings of attachment, and I am sure you know that my entire life is devoted to promoting the welfare of our beloved country. Our mutual confidence is

a guarantee for the future prosperity of Russia. I thank you
once more from the depths of my heart.

The Polish rebels, faced with such resolution and
confidence, must have capitulated at a much earlier
stage but for the encouragement held out to them by
England and France that there might be armed intervention on their behalf. The wavering Polish nobility
threw in their lot with the Red organizations. They,
therefore, shared in the consequent chastisement inflicted on Poland by Count Michael Muravief and
others.

Count Muravief, with the face of an exceedingly unpleasant bulldog, was a man whose character and career seemed to have been frustrated by the liberalism of
Alexander II. Heavy and resolute, but also hysterical
and brutal, he was well chosen for a task of ruthless
pacification. To him the words of Tacitus have been
frequently applied: "He made a desert and called it
peace."

Nicholas Miliutin, because of his experience in dealing with the serf question, was sent to coöperate with
Muravief. These two had been bitterly hostile to one
another but they found that they could work together,
and Miliutin admitted that the severity of Muravief
was justifiable and salutary, because it prevented much
more blood being shed. Miliutin's task was to regulate
the position of the freed Polish serfs, and make them
sure that Russia was their friend. They had stood aloof
from the revolutionary struggle and had not thrown in
their lot with their masters.

The confiscation of a great part of the land of the
Polish nobles facilitated the distribution of land among

their freed serfs. And changing Poland from a great feudal domain into a land of farmers and farm laborers would make future attempts at revolution more difficult. The nobles were not allowed to flee abroad: they must remain on their diminished estates.

Miliutin, having considered the whole problem of the Polish land settlement, had been loth to undertake the task, but Alexander had refused to hear of his objections. The Tsar had practically commanded him to go to Poland. But Miliutin did good work there as he had done on the committee of emancipation.

Nevertheless the unfortunate fact remained that as a result of insurrection the position of the Polish nation as a whole was worse than before, and the proud kingdom was silent and prostrate, a Russian conquered province. The hatred of the Russians remained but it was impotent. The common cause made with the Jews remained, and out of that came the revolutionary terrorism of a later era. There was no further bid for Polish national liberty until the outburst of 1906, after the Russo-Japanese War, and that was unsustained. Liberation from the yoke of Russia came as by a miracle, one of the unexpected secondary results of the great war between Russia and Germany in 1914–18.

Michael Bakunin

Count Michael Muravief

V.

THE NIHILISTS

ALTHOUGH there had been a Red movement with a republican tendency in Poland this was not Nihilist. It had little in common with the Nihilist movement among the Russians. The use it made of the churches and of religious feeling is proof of that. There have been fewer Polish anarchists and Nihilists than is generally imagined. The reason may be found in the deep hold the Roman Catholic Church has on the Polish people. There were a few freethinkers —but that was the whole of the atheistic movement there.

The strength of the Roman Catholic Church lies in the fact that when the individual is in difficulties regarding his belief, his superior takes the responsibility from him. The Church is a solvent for doubt. Roman Catholics were probably less affected by the rationalism and scepticism of the nineteenth century than the adherents of any other church.

When the simple childish belief in the miracles and cosmic explanations of the Bible is shattered the individual is either forced to rely on the faith and knowledge of others, as in the Roman Church, or he must make a transition from literal interpretation to spiritual understanding, from naïve materialism to mysticism.

"Nature abhors a vacuum," says the science manual, and the human brain shows its incapacity for religion. The mind, our mentality, which cannot conceive of a vacuum, equally abhors eternity and infinity. But in these matters ordinary reason completely contradicts itself. Eternity is absurd; but an end of time is inconceivable. Infinity—that the deep of space sown with planets and stars extends endlessly—is beyond human reason; but that there should be a limit to space, beyond which is *nothing*, is also an absurdity. It must be admitted that space and time are beyond ordinary reason. It is therefore not surprising that the ordinary mental processes of observation, measuring and deduction are very fallible means of dealing with religious belief.

The vainest spirit in Heaven was Lucifer who is the symbol of reason. He finally revolted against God, gained the adherence of Beelzebub, the flesh; and a swarm of petty angels, the world, was eternally hurled from paradise.

There was nothing new in the rise of the rationalists in the middle of the nineteenth century. It had been symbolized in ages past in myth which shows eternal repetition. And rationalism is never content with its own successes, such as deducing evolution from ape to man and onwards; it must pick a quarrel with religion and endeavor to substitute its own theory for creed. Vanity is the first characteristic of reason, as humility is the first characteristic of religion. As soon as the naïve believer has got into doubt and found courage to deny the literal sense of the myth of Creation in Genesis, he has a feeling of superiority over his fellows, and that is augmented when he throws overboard Jonah and the whale, and becomes a ribald triumph when he rejects the virgin birth of Christ. He was born into a civilization built apparently on a literal belief in the revelation of God in the Old and New Testaments; he must find a new basis for humanity and civilization, and that soon.

For the love of God the freethinker commonly substitutes the need for the preservation of the species; for charity, philanthropy; for the Christian ethic, enlightened materialism. It is more important for him that there should be *progress* in the world than it is for the religious man. Progress means defeat of disease and death, elimination of poverty, a higher standard of general knowledge for all. But religion puts these things in a second place. For the religious man the multiplication of the species is no addition; wealth increases no man's stature, neither does poverty decrease it. But the divergence of opinion between freethinkers and religious men is not merely separation and difference; it is war. It is commonly thought that the religious make wars on the freethinkers. But the reverse is clearer. The freethinker is always at war with the religious man, and at war with any system based on the assumptions of religion.

In the sixties Holy Russia began to be seriously menaced by freethinkers. The Russian intellectual, the *intelligent*, arrived on the scene.

Turgenief, hot upon the emancipation of the serfs, portrayed the type. He is Bazarof, a student of natural science, a man with a long lean face and greenish eyes who says, "The door of my room won't shut but there is an English wash-basin. Well, that ought to be encouraged, an English wash-basin stands for progress!" He is soon telling an old-fashioned romantic Russian who prates about Schiller and Goethe that "a good chemist is twenty times as useful as any poet." He meets a peasant girl with an illegitimate baby and his comment is "She's a mother—she's all right." He attaches no significance to marriage. "What matters is that two and two make four and the rest is foolery."

"Is nature also foolery?" asks his disciple. "Yes, nature is foolery in the sense you understand it. Nature is not a church, it's a workshop."

Bazarof had the realism of Lenin who, however, did admit that the revolutionaries sometimes added two and two and made it five. There is in fact a direct intellectual connection between the Nihilists of the sixties and the accomplishers of the Marxian revolution.

The name "Nihilist," supposed to have been coined by Turgenief, does not so much imply a man who believes in nothing as a man who takes nothing for granted, accepts no authorities or traditions. As regards the Russia of his time, all must be destroyed and cleared away for a new edifice built on a basis of common sense. He is told that for all his brave words he is not dangerous; there are few Nihilists, but there are many millions of traditional Russians who must always oppose them. Bazarof ironically remarks that "All Moscow was burnt down by a farthing candle."

Almost every opinion expressed by Bazarof in this famous novel, *Fathers and Sons*, has a prophetic significance which shows it to be a work of unusual inspiration. There is this laconic retort that Moscow was fired by a candle, and then in May, 1862, the Nihilists did almost succeed in burning down St. Petersburg. Bazarof said all must be destroyed—and we find bands of revolutionaries acting on that creed and Russia plagued for years by provincial incendiarism.

When the serfs had been freed there were many

propagandists who held that the best thing the nobility and officialdom could do was to quit Russia and leave the working people to govern Russia for themselves.

It is surprising if Nihilism was entirely due to the new facilities for university education granted by Alexander II. Some influence must be ascribed to the exiles whose return had been allowed by the Tsar, especially the exiles returning from western Europe, imbued with advanced ideas which had attracted them there. In England it was the time of Bradlaugh, then writing under the pen name of "Iconoclast." In Germany the physician and philosopher Büchner exercised an influence on youth. In the forties and fifties many listened to and were infected by the socialist theories of François Fourier. He considered the coöperation of individuals preferable to the system of free competition. He wished the abolition of marriage. But he was too sentimental and irrational for his influence to last. Büchner was much more attractive to the embryo Nihilist and especially his book *Kraft und Stoff* which Bazarof recommended as a much more valuable work than Pushkin's poems. Büchner was an utter rebel against the German mystics and romantics, a materialist who believed that in effect all action depended ultimately upon physical force. Hence perhaps some of the violence of those Russians who accepted him as teacher.

Education was an experiment which had not been tried in Russia before 1850. Peter the Great's education of his Russians was largely a workshop education. He did not start the masses learning their alphabet, nor did he regard education as book learning. Nicholas I limited the number of students in each university to three hundred, as there was not scope for the employment of more than about fifteen hundred educated men a year in Russia.

In his reign it could not be said that there was a students' movement in Russia. The undergraduates were drawn almost exclusively from the noble class, and a plebeian who obtained a university education must go to Dorpat or abroad. But at once when Alexander II came to the throne he opened the universities to all and sundry, and the only limit to the number of students was the capacity of the universities themselves. At the same time the entrance examinations were made much stiffer. But the fees were reduced to an almost nominal figure. Richer students were allowed to organize committees of assistance and there were funds for students without means. By amateur theatricals, concerts, collections, the funds raised for the help of poor students soon reached considerable dimensions. The unselfishness of Russians where education was concerned was, and indeed is, a national characteristic. The ideals of liberty and fraternity were realized under the uniform of the student. At a step university education became accessible to the nation as a whole—and not merely the privilege of the aristocrat's son. At some universities women students began to be admitted.

Higher education became a national hobby. There was some confusion and overcrowding in the lecture rooms owing to the invasion of the classes by outsiders. "It was not even necessary to write your name in the register upon entering," says Panteleyef. "You just came in to a lecture and listened." The universities of St. Petersburg and Moscow were crowded by people standing wedged to the doors.

Such was the position at the lectures of the historian

Kostomarof, and it is said that everyone was patient and no one complained of bad air, heat and lack of elbow room.

Apart from the activity in the universities there were many evening lectures and public debates, to which the students flocked in great numbers. A four-hour lecture followed by a two-hour debate was the mid-nineteenth century equivalent of the cinema.

Chernyshevsky, Dobrolubof, Mikhailof, Lavrof, and of course the revolutionary Herzen sitting in London, were the leaders of the young. *Sovremennik* was the favorite periodical. The ferment was predominantly liberal. A national philosophy founded on national institutions and traditions had not yet found expression. Alexander II had allowed the philosophical and theological faculties to be separated. It had been found impracticable to combine philosophy with Byzantine theology. It was at a much later date that they re-combined and the St. Petersburg and Moscow religious and philosophical societies held the stage. Dostoievsky was probing deeper than anyone into the national soul, but then his message had only begun to be heard. After him would come Vladimir Solovyof, Trubetskoy and many others to synthesize or interpret a combination of religious doctrine and pure philosophy.

The debates of the sixties were mostly critical and negative. The dark Russia from which the students had emerged seemed so hideous that the natural demand was that every vestige of it be forthwith removed. The students were neither speculative nor romantic. They craved action. They said a man who did a piece of good work was worth any number of men who merely talked about it.

The denial of the church with its miracles and relics and wonder-working pictures was natural to many. How could the rotting hand in the catacombs of Kief do anyone any good? The peasants must be made to believe in the living hand, not in the dead hand. What a waste it was to have a hundred-odd saints' days in the year and all the idleness these holidays entailed!

The two authorities of the peasants, God and the Tsar, must be scaled down, and the peasant must learn to believe in himself. As tsars go, Alexander II was a redeeming exception—but was not even he superfluous? Russia was not born yesterday: she had come of years. She ought to be allowed the power to rule herself.

The stumbling-block was the illiteracy of the masses. But in that illiteracy the craving for action found one objective. Many students swore to devote their lives to the education of the peasantry. No objection was raised by the authorities, and many peasants' schools came into being. Apart from that, a number of students and sympathizers took it upon themselves to be colporteurs and village propagandists, carrying pamphlets and progressive talk to the liberated serfs.

If the intellectual of the time were asked, "What is it in the long run that you require?" he would have answered, "A Russia that is devoid of superstition, well-fed, well-housed, educated, with just dealings between man and man, peace and happiness." Such fundamental questions as "Can a Russian free himself from superstition of one kind or another? Can all Russians live in peace? Are they capable of justice to one another?" were not asked.

The desire for action was characteristically Russian.

The immense spaces of Russia, the melancholy northern light, the peasantry fixed in a traditional mode of
life, prey on the will. Poetry, which is a natural expression in Russia, only aggravated the feeling of frustration and impotency. The endless debates in the cities
were a similar aggravation of the "pain of the soul."
We must do something.

In England and the West, *doing* comes naturally,
and talking about it is less easy. In Russia the desire to
act is the salient characteristic, but even to begin to do
something seems overpoweringly difficult. For one intellectual who went to the peasants to work out his and
their salvation, a thousand remained merely talking
about the necessity. The ferment which was not merely
a ferment of words, but of frustration, lifted the lid,
boiled over. There were repeated demonstrations, what
in England would be called contemptuously "students'
rags." There was petty action—the scrawling of revolutionary slogans on walls, the clandestine sticking of
red posters on palace walls at night. Policemen were
kept busy erasing the threefold cry:

> *Independence for Poland!*
> *The Land for the Peasants!*
> *Freedom for Russia!*

And then there were arrests, the required persecutions,
which at last seemed to justify the students' clamorous
condemnation of the old Russia existing in the new.

The year 1861, which saw the emancipation of the
serfs, was the year when the students' movement
reached its first crisis. The new Minister of Education,
Admiral Putiatin, decided to try conclusions with the
universities. The University of St. Petersburg had been

a sort of republic of letters. Its corporate life, its mode of government by consent through election, was distasteful to Putiatin. He began to exercise his right to control university appointments, and at the same time to regulate the matriculation examinations and exclude from the university all who had not matriculated. He forbade students' parades. The students defied him and the university was temporarily closed. Professors resigned as a protest and student youth came out in the street singing and shouting its slogans in disorderly parade. As a result, some three hundred of them were captured by the Preobrazhensky Guards and clapped into the fortress of St. Peter and St. Paul. Alexander, who was in the Crimea at the time, hurried back to the capital. On his way back the first of a series of attempts on his life was made, someone firing a pistol into his coach as his horses galloped along—the railway between Moscow and the Crimea was not at that time completed.

The Tsar ridiculed the officiousness of the St. Petersburg authorities and at once set the imprisoned students free. But his clemency did nothing to appease the rebelliousness of the undergraduates. Serious measures had to be taken to regulate university life and the cause of higher education had suffered a set-back.

Curiously enough, all Russia became possessed by revolutionary ideas directly after the emancipation of the serfs. At the end of 1861, the nobles and provincial gentry presented an address protesting their ruin through the partial expropriation of their estates and demanded an extension of privileges. The necessity for a constitution and a limited monarchy was openly proclaimed by some of the disgruntled landowners. Later, in 1863, another address was made, demanding representative government—in order that the landowners might not be robbed again at the caprice of an absolute monarch. One may remark the curious lack of judgment here. A democratic regime in Russia would almost certainly have taken more from the pockets of the owners and improved the lot of the liberated serfs. The Tsar replied:

> The reforms prepared, and those already realized, prove my anxiety for the improvement, as far as possible, of the political organization of the country. The past must be a guarantee r the future. The right of initiative in the various parts of the work of gradually perfecting those reforms belongs only to me, and is indissolubly united to the autocratic power confided to me by the Almighty. Those who would frame the laws in future should begin by observing them. I am sure I shall never meet again with such obstacles from my faithful nobles.

Alexander's firmness aroused murderous animosity, and while on the one hand there were Nihilists who wished to kill him, there were gentry who whispered also of murder. Two plots to assassinate the Tsar were discovered in 1862 and 1863. Liberators may be popular but their good deeds are no guarantee of personal security. Quite the reverse: they unloose passions and make mortal enemies. In America on April 14, 1866, a Good Friday, Abraham Lincoln was assassinated. The same day in the following year was selected by the Nihilists for the taking off of Alexander. The student Karakozof, one of a small group of fanatics, made up his mind to the dastardly attempt. The Tsar was taking his morning walk in the Letny Gardens in St. Petersburg. His carriage, with the coachman in the box, was pulled up near the main gates of the gardens. At the carriage door Alexander stopped to put on his cloak, and Karakozof, who had been waiting his moment, raised his pistol to fire. A passer-by, a certain hatter, rushed in and hit the pistol upwards as the Nihilist fired, and the shot went wide. There was a rush of people to the scene, Karakozof was seized and might have been lynched on the spot but for the Tsar's remonstrance. The Tsar was quite cool: he was no coward. He asked Karakozof why he had wished to kill him. "Because you refused to give the land to the people," he replied.

It may have been that Karakozof was acting independently, on his own responsibility, and without mandate from organized Nihilism. He was bullied in prison by Count Muravief and his inquisitioners, but the incoherent babbling of a fanatic doomed to die, no matter what he say, is a poor basis for establishing the circumstances of a crime. During the trial that followed, evidence of a widespread organization of Nihilists was traced working partly in Russia but having the great part of its strength and support in Switzerland and in London. According to the Russian prosecutor, this organization was leagued for the destruction of all authority of Church and State, the abolition of private property, civil law and marriage. It was easy to gather together various statements of Nihilists and frame a formidable indictment of Nihilism, but it is doubtful whether at that time any such sweeping program had been formulated or agreed to by any organization of revolutionaries.

The dangerous anarchist, Michael Bakunin, arrived in London in 1861, where he was welcomed with open arms by Herzen, Ogaref and other revolutionaries as a veteran heroic leader. England was the traditional refuge of political exiles and the right of asylum was jealously guarded by the British public. Bakunin was quite safe in London as long as he did not threaten British institutions. With his arrival London became the headquarters of the Nihilists.

Bakunin had had an adventurous and stormy career. He was by birth an aristocrat, strongly connected in Russian society. His family had owned many serfs; he had been a cadet at the School of Artillery in St. Petersburg; designed for a commission in the Guards, he was bitterly disappointed when he found himself gazetted to a line regiment. The duties bored him and he resigned his commission. He retired to live in Moscow. That was in 1836. In 1839 he went into voluntary exile in Germany and at Berlin became obsessed by the teachings of Hegel which he interpreted in a way peculiarly his own. Because he did not return to Russia at the command of Nicholas I, in 1843 the Russian Senate deprived him of nobility and rank, confiscated what personal property he had in Russia, and sentenced him to penal servitude in Siberia in case he should return. He was therefore cut off from the inheritance of his father's serfs and land. He became a socialist and a champion of freedom. He took part in the revolutionary movement in Paris in 1848. He was obliged to leave France but he threw himself with ardor into the struggles going on in Germany and Austria. Driven out of Austria, he went to Saxony. On May 9, 1849, he was the dominant figure in the defence of Dresden against the Saxon and Prussian troops. He was captured at Chemnitz on the following day after the crushing of revolution in Dresden. He was kept a prisoner in the fortress of Königstein for a year. The Saxon Government condemned him to death, but handed him over to the Austrian authorities. The Austrians kept him a year in prison and then condemned him to death again. But they in turn handed him over to Nicholas I, who shut him in the fortress of St. Peter and St. Paul. He remained five years in this dreadful prison. Nicholas I died; Alexander II came to the throne; there was a general amnesty for prisoners. But Bakunin was considered too dangerous to be set at liberty. Instead he was banished to eastern Siberia, not, it is true, to penal servitude there, but to freedom in exile. He used his opportunity and his influence to obtain permission to settle in the very lightly policed Amur territory. Thence it was easy for him to break *parole* and escape. So the year 1861 saw him in London, forty-seven years of age, unbroken, possessed of immense energy and strength of personality. He was a tall man combining unusual physical strength and power of endurance with a powerful intellect. He very soon dislodged Herzen from the leadership and when he began to edit *Kolokol* that journal ceased to be merely a reform sheet and became almost purely Nihilist in tendency.

Bakunin was naturally a life-long foe of tsardom, but he was more than that. He was opposed to all forms of government, even to Socialism and Constitutionalism, opposed to all laws except to those recognized as the laws of nature. He was a militant anarchist. His lineal successor was Peter Kropotkin, who though an anarchist was of a much more pacific temper. Alexander Herzen who sentimentally referred to his followers as the "children of Bazarof" was far from

belonging to the straight sect of anarchists and Nihilists. He was not indignant at acts of terrorism and destruction, never thought his cause was injured by these
outrages, but was violently indignant at the oppressive
and precautionary measures taken by the other side.
Herzen merely asked for reform and liberty, for more
reform and more liberty. He was not one of those who
demanded the complete destruction of existing institutions in order to enable mankind to live ideally. But
his one-sided sympathy gave a moral sanction to the
deeds of extremists and fanatics.

In the year following the attempt by Karakozof another attempt was made on the life of Alexander II.
As he was driving in Paris in June, 1868, in an open
carriage with the Emperor Napoleon III, Berezovski, a
Polish refugee, fired two shots at him. Like Karakozof,
he also missed his aim. Alexander did not seem to be in
any way perturbed: he was getting used to attempts on
his life. People began to say that the Tsar bore a
charmed existence.

VI.

THE PROGRESS OF REFORM

ALL that a nation should require is natural development, and the most it can ask of leadership is vision and judgment. But there is no reason why the progress of development should conform to a mathematical formula. It is not an arithmetical progression. Herzen characterized the Russian movement as "three paces forward and two back," but it was not as simple as that.

The Tsar was an autocrat, "self-upholding" as an Englishman has translated the word *samoderzhavny*. He was Emperor and there is a difference between an empire and a nation. A nation grows or dies; an empire increases or diminishes—it is an artificial aggregation. Empire represents force over others. The British Empire, as far as the self-governing dominions are concerned, is not an empire but a loosely-federated commonwealth. An empire may be powerful while the constituents, individuals and races are very backward. But Alexander II, both Tsar and Emperor, had inherited a diminished autocratic power and he voluntarily diminished it much further. For the first time in its history the Russian nation took a prior place. The nation was first, the sovereign was second. Tsardom in itself seemed to have no particular prospect of extension of power, but the nation seemed to have every possibility.

The nation had begun to have a voice and be aware of itself in the reign of Alexander I. It had still more voice in the reign of Nicholas I, in spite of the repressive despotism of that sovereign. In the reign of Alexander II there was a considerable volume of articulate sound coming from the nation. Definitely the nation had arrived on the scene, and there were two Russias: one, the old tsardom against which revolutionaries fulminated; and two, the emerging Russian democracy.

Gargantua, when he was born, cried lustily for drink, and it was natural in that Gargantuan prodigy, the Russian nation, that it should cry lustily for something. It was natural that it should cry out that it was the supreme monster in Russia and that the other pre-historic-looking monster must vanish. Whatever it was *given*, the Russian nation took as a right, and demanded more. It had suffered so much in the slavish bondage of empire that it could not look upon the monarch as the symbol of its unity and common interests, could not see that when the tsar gave something, the nation gave itself something also. The fact that autocracy parted with its privileges was more patent than that the nation assumed new responsibilities.

In the new Russia which had emerged we distinguish two types or groups. There was a Russia which was opposed to reform and a Russia that welcomed it. In the first were lumped together in the critical mind the "lackeys of tsardom," those who battened on the state revenues and enjoyed power and authority delegated by the tsar. In the second were the independent gentry and the *Raznochintsi*, plebeians, the writers, artists, professors, etc.

The first category remained powerful enough and militant, even aggressive in its determination to defend its privileges and perquisites. To say that it regarded

the awakening nation with suspicion would be to use
a mild phrase. Some were merely suspicious of it; some
were disgusted by it; many were obsessed by sheer hate
of it. They were, for the most part, men who ate and
drank prodigiously. Their highest intellectual pleasure
was the exercise of military or police authority or of the
social authority given by rank. They squabbled and
quarrelled among themselves; there was much intrigue,
place hunting, parasitism, sycophancy. There was not
much culture. Occasionally there was real administrative ability or military capacity. But the men of this
class were, in effect, the retainers and bodyguard of a
feudal sovereign. In theory, they were implicitly obedient to the tsar. They were instruments of the old-fashioned tsardom and if that tsardom relinquished its
power or delegated its authority to the nation, they
mechanically lost an equivalent amount of power, prestige and income. It was natural in them to believe that
the nation was the property of the tsardom, to be used
for the tsar's and their profit. Also they were jealous if
the tsar did anything for anyone outside their rank.
There were others whose character cannot be interpreted as gross, vulgar, selfish; there were ascetics, there
were some who had formulated for themselves a religion of absolute monarchy; but the general characterization stands.

Facing this old guard of Russian despotism was the
awakening Russian nation. It would be as easy to paint
the nation white as to paint the instruments of tsardom
black. Anything young and growing invites human
sympathy. But Holy Russia was not utterly saintly.
The dark pattern which had distinguished certain tsars

in Russia's history was not entirely lacking in the Russian people themselves. There were many destructive elements in their character which, once fully liberated, might make an end of the people as well as of the tsardom. An obvious feature of the life of the nation gaining freedom was the bitter conflict of egoists which ensued. It has been said that the meanest Russian peasant is a tsar. Remove the actual tsar and you have millions of petty tsars. When revolution was ultimately achieved and the tsardom destroyed, it was soon seen that freedom and democracy were impracticable in Russia. The nation must live under authority, if not under a monarch at least under a Communist dictator, and relinquish even the measure of freedom it had previously wrested from the tsars.

The question in the sixties and especially after the emancipation of the serfs was, "What is to be the future of the Russian people?" There was no such phrase as "nation planning," but there were enthusiastic workers whose activities implied a plan or at least an objective. There were those voiced in Turgenief's novel, starkly claiming bread as the objective, and there was Dostoievsky reminding man that he does not live by bread alone. There was Nicholas Miliutin, who went a little further in materialism and claimed that prosperity and domestic comfort were the inheritance of the masses. And there was Tolstoy, turning with avidity to the program of teaching the peasants to read and write. It is said that Alexander II warmly admired British institutions and envisaged the ballot-box and industrialism. Some wished the complete dispossession of the large landowners—the land for the people. Others in a very different political camp desired to see a nation of peasant proprietors, keeping the proletarian population at a minimum.

The greatest enthusiasm was displayed for the cause of teaching the masses, and that was allied with medical missionary zeal. The peasants and their families must have enough to eat. Their babies must not be allowed to die. Infant mortality must be checked. Those large families, so common in the village, a dozen or so children to each mother, must be kept alive and raised to be strong self-respecting men and women. To the question, "What work will there be for this multiplied population?" the answer was: "Give them more land, ever more land. Russia properly farmed can support four hundred millions. And what then? Then, Siberia, China, Asia, the world."

The chief object of popular education would seem to have been to help the peasants out of religious superstition, fit them to vote responsibly and with enlightenment, equip them mentally so that they could safeguard their rights and distinguish between friends and foes. "Progress in Russia," declared Tolstoy, "must be based on popular education!" But Tolstoy insisted that such education must not be compulsory. The peasant must first desire to learn, otherwise he would learn nothing of value.

Little was heard of what is called the "ladder of education." A ladder implies selection: all cannot get on the ladder. The new education was education in the mass, an attempt to raise the peasantry as a whole from the zero level of illiteracy. After the emancipation of the serfs the village communes were encouraged to start schools for the children of the serfs. In these there was scope for many university men to come and devote their lives to the cause of education. They came, flaming with enthusiasm, from the debates in the universities of St. Petersburg, Moscow, Kharkof and other cities. They were patient and devoted. But they certainly encountered a dullness and stupidity which would make most teachers despair. A child whose mind refused to take four rolls from five and give a one-roll answer caused even Tolstoy to lose patience. But that is not to say that there were not potentialities for book learning and mental training among the peasants' children. The majority remained where they were before the schools were opened; a small minority profited. It was not long before at least a few peasant-born students were on the way to the university. That at least was natural development: the intelligence of a nation should draw on all classes.

Alexander II has been generally known in Russia as the Tsar-Liberator, chiefly because he freed the serfs. But he has a further claim to the title. He was probably the only tsar who believed in Freedom. It may have been due to a rebellion of his spirit against the military authority assumed by his father and his father's subordinates over everyone and everything in the realm. Or it may have been simply the spirit of the time in Europe affecting a will which was predisposed to freedom through a belief in man. By virtue of his inauguration of freedom in Russia, he is entitled to be considered a great tsar.

The granting of political freedom consists firstly in the permission to choose one's own conduct, to arrange one's domestic and local affairs without interference from a superior authority. Freedom, it may be pointed out, is always freedom within certain limits. The freedom of the individual is bounded by the rights of neighbors and in all states the rights of the neighbor are protected by law. The freedom of a corporate group is likewise limited by the rights of neighboring groups, and the freedom of states by the rights of neighboring states.

There is another truism which is not quite so obvious. One cannot have the full benefit of one's own freedom while one denies freedom to others. The freedom of the individual is not complete while he denies freedom to others, the freedom of one race is not complete while it holds another in bondage.

The freedom which seemed promised Russia under Alexander II was a freedom within the bounds of authority, because there must be an authority to check infringements of the right of others. The tsar remained the supreme arbiter of rights. This conception of tsardom was destroyed by the revolutionary terrorism when it killed Alexander in 1881, and the ruins were swept away by his son and heir, Alexander III.

The institution of the zemstvos, the Russian county councils, by the statute of January 1, 1864, was the first important development after the emancipation of the serfs.

Rural councils were in existence, elected by the volost, that is, by small groups of villages, but the jurisdiction of these rural councils was vague and most of their decisions seemed to lack authority owing to the absence of clearly-defined limitations of the rights of the ex-serf-owners. Some superior local authority was obviously necessary, and to Miliutin was intrusted the duty of evolving a scheme. He was displaced owing to suspicion of his revolutionary tendencies, but the work went on under his successor, Valuyef.

The zemstvo was elected on a limited franchise. Landowners possessing estates valued at 15,000 roubles or over; manufacturers with an annual turn-over of 6,000 roubles or more; townspeople with a corresponding income or estate—each had a vote. The peasantry were allowed so many votes per volost, and business men could also club together to obtain a vote. This basis of representation worked out as follows:

Gentry,	43 per cent
Peasantry,	38 per cent
Others,	19 per cent.

Professor Vinogradoff in his book on Russian self-government, enumerates the departments of zemstvo activity:

(1) imposition and collection of provincial and district rates and services in kind; (2) the management of property belonging to the Zemstvos; (3) taking care of a sufficiency of food and other supplies and measures of relief in case of shortage; (4) the construction and keeping in good order of roads, canals, quays and other means of communication; (5) arrangements as to the mutual insurance of local bodies; (6) the rearrangement of hospitals, charity organisations, asylums, relief of the poor and of the sick; (7) measures of public health, of veterinary supervision and treatment; (8) the prevention and suppression of fires; (9) the spread of popular education and participation in the management of schools and other institutions of enlightenment; (10) assistance to industry and commerce, measures for checking the ravages of insects and the diseases of plants; (11) the performance of obligations imposed on localities for the benefit of the military and civil administration, e.g., the provision of barracks or the quartering of soldiers.*

* Vinogradoff, Paul, *Self-Government in Russia.*

The zemstvos did much for popular education. In the period from the institution of these local authorities until the end of the reign of Alexander II, some 14,500 schools were opened.

In other matters, the zemstvo relieved the central bureaucratic authorities of much cumbersome business and helped to consolidate the tsardom against revolutionary attack. Although the zemstvos were eventually swept away in the revolution of 1917–18, they had never been the target of revolutionary attack. The chief opposition they encountered was from the stalwarts of the old regime. Some of these still grudged the loss of privilege and position; others were chagrined by the disappearance of opportunities of graft and self-enrichment at the public's expense. That is not to say that the zemstvos were entirely free of corruption; no Russian institution could be entirely pure in this respect. Certain Eastern or Turkish elements in Russian character make incorruptibility a rarity. In Russia "every little bee takes a little bribe from every little flower." But the zemstvos gave hope to men of honor and integrity and these also have never been lacking in Russia. Alexander II set his face firmly against the ineradicable evil of corruption, and raised salaries all round, that the plea might not be made "we are too poor to exist without bribes."

The gain of local self-government was one of increased administrative efficiency, but it was also a strong moral gain for the Russian people. In a sense Russia had come of age. The nation had begun to wish to be responsible for its own affairs, and the wish was in part gratified. Local self-government raised the standard of the dignity of the people. The serfs had been freed. No man now was the property of any other man. The supreme local authority of the lord of the manor had gone. Gentry had to work on committees, devise plans for their own improvement, raise taxes for their own budgets, for schools, sanitation, hospitals, municipal enterprises.

Alexander did much to help Russia to believe in herself, to permit Ivan Ivanovitch to believe that indeed he was a man. For the slave-mentality existed after the slaves were freed. In his religion, the peasant persistently called himself a "slave of God" and knew nothing of the God "whose service is perfect freedom." The released serf was often slavishly humble with his superior neighbor, bestially humble. At a stroke of the pen the Tsar removed one sort of humiliation. He took the question of corporal punishment into his own hands and abolished it forthwith. He could not get it abolished by consent; too many Russians persisted in believing that there was biblical warrant for thrashing wrong-doers; too many believed that the knout was holy, an emblem of Russian national greatness. But flogging has worse moral effects than other punishments. After being flogged by his fellow man, even by an official in uniform, a man is hopelessly degraded, no matter what his offence.

The Grand Duke Constantine made himself responsible for the abolition of flogging in the navy. The new War Minister, Dimitry Miliutin, took steps to stop corporal punishment in the army. Peter Valuyef, Minister of the Interior, saw to it that the flogging of the peasants by landowners and by irresponsible police officers ceased. Indeed the minister most responsible for carrying out the new order was Valuyef. Valuyef was one of the most capable helpers of Alexander II. He had been a vigorous critic of the government of Nicholas I. Writing in retirement at Riga, he had made such a vigorous onslaught on abuses that it was generally thought he could have no official career in Russia. But Alexander had observed that Valuyef's ideas were very much his own. When in 1856 the governorship of Courland became vacant the Tsar struck out all the names in the list of candidates which was placed before him and wrote across the list, "I have got my own candidate." His appointment was Valuyef. At the same time this critic of the administration was made Privy Councillor. Some years passed and the aged Lanskoy resigned from the Ministry of the Interior. The post was given to Peter Valuyef.

Valuyef had a very difficult task steering a course between exuberant freedom and malevolent reaction, sometimes himself appearing to be a revolutionary, and other times appearing to be a reactionary. To him came the difficult problem of appeasing the student movement. He had to stop the arson of Nihilists and to curb the insubordination of the nobles. And although a liberal, he was bound to restrain the press, and upon occasion he was obliged to confiscate certain journals.

Among other reforms which Valuyef effected during his term of office, was the abolition of the local governmental monopoly of the sale of spirits. What he was chiefly opposed to in the monopoly was the system of *otkup* whereby the privilege of manufacturing and selling vodka was farmed out to certain individuals. This had resulted in much corruption, leakage both of money and of spirits, cheap bad vodka in many districts and a deplorable condition of drunkenness among the peasants. He declared that the vodka leaseholders had the whole body of police in their power and that with their help they were not only in a position to poison the life of the lower classes but to upset all arrangements of the Government which did not suit their purpose.

Valuyef had also seen the necessity for a reform of the courts. By all accounts, there was little justice to be had by a poor man in Russia before the reign of Alexander. "At the thought of the old courts my hair stands on end, my blood goes chill," wrote A. S. Aksakof. While the serf-owners had the right to punish their serfs and even to banish them to Siberia upon a personal accusation alone, there obviously could be little national justice. The laws were confused by innumerable privileges and traditions. A law which held for one class did not hold for another. At the best a rough and ready *equity* was administered; at the worst, judgment was dependent on caprice, brutality, prejudice. Cases were tried behind closed doors, often in the absence of the prisoner, and punishments were often awarded without a statement of the crime.

After the emancipation of the serfs, Count Panin was replaced at the Ministry of Justice by Zamiatin. In 1862, a plan of reform for the courts was submitted to the Emperor. This laid down the principles of impartiality of judges; equality of all citizens of whatever class in the eyes of the law; independence of the courts from administrative interference; good pay for judges, but they must possess the necessary legal training and education; appointments to be permanent; public hearing of all cases. Magistrates for the hearing of petty cases of law infringement were to be elected by the zemstvos. In more important cases, trial by jury was instituted. Counsel for defence was allowed.

An energetic worker for this great reform was Zarudny, State Secretary of the Senate. The whole plan was approved by the Tsar and became operative shortly after the constitution of the zemstvos. The opening of the new courts with the reformed procedure was in the year 1866.

To a sense of freedom was added a sense of security. Security is no doubt an aspect of freedom but it is not the same thing. There is another aspect which may be differentiated as liberty. There was freedom; there was increased security, but liberty lagged. Men and women must be careful in the voicing of their political opinions; authors and editors of journals must submit all they wished to publish to the scrutiny of a censor. The granting of liberty of opinion was bound to be the most difficult of all the reforms carried out by Alexander II.

The history of the press runs between liberty and license. Absence of liberty is so great an evil that it commonly blinds the critics to the other evil of license. Public opinion through the channels of the press cleanses public morals; but who shall cleanse the press? The river Rhine cleanses the city of Cologne,

> But tell me, nymphs, what power divine
> Shall henceforth wash the river Rhine.

The complete liberty of the press is ideal when the control of the press is democratic and impartial. When it voices violently the opinions of a minority, its continued immunity from restraint becomes a problem for authority. Alexander II and his functionaries swayed back and forth between the granting of freedom to journalism and the withholding of freedom. When Alexander came to the throne he relaxed the control of censorship. The newspapers were allowed to discuss domestic and foreign politics and at once ceased to have that purely literary interest of the previous era. The modern political newspaper made a beginning in Russia. Certain subjects were still banned. From 1857 onwards discussion of the serf problem was allowed in the press. The Tsar ordered that nothing should be censored unless it displayed a distinctly dangerous tendency. Literate Russia buzzed with political journalism, the greater part of which was of a liberal and idealistic character.

But in 1861, due to the students' movement, there was a manifest revolutionary tendency in the radical journals, and the new Minister of the Interior, Valuyef, persistently harassed the censor Golovin to be more strict; Golovin, a liberal, entreated the Tsar to separate the function of censorship from the authority of the Ministry of the Interior. This was allowed and he was invited to present a charter for editors and publishers, setting forth clearly what was permitted and what was not. Most newspapers were then allowed to appear without previous submission to the censor's office. The date when these new regulations came into effect was September 14, 1865. But after the attempt on the life of the Tsar in 1866 there was again severe repression of the radical press.

Liberty in Russia should have meant liberty also for the subject races living on the borders of the Empire. It was the intention of Alexander II that there should be equal freedom in these regions. We have seen how his plans miscarried in Poland. It was impossible to conciliate Poland by qualified freedom. A caged people cannot be conciliated. In Finland, the Tsar's efforts were more fruitful. Alexander was partial to Finland and one of his early acts was to restore home rule to the Finns. On September 17, 1862, he opened the Finnish Diet. From a throne set up in the House of Legislature in Helsingfors, he declared:

I desire to guard the inviolable principle of constitutional monarchy ingrained in the character of the Finlanders, and stamped on their laws and customs. Representatives of the Grand-Duchy, it is for you to prove by the dignity and the calm moderation of your debates that in the hands of a discreet people, resolved to coöperate with its sovereign in a practical sense, liberal institutions, so far from being a danger, become a guarantee of order and prosperity. I declare the session of the Diet opened.

The Finns have not the history and tradition of the Poles. They have not been a nation. They were content to be free of Swedish dominance and to manage their own affairs under the Russian crown. It was left to Nicholas II, by a repressive policy of Russianization, to make the Finns violently antagonistic to Russia.

There were other racial minorities in Russia, the chief of which was the Jews. It cannot be said that Alexander II was in any sense Judophile, but he was more reasonable and tolerant in dealing with the Jews than any other tsar before or since. He abolished many of the disabilities of the Jews, making their position better in Russia and Poland than in most other countries of central Europe. There was considerable Jewish migration into Poland from Germany and Austria, and thence into Russia proper. The Jews were allowed to reside in Russian towns, but they were still kept from possessing land except within the pale of settlement. They were still not allowed to settle on the land in central or eastern Russia. But they were allowed scope in business, which seems to be their special *milieu*, and they did much to organize and increase Russian commerce and industrialism in Alexander's reign.

Jews were allowed in the universities, and in Alexander's reign the first Jewish professor was appointed. They had access to some of the learned professions. Anti-Semitism smouldered but it was kept within bounds by the common belief that Alexander II was partial to the Jews. That is not to say that there was not a Jewish movement for the complete removal of the irksome disabilities which still prevailed. An interesting result of this movement was the visit of the aged and patriarchal-looking Sir Moses Montesiore in 1872. He was ninety years of age and came to pray the Tsar for more freedom for his people. He was received in audience by Alexander II, who listened to him sympathetically and with a certain warmth of admiration. Sir Moses said he was enchanted with his audience. He did not expect any immediate result of his appeal but was content to leave it to the impression produced and the working of time.*

* *See* Loftus, Lord Augustus, *Diplomatic Reminiscences.*

VII.

THE FINANCING OF REFORM

THE expense of the Crimean War had caused the first fall in the value of the rouble. In the two years following the conflict, there was a great increase in Russia's imports accompanied by little increase in exports, an unfavorable trade balance which caused the devaluation of the currency to continue. Seven hundred and eighty millions of currency were backed by one hundred and nineteen millions of gold and silver in 1858. The paper rouble could not be exchanged for gold in St. Petersburg. It began to be the sport of speculators in exchange.

It is said that the instability of the rouble was aggravated by the exodus abroad of numbers of rich Russians, using their fortunes to live extravagantly in Paris and elsewhere. Large quantities of paper roubles were on offer in western Europe. Nicholas I had held his subjects severely within the bounds of the Empire. Passports for travel were difficult to obtain and were only for limited periods. Failure to return to Russia upon the expiration of the visa commonly resulted in a confiscation of estate in Russia; thus the drain of Russian extravagance abroad was averted. But Alexander II lifted the ban on foreign travel. In his reign it was comparatively easy to obtain permission to go abroad. Not only the rich went out of the country at will, but masses of student youths flocked to Geneva and the

universities of the West. After the emancipation of the
serfs, the rush to the gay cities of the West by young
aristocrats and squires with the redemption money in
their pockets did much to weaken the currency. At the
same time, the great reforms inaugurated by Alexander
II made immense demands upon the financial resources
of the state. The menace of war on Russia by England
and France on behalf of Poland in 1863 also depressed
the speculative value of the rouble.

But in 1862 the Tsar found a capable and energetic
Minister of Finance in the person of Count Michael
Reitern. Reitern was forty-two years of age and he remained finance minister for almost the whole of the
rest of the reign of Alexander II. He was a travelled
man who had visited both England and the United
States at the behest of the sovereign. He had been
largely employed by Nicholas I and Alexander II, and
had made himself a specialist in railway business and
banking. He had already done much in the reform of
the banking system and of the procedure of the State
Bank. On him devolved the problem of adjusting the
financial difficulties caused by the failure of some of
the peasants to pay the whole of their redemption
money. He was a liberal-minded man of culture and
attainment, who loved his country and was in soul and
will committed to change and reconstruction. His able
administration set the seal of genuineness upon the
Tsar's achievements. Count Michael Reitern, however,
commenced his career as Finance Minister by a failure,
attempting to raise the value of the rouble by a mechanical operation. There resulted a commercial and
financial crisis which almost amounted to a crash. But
he saw his error and admitted that the rouble could

only be raised by increasing the exports of Russia and obtaining a favorable trade balance.

With a view to organizing a greater export of wheat he made it his first task to build more railways and extend those already existing. Railway construction under the direction of General Kleinmichel in the reign of Nicholas I had been costly and little had been achieved beyond the St. Petersburg-Moscow line. The Crimean War retarded the development, which in any case had been slow. After the war a company registered in Paris took large contracts but its capital was not fully subscribed. The main function of the company would appear not to have been to construct railways but to graft on the Russians. International capital might hold benefits for Russia in exploiting its resources, but from the first it showed itself as merely predatory.

In 1861 the agreement with the French company was cancelled by mutual consent of the company and the Russian Government. As the capital of this concern was held more in Russia than abroad, the headquarters of the company was transferred to St. Petersburg. In 1863, Reitern in coöperation with Melnikof, Minister of Communications, advised the Tsar to resume construction. The lines which ended in fields must be taken to towns. The agricultural centers must be properly served. A new plan of development of railroads, based on the necessities for the export of wheat, was submitted. The most important proposals were those for lines from the black-earth regions and Kief to Odessa. The Moscow-Sebastopol railway would also be carried through as originally planned. All the great ports must be served, not only those of the Black Sea, but Riga and Libau on the Baltic. If by means of railways double the amount of wheat could be got out of the country—the rouble would be saved.

But it was not found possible to attract foreign capital for railway enterprise. English financiers hung back even when offered extremely advantageous terms, including the entry of British goods to Sebastopol free of tariff. It was said abroad that railway construction in Russia presented great difficulties and that when railways were constructed they proved to be completely unprofitable—false judgment in both instances. The Russians were forced to carry on the work on their own resources. That was fortunate for them. They found they could build at a cost of 50,000 roubles per verst, whereas the Paris company had been building at a cost of 100,000 roubles per verst. The first new railway especially that connecting Moscow and Riazan at once produced good dividends. The Government, though guaranteeing a minimum dividend of 5 per cent, was not called upon to pay any money to the Russian concession-holders. A new faith in railways sprang up, and rich Russians were eager to invest in them. The new zemstvos also began to help to undertake railway construction. The modest program of adding 5,000 versts of railway between 1865 and 1875 was easily achieved. Actually 12,000 versts of railroad were added during the ten years. By 1875 Russia already possessed a total of 17,000 versts of railroad, nearly 13,000 miles.

Nevertheless the Russian budget showed a heavy deficit every year. It was not until 1875 that a surplus was realized. There was a long period of forced sales and departmental economy. The reorganization of the army, very necessary after the Crimean War which had shown Russia to be out of date in military equipment, was postponed indefinitely. Every minister was invited to reduce the expense of his department. Reitern insisted on an honest administration and did much to reduce the extent of the appalling corruption which had been prevalent. He welcomed the separating of the judicial from the administrative authorities because that stopped the buying of justice and the intimidation of witnesses. He was a stickler for the correct presentation of accounts, check and counter-check, on financial control everywhere.

As was natural, Reitern made many enemies among those who were denied the opportunity of enriching themselves at the public expense. In the reaction which took place after the attempt by Karakozof on the life of the Emperor, the intrepid Finance Minister came near losing his post and the confidence of the Tsar. In that year, 1866, several liberal ministers were replaced by men of a different stamp. Golovin left the ministry of Education to be replaced by Count Dimitry Tolstoy. Prince Dolgoruky ceased to be head of police and his place was taken by Count Shuvalof. These men were conservative functionaries, regarded by men of the Left as reactionaries and by those on the Right as philanthropists. In any case they both sought the downfall of Reitern. The Finance Minister was obliged to make a strong personal appeal to the Tsar which he did in a long and notable memorandum on September 29, 1866. He wrote as follows:

Your Imperial Majesty has laid upon me the duty of dealing with the present financial difficulties and devising those measures which seem necessary for the betterment of the financial and economic conditions of the State.

The financial and economic condition is complicated, depending not only on fiscal measures, but on the general development of state and people. While, on the one hand, it is undoubted that extravagance, bad administration, and ill-calculated and repressive fiscal measures must disorganize finance and the economic conditions of the state, yet on the other hand, it is also true that financial difficulties are the inevitable result of the circumstances of an epoch of reform, a symptom of the process taking place within the social organism. Russia emerged from the Crimean War tired by the gigantic struggle, exhausted financially, having issued some 400,000,000 rouble credit notes. The moral authority of the Government was undermined. The war had disclosed many defects both in the civil and military administration. The country seemed to lose that dominant position in Europe which had been hers after 1815; her influence was impaired abroad, while in Russia itself there was distrust in the power and capacity of the Government.

After the Crimean War, had the Government wished to return to the administrative tradition of the early part of the century, opposing the march of the new era, it would have had to face an insurmountable obstacle, if not in open, at least in passive opposition, which might have shaken eventually the loyalty of the nation, the broad faith on which is founded the monarchic principle. To the good fortune of Russia, your Imperial Majesty has chosen a different road. The history of all nations demonstrates that revolutions can only be averted by timely reform, granting to the nation in advance in a peaceful way the things which it demands in revolutions. The reforms which render immortal the reign of Your Imperial Majesty have not been simply those superficial social changes which are, in general, undertaken by governments. The roots of the evils have been boldly and manfully attacked. Millions of people have been called to citizenship; the system of graft, tolerated and even encouraged officially, has fallen, and for the first time an honest administration has been made possible; legal authority has been made independent of the Government; the principle of popular self-government has been established by the institution of the zemstvos. These reforms and many others, in their infancy, have changed Russia, and I make bold to say, changed her for the better; but still they have not been entirely assimilated. Much time, much labor, much sacrifice is still necessary before Russia can emerge from the transition stage and establish herself firmly on the new and reasonable foundation. Only when economic development has sufficiently progressed will credit be established and financial stability ensured.

Count Reitern went on to characterize his financial measures during the years 1862–66, and concluded:

In view of this line of action, it is possible to hope that in the course of a few years the economic forces of Russia will be strengthened and that transformation of Russia which constitutes the glory of the reign of Your Imperial Majesty will not be stopped by lack of financial resources, but will, on the contrary, yield abundant results, and at last Russia will emerge from these transitional and troublous times stronger and richer than ever.

It is probable that Count Michael Reitern was never in danger of being dismissed from his post. Such a man could not easily have been replaced. Alexander II was pleased, perhaps flattered, by the memorandum. The Finance Minister was still allowed a free hand. In the following year an important deal was made with the United States: Alaska was sold for $7,200,000 gold.

Russian America, discovered in 1731 by Behring and Chirikof, had been in the control of a trading concern, the Russian American Company, probably kindred to the Hudson Bay Company. Its object was profit; its means, the selling of furs and skins. How rich the region was in gold had not been surmised; no Klondike was in view. The company bore the responsibility of Russian sovereignty and government, but it cannot be said that its authority yielded much credit or honor for the tsars. In 1860, however, the Russian American Company refused to carry on without military or police assistance from the Russian Government. This extension of Siberia on the American continent began to prove an expense to Russia. It was therefore decided to offer Russian America for sale. The United States bought it for cash. William H. Seward renamed the region Alaska.

But the $7,200,000 was not simply absorbed by the Russian state treasury; it was allocated by Reitern to the fund for railway development. That was a characteristic economy; a source of loss was converted into a source of gain. Railway development came first; railway development meant increased exports. Increased exports meant a reduction of the unfavorable trade balance and an enhancement of Russia's international credit. A similar state sacrifice had been made previously when the St. Petersburg-Moscow Railway was sold and the proceeds allotted to the fund for the building of more railways.

The years 1866–70 represent a period of revision. Some privileges were taken away, some excess of freedom curtailed. Critics of Tsar Alexander II say that following the attempt on his life in 1866 he became a reactionary. That is an exaggeration. The character and temperament of Alexander could not have been greatly affected by attempts on his life. He was cool in danger and was ready to die when Fate demanded it. Actually Russia in freedom tended to get out of hand. Some restraint was required.

But with Reitern still controlling the finance, the work of the consolidation of reform proceeded steadily. The development continued.

In 1870 the towns which had had a measure of municipal self-government since the reign of Catherine II were made financially self-dependent, with the power of raising taxes and loans, and of budgeting for their own local requirements and expenses. The reasons for this reform would seem obvious. Cities must have immediate responsibility for their own development. But the necessity was increased by the fact that towns were not expanding at a rate proportionate to the rapid development of industry and commerce. The cities tended to be aggregations of dwellings and factories rather than organized and spacious communities.

VIII.

BISMARCK IN ST. PETERSBURG

IN April, 1859, on his forty-fourth birthday, Bismarck became Prussian Ambassador at St. Petersburg, and remained until the spring of 1862. While it cannot be said that in itself his mission was marked by events of great importance, yet the presence of such a statesman of genius at the Russian court could not be without significance in history.

The north German kingdom of Prussia was nearer and more neighborly to Russia than the subsequently expanded state of Germany, the German Empire, could ever be. The Romanofs, besides being dynastically allied to the Hohenzollerns, had a strong Prussian support in the Baltic barons and landowners. Society in St. Petersburg itself was more Prussian than Russian, or let us say more Baltic. Russia was governed from the northern fortresses of Peter the Great.

There was considerable glamour in this fortified life, great houses fortified against the rigors of winter, institutions fortified against the intrusion of the talkative and vulgar middle class of Russia. Bismarck was no democrat; he liked the Russian atmosphere. He had been an admirer of Nicholas I and while he did not share Alexander's belief in social reform, he found enough authority and discipline in the Russian capital to satisfy any Prussian.

In Bismarck's opinion, the Russians, the Slavs generally, were good material for nations, that is—interbred with Prussians they would become nations. What the feminine, impulsive, self-contradictory Slav required was breeding with the male German type, *par excellence* with the disciplined, logical, sure-footed Prussian. The dominance in the army and in the court of Russians with German names seemed to prove that. He ignored the fact that in the arts, in all true modes of self-expression it was the Russian Russians and not those of German extraction who were announcing themselves. Between the Russian nation, finding expression in political institutions and in the arts, and the German element in court and administration, there was a strong racial antipathy, masking itself generally in lurid political discussions. The persistent coldness of a great part of educated Russia towards their Tsar must be held due to the fact that, consider the latest Romanofs how one would, there was much more German blood than Russian in them.

Bismarck was more at home in Russia than he could have been in any other country outside his own Prussia. St. Petersburg society liked him also.

The tall figure of the Prussian Minister who showed himself almost daily on horseback soon became familiar and welcome to the whole city. No other foreign diplomat was more warmly received by the Emperor, or so frequently invited to the weekly court hunts as Herr von Bismarck, who was not only a sportsman but a genuine lover of nature. The Prussian Legation—theretofore the abode of decent dullness, the scene of rare and then pretentious entertainments—now became one of the most charming and frequented resorts in the capital. Everybody knew that the Prussian Envoy was unable to compete with his French, English, and Austrian colleagues in splendor and display; but everybody also agreed that this drawback could not have been more happily and gracefully dealt with than it was by Herr and Frau von Bismarck. Society was unanimous in declaring that this diplomat formed a marked contrast to his stiff, would-be wellbred, buttoned-up and pretentious predecessors. The fresh, unconstrained and yet self-possessed manner of the newcomer accorded in every respect with the social demands of our aristocrats. Business people were impressed with the offhand readiness of the diplomat who proved himself at home on every subject; while the lions and lionesses of our drawing-rooms were charmed with the unfailing good temper, the flowing wit, the distinguished yet simple manners, and the excellent French of the man of the world. Here at last was a German with whom we could associate as easily and pleasantly as with other people.*

The political object of Bismarck was to preserve a united front of Prussia and Russia towards the West, to weaken Austria, to counter the intrigues of Napoleon III insofar as the French Emperor's policy was directed against Prussia. He was particularly popular in St. Petersburg because of his antipathy towards Austria, that ungrateful Austria which had gone against Russia in the Crimean War after having been saved from revolution by Nicholas I. Bismarck confessed his conviction that the liberation of Italy from Austrian influence was a European necessity, which formed the first stage in the emancipation of German and Prussian from the tutelage of Vienna.

Some commentators are of opinion that at this period Bismarck was friendly towards France, but he does not seem to have been unaware of the readiness of Napoleon III to embark upon a war with Prussia. In July, 1859, he wrote:

If we fire one shot on the Rhine the Italo-Austrian War is over, and in place of it we shall see a Prusso-French war, in which Austria, after we have taken the load from her shoul-

* Eckardt, Julius, *Aus der Peterburger Gesellschaft.*

ders, will assist, or assist so far as her own interests are concerned. That we should play a very victorious part is not frankly to be conceded. Be it as God wills! It is here below always a question of time; nations and men, folly and wisdom, war and peace, they come like waves and so depart, while the ocean remains! On this earth there is nothing but hypocrisy and jugglery.

It was partly owing to the ill feeling existing between Prussia and Austria that in the Polish dispute of 1863 Austria lined herself up with England and France in demanding better treatment for the Poles. It also must be considered as partly due to the influence of Bismarck that Prussia supported Alexander II against the insurgent Poles. According to the historian Pokrovsky, writing under Soviet auspices, there was much more in the Prusso-Russian understanding than mere support in quelling Poland. It enabled Russia to feel stronger, to fear interference less, and to proceed with her campaigns in Central Asia. In 1859 Russia had consolidated her hold on the Caucasus by the defeat and capture of Shamil. That same year Russia moved against the Khanates of Transcaspia in order to punish them for attacks upon her mercantile caravans. It appeared to England that Russia, thwarted in the Balkans, was already seeking compensation in Central Asia. In the succeeding twenty years Russia made herself master successively of Tashkent, Samarkand, Khiva, Bokhara, and the British press discovered a new bogey in the Russian menace to India. Prussia was not concerned one way or the other regarding a menace to India. And the other continental powers could not be made interested in a development that concerned them so remotely.

Bismarck, apart from his diplomatic work, enjoyed his life in Russia, especially the hunting. There was no lack of sporting parties; he hunted the elk, the bear and the wolf. He avoided the everlasting balls and late parties of the Russian court, but he was untiring as a Nimrod, often out in the snow alone with one Russian servant, sometimes getting lost in the woods or the blizzard. One day he seemed quite lost. He turned to his Russian peasant servant and asked what would become of them.

"*Nichevo*," said the peasant. "We'll get out somehow."

That word *Nichevo* amused Bismarck exceedingly and remained with him after he left Russia. He pronounced it "Nitzchevo" and sometimes puzzled statesmen at the council board by his exclamation, "Nitzchevo, we'll get out somehow."

Russian character, so different from Prussian, surprised Bismarck often, but he met it with a good-natured indulgence.

I am waiting for the samovar and behind me a young Russian, red-shirted, is troubling himself with entirely fruitless attempts to heat the stove; he sneezes and sighs but it won't burn. Nitzchevo! I ordered my carriage two hours ago; to every inquiry I have made at ten-minute intervals for the last hour and a half, the reply is "Directly!" with stolid, friendly quietness; and so it remains. You know my pattern-like patience in waiting, but everything has its bounds.

Bismarck's impression of the new railway shows that from the first railway travel in Russia was characteristic. He wrote:

No German train conductor could imagine the amount of

luggage brought into a railway carriage. No Russian travels without two pillows, children in baskets, and masses of provisions of every kind.

These years at St. Petersburg enabled Bismarck to take the measure of the Russians whom as a military force he flattered but never feared. At a much later period of his career he made the mistake of retiring the Prussian friendship with Russia in exchange for an Austro-German defensive alliance, as if the support of Austria were worth more to Germany than the support of Russia. Not that such a *volte face* occurred to him in 1862: Austria must be beaten first and brought to her senses. The moral support of Russia was valuable while in turn Prussia thrashed the Austrians and thrashed the French.

In 1862 and for more than a decade following it, Bismarck respected the Russian Chancellor, Gorchakof. There was a great difference in age and in ornate accomplishment. When Bismarck and Gorchakof were together Gorchakof shone. To some extent Bismarck admired the old-fashioned diplomatic chicane of Gorchakof. Possibly he came under its influence, for at a later stage Bismarck became cynical in his dealings with the representatives of other powers and was far from being the frank downright man of his word that some admirers have taken him to be. But when Gorchakof became senile Bismarck had no difficulty in seeing through him and he held him up to ridicule on every possible occasion. He not only found no difficulty in deceiving Gorchakof but he wrecked the Russian Chancellor's credit in Europe by making every other statesman understand that Russia in her foreign policy was represented by a silly vain old man. Bismarck was a much greater man than Gorchakof; at the same time it must be admitted, in the light of history, that he did not benefit Germany when he made an enemy of him.

IX.

PRINCE ALEXANDER GORCHAKOF

THE progress of Russian domestic reform was accompanied by intermittent thunder and threat of storm in western Europe. The comity of the nations was constantly in jeopardy. The risk of war was always present. It cannot be said that the threat to peace was due to a vast increase in armaments. Europe was not the armed camp she was in 1914. It was due to national and individual quarrelsomeness and ambition, through a general lack of neighborliness and of international sympathy. Probably that is always true. The causes of war must be sought in national psychology. The modern assumption that war is due to excessive armaments is merely vulgar materialism; that assumption is for the most part an Anglo-Saxon assumption, bespeaking an intellectual indolence which finds it easier to deal with things mechanical than with motive and character.

After the Crimean War Russia under Alexander II had great need of peace. A European war in which Russia was involved would undoubtedly have halted the progress of reform and might conceivably have resulted in a Russian revolution. Alexander II was a pacific tsar, the nearest approach to a pacifist on the throne. He did not wish war; he had no personal military ambitions. But he was no coward, neither was he lacking in dignity. Though his people had been worsted in conflict with England and France at the moment he came to the throne, he was not prepared to eat humble pie in Europe and do the bidding of a brow-beating Englishman such as Earl Russell or a cynical schemer such as Napoleon III. The West was confronted by an utterly honorable personality.

On the other hand, Russia under Alexander II had lost nothing of that self-esteem which has always seemed excessive to Western nations. Doubtless as a military force Russia was not redoubtable. Despite her almost inexhaustible man power, the Crimean War had proved that. But the Crimean War had also demonstrated that Russia was invulnerable. The combined efforts of England and France in the Crimea only resulted in penetrating some five miles from the coast. It was never forgotten that the great Napoleon was ruined by his march to Moscow in 1812. If the tsardom was to fall it must be through disorder and revolution within Russia, and not as a direct result of foreign military pressure.

The encouragement of Russian revolutionaries by sympathizers in England must be held due to an instinctive desire to see the power of Russia reduced. The reforms carried out by Alexander II were little understood at the time, but in so far as they were understood, they were regarded with suspicion. Many condemned publicly the project of liberating the serfs. It seemed better that the tsardom collapse than that it should be bolstered up by reform. The agitation in favor of Poland was characteristic of the interference of the West. In its ostensible object it failed in every way. It encouraged the resistance of the unfortunate Poles in the belief that there would be armed intervention on their behalf, as there had been on behalf of Turkey in 1855.

It overlooked the fact that the Poles had more to hope
from Alexander II in peace than they could have in
conflict. It caused the destruction of Polish liberty. But
it also had other unfortunate effects. It caused the Tsar
to mobilize an army of defence; it caused a commercial
and financial panic in Russia. It rocked the financial
foundation on which the reforms were based. It played
into the hands of reactionary nobles and politicians
who held that Alexander's liberalism was untradi-
tional, un-Russian and a danger to the stability and
integrity of the Empire. It slowed down the *tempo* of
the liberal movement in Russia generally. It turned the
attention of Alexander II from internal to foreign politics. His interest in the intrigues of western Europe
may have been slight at that date; but from 1863 onwards that interest grew steadily—to the detriment of
domestic administration.

In the negotiations of 1863 the Western Powers encountered for the first time a new personality in Russian affairs. It was not Alexander himself, but his Foreign Minister, Prince Alexander Gorchakof, certainly
a man of outstanding ability—excepting Bismarck,
probably the strongest personality in the chancelleries
of Europe.

Alexander Gorchakof was a cousin of Prince Michael Gorchakof, who as Governor-General of Poland
had attempted to cope with the Polish patriotic movement. He was born in 1798, and at the time of the
Crimean War he was already some fifty-seven years of
age. As he only died in 1883, his life and activity may
be said to have covered the greater part of the nineteenth century. He was a contemporary of Lord Salisbury but he had been at the coronation of George IV

and had long conversations with Sir Walter Scott. His fame in Russia relates to a time when he was, comparatively speaking, an elderly man. He had a venerable appearance which was deliberately increased by the studied wearing of old-fashioned garments, by his high cravats and heavy velvet waistcoats. In this he was in contrast to the foppishness of most other prominent Russian statesmen of the time. It was his tacit protest: "I do not need to dress, I am clever. I do not need sartorial ornament, I read Horace in the original."

As a child he had been a playfellow of Alexander Pushkin who was to become the great national poet of Russia. In his boyhood Alexander I was still on the throne and education was more esteemed than it became in the reign of Nicholas I. He had the advantage of a good schooling at the Lyceum of Tsarskoe Selo. He grew up to take an intelligent interest in national literature as well as in affairs. But he had an aptitude for book learning. Someone has said he never enjoyed life as much as he did his running commentary on life, his criticism of it derived from reflection. His first post was that of secretary, under Lieven, at the Russian Embassy in London. He won there the reputation of being *un homme capable!* Some time after that he was accredited to Stuttgart. Then he became Russian Ambassador at Vienna. He formed a prejudice against the Austrians, whom all his life he either hated or distrusted. It is suspected that in the outbreak of 1848 his sympathies were more with the revolutionaries than with the Emperor of Austria. He did not forgive Austria for siding with England and France in the Crimean War. Nevertheless he had advised in 1854 that the foreign opposition to Russia was too great and that it would be better not to commence hostility against Turkey rather than to incur the almost certain risk of almost certain European war. But this advice was not heeded. At the peace conference in Paris in 1856 he avoided giving his signature to the treaty signed for Russia by Count Nesselrode, and evidently made personal provision for denouncing the more onerous terms of that treaty, should he ultimately be in a position to do so. Alexander II recognized his ability and made him Foreign Minister in place of Nesselrode. Count Nesselrode was a weary old man who did not care for the new ideas of Alexander II. He was glad to withdraw to private life, the writing of his dull memoirs, the tending of his gardens, long evenings at whist and petty gossip in the small circle of the Dowager Empress.

Gorchakof was an accomplished scholar, especially versed in the Latin classics and elegantly facile in the use of the French language, and his *mots* had a *réclame* all over Europe. His first and perhaps most famous was his definition of Russian policy after the Crimean War in the words *"La Russie ne boude pas; elle se recueille."* One of the cleverest of these *mots* was *"L'Autriche n'est pas un état, ce n'est qu'un gouvernement."*

Gorchakof met the Anglo-French note on Polish affairs by a counter-proposition as sagacious as it was discomfiting. That proposition was that the Powers who had originally partitioned Poland should confer as to the future status of Russian Poland. Russia and Prussia and Austria were the Powers. England and France were merely privileged outsiders to whom, however, the results of the conference would be communicated.

Gorchakof profited by being a close friend of Bis-

marck. Thanks to that and to dynastic ties the support
of Prussia had been obtained in the Polish dispute. At
first after the conclusion of the Treaty of Paris Gorchakof cultivated France and led Napoleon III to
think he might find a friend in Alexander II, but later
he came to the conclusion that Bismarck and not Napoleon III, or the Emperor Franz Joseph, and certainly
not England, was the coming arbiter of central European history. Gorchakof was talkative, vain, even upon
occasion pompous, but he was sagacious. He was capable of weighing in the balance all the potentialities in
the Europe of his day. He soon learned to distrust the
showiness of Napoleon III; he was steadfast in his low
estimation of the power of Austria; he discounted the
moral self-righteousness of England.

The success of Russia's Foreign Minister during the
decade following the humiliation of the Crimean War
must depend on an ability to sort out the personalities
and forces of Europe and to associate Russia's sympathies with strength rather than with weakness. While
he was disposed to accept the olive branch from France
and favored the anti-Austrian campaign in Italy, he
kept the Tsar suspicious of the personality of Napoleon
III. Napoleon in false humility said that he came before Alexander like a slave with a halter on his neck,
but the Tsar's secret thought was "you treacherously
fought my father."

Napoleon III was sufficiently cynical to imagine that
he could obtain complete friendship and military alliance with Russia on the morrow of a sanguinary war.
He wished Russia's support in order to thwart Prussia,
for he was in love with his own secret tragic destiny
which must ultimately fulfil itself in the Franco-Prus-

sian War. He must take revenge on Prussia for Waterloo, not foreseeing a second Waterloo at the battle of
Sedan.

Napoleon's hope for an alliance against Prussia persisted even after he had espoused the cause of the Poles
in 1863. Prussia, alone of all the European powers, had
supported Russia in the coercive policy in Poland, and
yet Napoleon III thought that the practical friendship
of Bismarck could be rewarded by Russian enmity. But
the Russians stood by their friend and would not
thwart Prussia in her war against Denmark in 1864.
And Gorchakof, at least, had rejoiced when Prussia
fought Austria in 1866. Austria had proved herself the
most treacherous power in Europe as far as Russia was
concerned. When the Austrian Empire had been in mortal danger after the revolutionary storm of 1848, Nicholas I had saved it by sending an army into Hungary.
But Austria never showed any gratitude for that support. On the contrary, in the Crimean conflict, she used
her opportunity to occupy Slav territory to extend her
sway and to mobilize an army which kept a considerable force of Russians engaged in garrison duty upon
her frontiers. Then in 1863, though she was equally
with Russia a despoiler of Polish liberty, she had had
the impudence to join in the remonstrance of the Western Powers against the Russian action of suppressing
revolt in Russian Poland.

King William I of Prussia, aided by the statesmen
Bismarck and that soldier of genius, Von Moltke, was
a force in the ascendant. It was not generally grasped,
unless by Russia, that in 1866 Prussia had already become the greatest military force in Europe. In 1858 the
whole of the Prussian infantry was armed with the new

needle-gun; by 1866 the army had been developed to such an extent that Prussia with a population of only eighteen millions could nevertheless put five hundred and fifty thousand men into the field. Austria with twice the population could not mobilize as great a force. But of more significance than numbers and equipment was the fact that in Von Moltke Prussia possessed a chief of staff of more ability than any other soldier in Europe, one of tremendous foresight who made war his trade and who had taken not only the measure of Austria but of his ultimate antagonist Napoleon III.

The Austro-Prussian difference arose out of the joint occupations by Prussia and Austria of Schleswig-Holstein and the desire for territorial compensation by Austria, should Prussia annex the Danish provinces. But the real cause of the war may be set down as Prussian ambition. The German states and peoples were divided in leadership as between the Protestant north and the Catholic south. Prussia under Bismarck was increasing yearly in her national pretensions and consciousness of leadership as the dominant German state. A trial of strength between her and the somewhat moribund Austrian Empire was inevitable.

Bavaria, Saxony, Hanover and Austria were lined up against Prussia aided by Italy; and the German civil war, the memory of which still rankles, broke out in the summer of 1866. On July 3 the Austrians were crushed at the battle of Königgratz in Bohemia. The war was soon over. Austria sued for peace, and the southern German states became virtually within the control of a north-German confederation under the dominant leadership of Prussia—the beginning of modern Germany.

One of Russia's enemies had been reduced in power and arrogance. Alexander II was not displeased by the course of events. William I and Bismarck were congratulated on their success. It cannot be said that the Prussians were popular with liberal Russia but Austria was more disliked. The Tsar said openly that while he lived certainly Russia and Prussia would never come into conflict. He warned Napoleon III several times that he could not expect help of any kind if he made war on Prussia.

One of the chief defects of the French Emperor was an inability to form correct judgments. His assumption in his letter to Queen Victoria that the Treaty of Vienna had lapsed was an example. His shallow approach to the Tsar in 1857 was another. His notion that both Austria and Prussia would reward him for his neutrality in 1866 was another. His assumption that all men were opportunists must have been derived from his own opportunism. It was difficult for him to understand the steadfastness of Gorchakof and Alexander II. When the latter in June, 1867, accepted his invitation to the Paris exhibition, he could still imagine the project of a Franco-Russian military alliance to be feasible. He could imagine it even in the presence of the King of Prussia, Bismarck and Von Moltke, who had also arrived in Paris to view the exhibition. He could imagine it while French people booed Alexander in the streets of Paris and shouted *Vive la Pologne!* after his carriage. His police had not taken sufficient precaution to prevent an attempt being made on the life of the Tsar in Paris, but even after the revolver shot of Berezovski he could still nurse his favorite project. In September of the same year he sent Thiers to Alexander imploring him to place himself at the head of a league of European states pledged to restrain the ambition of Prussia. The Tsar received the Frenchman warmly and afterwards expressed his admiration of his personal character, but naturally he took no steps to realize the absurd proposal. Napoleon III came to understand that if he fought the King of Prussia he would have to do so single-handed. He had his army with him; the army greeted him with shouts of *Vive la Guerre!* and *Au Rhin!* The army had a mistaken belief in its ability to win victories over the Prussians. The officers of both nations became busily engaged in spying. In the spring of 1868 Von Moltke made a careful inspection of the whole of the French frontier and drew up a detailed plan for an invasion of France. Meanwhile Prussia and Russia exchanged assurances of friendship. The King of Prussia and the Tsar of Russia exchanged decorations. They drank in memory of the great epoch of 1814 and 1815 when they had been allied against the common enemy Napoleon I.

Gorchakof visited Bismarck in 1869 and gave him assurance of Russia's neutrality in case of war, a condition being Prussia's support of Russia should the latter denounce certain clauses of the Treaty of Paris of 1856. Gorchakof intended to use the opportunity of the war to obtain the freedom of the Black Sea for Russia.

This was probably the reciprocity for Russian neutrality during the war with France and was very inopportunely acted on before the close of the siege of Paris by a notification to the European Powers that Russia repudiated that article of the

Treaty of Paris and resumed full liberty of action as regarded the Black Sea.*

In July, 1870, commenced the tragic war between France and Prussia.

It may be noted that in Russia, while the sympathy of the Tsar, his court and ministers was with Prussia, the greater part of those who took an interest in foreign affairs were on the side of France in the great conflict. The Russian newspapers were mostly hostile to Prussia; some Russians volunteered and went to fight for France; large sums of money were subscribed while Red Cross workers and field ambulances were sent out to take care of the French wounded.

Although Russia has repeatedly come under strong German influence there is no doubt that the Slav is more sympathetic to the French than to the Germans. This is perhaps natural. It is a preference of liberty to discipline, art to materialism, and of emotion to conscience.

In June, 1870, on the very eve of the outbreak of the Franco-German War, Alexander was at Ems in the province of Hesse-Nassau in Prussia, taking the waters, and his mistress the Princess Catherine Dolgoruky was there also.

In this month of June Catherine's villa heard secrets which the French Government would have paid heavily to know. To the Princess Dolgoruky was confided at first hand the grave conversation, stretching over four days, between Alexander II, William I, Prince Gorchakof and Bismarck. The Tsar explained to her the whole European chessboard, the adventurous policy of France, the suspicious attitude of Austria, the imminence of a conflict and, consequently, Russia's obligation to

* Loftus, Lord Augustus, *Diplomatic Reminiscences.*

renew her traditional alliance with Prussia . . . after assuring
for herself some advantages in the East. A month later the
Hohenzollern candidature set a match to the powder; Alexander said to Catherine: "You see, I was right! In this business
all the blame lies with France."*

England refused to be drawn into the Franco-Prussian War unless one of the belligerent nations infringed
the neutrality of Belgium. In effect she stood by and
saw Napoleon III whipped, France crushed, the ravish-
ment of the provinces of Alsace and Lorraine, complete
French humiliation. Carlyle was pleased that the "va-
pouring" French had been taught a lesson. Queen Victoria was pleased that kith and kin in Germany had
proved their righteousness by the sword. The "brother"
and "sister" letters of Napoleon III with their *épanche-
ments* went for nothing. It was likewise nothing that
French and English had fought shoulder to shoulder
fifteen years earlier in the Crimea.

France had no call upon British support and yet it
is not surprising that after the war the legend of *perfide
Albion* grew and that obscene caricatures of Victoria
appeared in Parisian journals. Not surprising that England looked upon France as a power proved to be de-
generate.

The Russian court and government were not displeased. Prussia had shattered the power of France.
England had no potential ally to use against Russia in
European politics. The Prussians were pleased by the
benevolent neutrality observed by Russia. Alexander
had kept an army in readiness to check Austria should
the latter have seized an opportunity for revenge. Wil-

* Paléologue, Maurice, *Le roman tragique de l'Empereur Alexandre
II.*

liam I wrote to Alexander II, "Never will Prussia forget that to you it is due that the war did not assume larger proportions. May God bless you for it! Your grateful friend for life."

In the Hall of Mirrors at Versailles, on January 18, 1871, William I of Prussia had announced himself, through Bismarck, German Emperor. Germany became the strongest military power in Europe. England became more isolated, began to live in "splendid isolation." Russia regained something of that position in Europe lost by the Crimean War. After every conflict in Europe there is an adjustment of the balance of power which affects not only belligerents but neutrals.

On October 31, 1870, Russia denounced the Black Sea clauses of the Treaty of Paris of 1856. England sought Prussian coöperation to bring the Russians to task—but that was naturally a fruitless effort. The treaties imposed by the victors in a war become a dead letter when the victors cease to have power to continue to enforce them. England by herself could do little to stop the fortification of the Black Sea ports, the building of new warships and the resumption by Russia of a championship of the Slavs of the Balkans under the yoke of Turkey.

At the London conference in 1871 the British cabinet wished to know whether in case of a war with Russia to enforce the Treaty of Paris Prussia would remain neutral. Bismarck replied:

I am no friend of conjectural politics; it would depend on circumstances. I am not of opinion that gratitude is without its place in politics. The present Emperor of Russia has always shown himself friendly and well-disposed towards us, while Austria has never shown herself trustworthy. As to the Black

Sea, the Treaty of Paris contains unjust stipulations; for its coast-line really belongs for the most part to Russia. People say the Russian policy is diabolically artful, full of shuffles, and quirks and dodges. It is nothing of the kind. Dishonest people would have made no such declaration. They would have gone on quietly building warships in the Black Sea, and waited till somebody asked them about it. Then they would have said they knew nothing about it; they had sent to inquire; and they would have wriggled out of it. They might have kept that sort of thing up in Russia for a long time, till at last people got used to things as they were . . .

The Black Sea clauses were a hindrance to the development of Russia, to its trade as well as to its foreign influence. Complete freedom from interference must be obtained for the great grain port of Odessa. Denouncing the treaty may have been a breach of good faith, but no nation is likely to remain passive where natural development is hindered by a treaty of peace imposed by victors.

Gorchakof was not a convinced Easterner in politics. For him the sphere of Russian influence was the West rather than the Near East. But his defence of Russian policy in Poland in 1863 won him great popularity with the Slavophile or national party in Russia. It is said that at that time he held up one finger to them but they took the whole hand.

After the Moscow newspapers had once done honor to Gorchakof and had declared him one of the greatest Russians of all ages, after the irresistible influence of the Moscow publicists had carried matters to such a point that no banquet could be given at which the health of the most noble vice-chancellor was not drunk and telegrams despatched to him—the chancellor could no longer forbear concluding a tacit compact with the founders of his popularity; a compact which imposed upon him the duty of forwarding, or at any rate of not disturbing, the plans of these men even if he could not approve of them. One peculiarity of the Prince, which had always been recognized but which hitherto had been smiled at as innocence—namely, *vanity*—now for the first time appeared to its full extent; being indeed so unrestrained and extreme that it seemed to pervade the whole man. Just as boundlessly as the delight of the Chancellor increased in the hymns of his publicist admirers, so insatiably did he demand the homage which was awarded him by the influential Moscow newspapers; he not only overwhelmed Katkof and his colleagues with acts of courtesy, inviting them frequently to St. Petersburg,*

but he became tolerant of the brutal repression carried out by Muravief in Poland. The nationalists were so numerous, so gifted and so strong in Russia that they provided almost the only popular backing for a chancellor who wished to be something more than servant of the Tsar.

This backing of popularity was even increased when the Treaty of Paris was denounced in 1870, and the Tsar seemed to approve Prince Gorchakof's glory by giving him the title of "Most Serene."

* Eckardt, Julius, *Aus der Peterburger Gesellschaft.*

X.

POLITICAL MOVEMENTS

AS regards the various political movements agitating mankind within a given period, we should do well to inquire as to their objective. The means employed by a movement such as the Marxian revolution in Russia are not so important as the end in view. Adherence to a new movement is often merely a negation of the existing order: "I think that democracy is played out: therefore I have become a Fascist," or "Capitalism is the law of the jungle, I have become a socialist." Or it is response to leadership, a pricking of the ears as at the sound of martial music in the streets, a surrender of personal judgment to follow blindly someone of striking personality.

And the history of movements is plagued by fanaticism; not only by the fanaticism of those in the movement but of writers giving an account of them. Russian historical works dealing with the nineteenth century are remarkable for their spirit of *parti pris*. Anything in the nature of an impartial account of the great era of the reign of Alexander II is a rarity. Apart from a few adulatory volumes bearing an almost official stamp there is nothing that is not written in a bitter and grudging spirit. The revolutionary virus of the universities infected almost all the historians. The censorship on historical writings was never severe. The chief historians of the time, Pokrovsky and Kornilof, are both so intent on disparaging Alexander II that it is difficult to elucidate positive elements of any kind. Had they written in as biased a way of the revolutionary era which followed tsardom they must assuredly have been banned by the Soviet, if not imprisoned or executed.

The histories of the reign are themselves part of history in that they indicate a mood, a persistent discontent, a desire for institutions other than those they described.

Pokrovsky is a historian of considerable reputation. He had a high standing already in the reign of Nicholas II. He was born during the epoch of Alexander's great reforms, graduated in Moscow in 1891, abandoned the even tenor of professorship and historical writing for politics in the revolutionary struggle of 1905–6, became a Marxist, continued his historical research in Paris, returned to Russia with the Bolsheviks in 1917, was personally blessed by Lenin and became the chief historical professor under the Soviet regime. His career is not irrelevant to the biography of Alexander II, because the movement which began in Alexander's reign obtained free play in the revolution of 1917 and in the regime in which Pokrovsky became what might be called the Red dictator of history.

In the reign of Alexander, as in most other eras, the "haves" were ranged against the "have nots," the holders of privilege against the common people, the rich against the poor. That may be put to one side because selfishness, greed and covetousness are constant factors in human society. The bickering of privileged and unprivileged is not so much a movement as a chorus. When there is movement and change one set of privileged persons supplants another and the chorus of recrimination continues. Genuine political movements arise from stronger motives than selfishness.

In the reign of Alexander II there were two great movements, the Slavophile or nationalist movement, and the revolutionary or cosmopolitan movement which merged into Marxism. We will consider the second first because it seems to have lasted longer, and by common consent what seems to endure is held to be more important than what seems to be dead.

The attempts made on the life of Alexander II by Karakozof advertised the extent of the revolutionary movement in the sixties. Pokrovsky called the attempt of Karakozof, "the first heroic action of the Russian revolutionary socialistic movement." The subsequent persecution of suspected persons was a natural enough result. To quote Pokrovsky again, "The extermination of the Romanofs, including Alexander, was but a detail in a vast revolutionary plan." In political warfare it is not unfair when the party which is attacked counter-attacks with ferocity.

One of the suspected persons was Lavrof, a professor of philosophy and mathematics. He was banished and in banishment formulated for himself a creed of revolution. He escaped from Russia and resumed political activity abroad. He is said to have had very considerable influence as a propagandist, especially among students. His objective was a state, the apex of which should be the intellectuals, a feudalism of brains to supplant the feudalism of brawn. For Lavrof the masses did not make history: They were only the manure of history, the rich manure on which the crop of "critically seeking individuals may be grown." "But," he said, "revolutionaries must never forget that nevertheless this rich manure is human."

Obviously a theory of this kind appealed to those who thought themselves intellectual rather than to those who knew frankly that they were just uncouth working men and peasants. It is not surprising that Lavrovism did not go far. The most that can be said of it is that this movement imparted momentum to the greater movement of which it was a part—Marxism.

Marx held that the toiling masses controlled history, a theory that obtained its first striking confirmation in the Bolshevik revolution of 1917. Marx, however, was not troubled by the doctrine of eternal recurrence, and did not predict that as soon as the masses had obtained control by an executive called the Communist party, individuals would in turn gain control of the executives and turn the masses back to the bondage of authority.

The Marxian movement in the late sixties tended to develop through Bakunin rather than through Lavrof. Karl Marx published the first volume of *Das Kapital* in 1867. Bakunin must be regarded as an instrument rather than a disciple of Marxism; on many points he disagreed with Marx. The movement reached a peak abroad in the ferment in France after the seige of Paris, the fall of Napoleon III, and the humiliation of the French by the Prussians. There were barricades and red flags once more in Paris—March 18, 1871, one of the red letter days of Bolshevik Russia to-day. The Paris Commune was set up, and lasted two months. It was broken because as Bakunin said, "The highly paid workers of the West have a *bourgeois* mentality."

Bakunin looked to Russia for the real lasting triumph of Communism, because, "the peasant is a born revolutionary; he is constantly in revolt and his revolt finds expression in banditry which the revolutionaries must learn to utilize. When these two forms of revolt meet—the bandit's and the peasant's—then a popular revolution is born."

There ensued in the seventies a new movement towards the people. The earlier movement, that of the sixties, had been chiefly to bring education to the peasantry; the new movement was one more of incitement than of improvement. Actually it had no success of any significance. The majority of converts to revolutionary doctrine were of the same class as the propagandists, intellectuals of slight intellect and unlimited pretensions. Had no revolution eventually taken place it would have been difficult to deduce the ultimate objective of these woolly-pated propagandists. But fortunately for the historian, Germany in 1917, delivering a death-thrust at tsardom, enabled the revolutionaries to destroy the old Russia and produce or attempt to produce the objective of all their revolutionary striving—the dictatorship of the Communist party, the Five-Year Plan, mass production of grain and of raw materials. The main objective proved to be *bread*.

The tsardom and what was called *"bourgeois* culture" were thrust away in order that there might be more bread.

This Red movement won its way: the other movement, Slavophilism, perished.

Slavophilism may be thought, by the year 1914, to have become extinct because no one at that time was identified as a Slavophile. The expression had become old fashioned. The word characterized writers of sixty years previously, Pogodin, the poet, Khomiakof and Tiutchef, the brothers Kireyevsky, the indefatigable worker for the emancipation of the serfs, George Samarin. The movement became side-tracked in Panslavism, the championship of "brother Slavs" in the Balkans. But it persisted actually as Russian nationalism, a faith in everything characteristically Russian, a faith only shattered by despair in the war of 1914–18.

The origins of Slavophilism must date round about the time of the menace of Napoleon Bonaparte in 1812. Bonaparte became for the Russian peasant antichrist; cultured patriots interpreted antichrist as the power of this world incarnated in one man of diabolic energy and leadership. Russia in counterbalance became Holy Russia. The Russian army became the "Christ-serving army." In the rush of volunteers to serve against Bonaparte there was a movement of national self-consciousness. Apart from the question of tsars and modes of government, the Russian fatherland was aware of itself as something infinitely worth protecting from the French, and if from the French in particular, then by association from the West in general.

Among those volunteers who served against Napoleon was the Slavophile Zhukovsky who afterwards as poet and as teacher of Alexander II in boyhood did much to give the whole court of St. Petersburg a complexion of Slavophilism.

The Slavophile doctrine or faith embodied: (1) a national protest against the imitation of Western civilization; (2) a philosophical historical theory of national originality; (3) Panslav sympathy. The objective of the movement was national expression undefiled by foreign influences. It was decidedly opposed

to cosmopolitanism and therefore to Jewish culture
which always tends to be European. Much of the later
anti-Semitism must have arisen accidentally from Slavophilism. Slavophilism in Russia was as exclusive as
at a later date Hitlerism is in Germany. The Jews
wished Russia to be European; the Slavophiles wished
her to remain Russian. Jews are instinctively interna-
tionalists; and Slavophiles were passionately Russian.

The Slavophile movement also ran counter to the
opinions of most Russians living abroad and especially
of those who thought England a happier place than
Russia. It was a movement that denied the point of
view of Herzen, Kropotkin, Stepniak and the rest who
painted Russia black for the edification of the English
and England white for the edification of the Russian.
It found characteristic expression in Dostoievsky after
his visit to London in 1863. No doubt the picture he
gave of the drunken brawling crowds of working men
and the prevalence of prostitution is presented somewhat out of focus. Dostoievsky saw London as rather
worse than it was because he was prompted by the desire to refute effectually the opinions of all those who
thought England an example of godly life. In his mind
ideal Holy Russia was enthroned and in the West he
saw only "the triumph of Baal."

He saw English civilization as "a colossal decoration of wealth and luxury before whose gigantic pride
and massive grandeur the hungry soul bows, makes
peace, seeks salvation in debauch, and tends to believe
that that is the way for all." He was appalled by the
public houses, "illuminated and decorated like palaces," by the women in the saloons and the little children running about at their knees, by the foul language

and the fighting. When Russians drink they turn to dancing and song, but the English working man to obscenity and insult. He saw the district of the Haymarket swarming with prostitutes and even girls in their teens pressing their hands into the hands of strange men and asking to be led away. Desperate poverty mingled with irresponsible wealth.

He wrote:

> Once in the crowd in the street, I saw a little girl, six years, no more, all in rags, dirty, barefooted, emaciated, worn out. Glimmering through her tatters her body was all bruised. She walked as if not thinking where she was going, not hurrying anywhere. God knows why she tottered in that London crowd; perhaps she was hungry; no one paid her the slightest attention. But what struck me most was the grief, the hopeless despair written in her face, so that to look on this little creature already bearing such a burden of unhappiness was an anguish to the heart. I gave her sixpence; she looked at me for a moment with frightened eyes, then took to her heels and fled for her life.

Instead of Britannia with helmet and trident, Dostoievsky saw this little girl, and saw her as more representative, as if she were the English *Psyche.*

Out of this impression by the Russian novelist one may deduce that St. Petersburg and Moscow in 1863 were at least better than London and that there was no warrant in English life for the assumption that all would be changed for the better in Russia by imitating the life of the West.

Slavophilism had much in common with modern nationalist movements. It encouraged the wearing of national Russian dress. It raised the Russian language to a pinnacle, as a greater language than German or

French, and in any case the proper language for Russians to talk and write in. It broke the pretensions of those who thought Russian unrefined and that if one had anything serious to say one must say it in a foreign tongue.

The Slavophiles were not critical of the Orthodox Church because the Church was national. The Church was neither Greek nor purely Byzantine; it was what the Russian people had made it. It was part of the national expression. The peasantry, the people as a whole, loved its Church, and as Dostoievsky said, "the people is the final judge." The Russian people was the "god-carrier." It carried God in its midst, like the sacred Ark. That at least was Dostoievsky's vision. When revolution ultimately came it was attempted to abolish the Church, but the Church persisted in the face of incredible persecution. Some aver that the religion of the peasants was only skin deep but it is not clear that that has been proved.

The greatest success of the Slavophile movement was undoubtedly in the arts. The music of Russia is almost entirely national, derived from folk music and that from the depth of the soul of the people. Fine art, all of it that matters, is purely Russian, and most Russian painters became leagued together to depict only Russian scenes, to take only Russian subjects for their canvases. Thanks also to the nationalist movement Russian literature developed on purely Russian lines. There was little straying from Russia to Paris, Monte Carlo, Venice, New York for local color for novels and drama. Turgenief wrote novels whose scenes were sometimes laid abroad; he wrote sometimes in French rather than in Russian, and for that earned the scorn of Dostoievsky who offered to send him a telescope that he might see Russians more clearly.

The national movement in literature is best expressed by Tolstoy who would have shrunk from the label Slavophile. But he also renounced the greater part of Western civilization. His novels and dramas all concern Russia and Russian only. He believed in the peasants as the *source* of language. It is often said that the characteristic peasant of any nation has a limited vocabulary of say some thousand words, but that is probably untrue. It is certainly untrue of the Russian peasant who had a larger vocabulary than the intellectuals. It is probably the factory worker and the clerk who have the most limited vocabulary. Tolstoy abjured the jargon and clipped expressions of the city and took his language from the people. His style is one free of latinisms, German importations, newly invented words and expressions. It is the peasant language without dialect and localism, elaborated and made literary but nevertheless original. This peasant language movement did not die with the revolution, but persists in the work of Remizof and other writers under the Soviet regime.

But all Russian writers of prominence are national and derive from Slavophilism and a preoccupation with Russia itself. No one claims a place in immortal literature for the work of Lenin, Trotsky, Kropotkin or even for the diaries of Herzen. In a sense Slavophilism is dead and Russian internationalism lives, but something still lives and cannot die in the arts.

XI.

RUSSIA AND ENGLAND

FROM the time of the Crimean War until 1874 when the second son of Queen Victoria married the Tsar's only daughter, England remained hostile to Russia. The Queen must have believed most of the lies written about Russia during the Crimean War and she had a strong Protestant dislike of superstition and Byzantinism. Her conscience had demanded that in fighting the Russians in 1854 she had been a sun of righteousness opposing the forces of darkness. She remained all her life *suspicious* of the Russians. And this feeling she communicated to her eldest son. Albert Edward, afterwards Edward VII, was also suspicious of Russia, though in course of time his antipathy to Prussia caused him to become more friendly. For twenty years the Prince of Wales believed in the Russian menace to India, followed Russian operations in Central Asia on large-scale maps and kept urging responsible British statesmen to take action. He was amused, even cynical, when he heard that his younger brother Alfred was going to marry a Romanof.

But the marriages of royal houses inevitably cause modifications in court sympathies. The Prince of Wales could hardly have imagined, when on March 10, 1863, he married Alexandra of Denmark, that the union was destined to bring him nearer in sympathy to Russia. Yet it was so, because three years later the Grand Duke Alexander was married to Dagmar of Denmark. The heirs to the thrones of Russia and England were married to sisters. The Prince was very eager to be present at the Russian marriage though Queen Victoria did not wish him to go. The Prince used remarkable words when writing to the Prime Minister regarding this visit: "I should only be too happy to be the means of promoting the *entente cordiale* between Russia and our own country." After the wedding he invited his brother-in-law to England and lavished hospitality upon him. A little later the Tsar wished to bestow on the Prince of Wales the honorary colonelship of a Guards' regiment. Albert Edward was exceedingly keen to accept, but the Queen was adamant. Such a thing was unheard of; Victoria repeatedly refused to allow it.

Still, apart from the feelings of Queen Victoria and the sympathies and antipathies of the Prince of Wales, there remained a national hostility to Russia which it proved difficult to overcome. This enmity may be explained under several heads. First there was a jealousy such as generally exists between England and any great power which is constantly expanding territorially. There was the animosity of two fighting roosters challenging one another from distant farmyards. Even after the Crimean War there was no other great rival power in Europe. The impression of the victory of Waterloo remained and it was not necessary to thrash the French again. France was regarded with tolerance and patronage. The new Prussia of Bismarck and Von Moltke had barely announced itself. It has been said that in 1863 when England threatened to make war on Russia on behalf of Poland, Queen Victoria was almost the only influential person in Great Britain realizing the significance of Bismarck. In Russia was descried a menace to the future of the British Empire, a hazard to India if her Central Asian expansion continued, a threat to maritime connections in the Mediterranean should she ever gain control of the Dardanelles.

Whether England's instinct for world power and her jealousy of rivals may be held to include and explain all other motives is open to controversy. The second head under which England's enmity towards Russia may be explained is that of political righteousness.

The oriental despotism of the tsars was disliked. England appeared to have a conscience which distinguished her from countries on the continent. And conscience is often linked to credulity as cynicism is often linked with incredulity. The stories of Russian misrule and tyranny found ready ears in London, evoking bursts of indignation. The same stories told in Paris were just "good stories." In London stories of the "dreaded police," of men laden with chains toiling through the snow to farthest Siberia, of patriotic girl students stripped naked and flogged by brutal soldiery, could always be reckoned upon to rouse a considerable section of the English public. This section was duly fed by those wishing the downfall of tsardom. People with a morbid need of horrors to compensate their souls for a too placid existence were glad to escape from complacency and ask God for vengeance on tyrants. To doubt the stories, to inquire into them was abhorrent. It is true that the Russian Government did nothing to refute them. Judgment went by default and the Russian masses were considered the most unhappy and downtrodden people in the world. For that reason the Poles in 1863 had such wide popular support in England. The barbarous tsars had no moral right to govern a cul-

tured and æsthetic people and to impose on another
nation the tyranny which degraded the Russians themselves.

The enmity against Russia may also be explained
under a third head: the animosity which exists between
Englishman and Slav, the English temperamental dislike of the Slav on the grounds of character. Englishmen are willing to admire certain Russians at a distance
but in personal contact distrust them, fail to understand them, dislike them. It ought to be stated that the
converse is not true; Russians do not dislike Englishmen. On the contrary they are greatly attracted by the
English and are seldom found to be personally hostile
to England.

The Russians are just too foreign—they have not the
supposed truth-telling habits of the Germans, nor the
logical simplicity of the French. They are abominably
talkative. They are crafty, not to say "tricky" in all
business deals. The educated men are, or were, unnec-
essarily cultured. The educated Russian with his fluent
knowledge of languages and his ready opinion con-
cerning all the cultural movements of Europe went to
make the average English university man seem colorless. But the same educated Russian, though he may be
a good sportsman, is apt to appear strangely effeminate.
In excitement he has been seen to cry. In agreement
with another man he may want to kiss him. Russians
eat and drink too much. They are fantastically improvident, not careful people, not savers, scandalous
wasters of other people's savings. They take bribes
from the highest to the lowest. It was the same in the
period of alliance, 1914–18. The English in personal
contact with Russians were repelled by Russian charac-

ter. They felt instinctively that people with such character had no right to be a great power in Europe.

On the other hand it was not forgotten that the Russians fought with uncommon bravery in the Crimean War. And they behaved well towards the wounded and the prisoners. Although they lost the war they gained a modicum of respect in certain quarters. The England of the sixties was not entirely hostile to Russia. Some began to grasp that not everything said against Russia was true. Kinglake, writing the history of the Crimean War, became Russophile. Lord Napier, Ambassador at St. Petersburg in 1863, though doing the will of Lord Russell in presenting angry notes to Gorchakof, was not absolutely at one with the Foreign Office. He wrote to Olga Novikof in July, 1863:

> How strange the people are. I have laboured sincerely and reasonably with application and argument, to show the falseness and hollowness of Polish pretension and to defend the Russian Government where I think it can be with justice defended, blaming it temperately where I think it is wrong; and I reap nothing but incredulity! Now, because in a despatch from Russell it appears that I have sent home an extract from the *Journal de St. Petersbourg* they turn round and salute me as a friend.

In a speech in St. Petersburg in 1864 Lord Napier said:

> If the political relations existing between Russia and England do not offer the basis of an exclusive and constant friendship, they yet afford much cause for mutual good offices. We cannot flatter ourselves with the hope that the interests of the two so differently constituted powers, whose expansive sources in regard to influence, trade, and strength nearly approach each other on many sides, should never come into collision. It is the duty of diplomacy to obviate, or at any rate to weaken, the

motive for differences which might arise, and to seize every legitimate opportunity for friendly co-operation. Pressing circumstances impose upon most powers the imperative necessity of pursuing a peaceful policy. It appears to me that the opinion of most thoughtful Russians, whether servants of the state or private individuals, is favourable to England. It would be useless to deny that there are things with regard to which the honest and deliberate feelings of the majority of Englishmen are opposed to Russia. I expect to witness a remarkable change in this respect.

Katkof in the *Moskovsky Vedomosti* praised the pacific speech of the British Ambassador highly.

It would appear that Russia at the time owed much to a brilliant young woman, Olga Novikof, who had become a close friend of the British Ambassador and had done much to interpret Russia to him. Olga Novikof was one of the Kireyefs, an ardent Slavophile. She had married General Novikof in 1860. She knew English but had not then lived in England, a society woman much under the influence of the Grand Duchess Helen, whom she would have liked to imitate.

Madame Novikof's career as a maker of friendships between England and Russia is remarkable. Lord Napier and Ettrick was the first of her conquests. He was moved to Berlin in 1864 but he wrote to her from the Prussian capital:

When I left Russia I wished to say something to the English and the Russians. The merchants gave me an opportunity of doing so. I might have said something merely civil, courteous, and colourless. That would have had no effect one way or the other. I might have said something highly coloured with praise of Russia that would have called forth in England abuse both of Russia and of myself, and many Russians would have said it was mere diplomacy and hypocrisy. I thought the best

Vasilly Zhukovsky

Olga Novikof

compliment I could pay to Russians was to tell them the *truth*, to hold up to them a *true* picture of the relations between England and Russia. To say to all publicly what I have constantly said to *many* privately. You are one witness that I have done so. . . . The English are still generally adverse to Russia, the feelings about Poland, Turkey, Circassia, etc., are still very active with us. To bring England to a better and juster feeling towards Russia great prudence and moderation must be used. The English must be accustomed to hear good said of Russia gradually. You may say that we are very stubborn and unjust. I admit at least that the English are very tenacious of resentments. It is the nature of our nation. That nature must be recognised and dealt with accordingly.

That the "English must be accustomed to hear good said of Russia" was a new line of thought in Anglo-Russian relationship.

Muravief pacified Poland, wreaking some extra vengeance on the Poles because a Don Quixote had taken their part. England had decided not to make war and then overlooked most of what Muravief did. There was a quiet spell until 1866, when Russia took the part of the Christian Cretan insurrectionaries against Turkish rule in Crete.

Charles Villiers, the celebrated M.P. for Wolverhampton, wrote to Olga Novikof—he had just met her at Ems:

In one respect I wish you would be less reserved, and tell me what your country is going to do about Crete. I see the fighting has begun in Crete, and all the world, of course, say that Russia is at the bottom of it all, and Louis Napoleon complains that things are not less quiet in the East! The Russophobia however is all ready to break out again, so tell me that there is no reason for it or perhaps no good reason for it—for with such an Emperor as you have now, we ought to prefer Russians and Christians to Turks.

In October of the same year Villiers appealed to Madame Novikof to assume the rôle of interpreter of Russia and the Russians to English statesmen. This was a piece of advice which Olga Novikof was ready to assimilate, but she was only twenty-five years of age and it was rather much to expect that she should tackle Gladstone and Disraeli at that tender age.

In November, 1866, the Tsarevitch Alexander, heir to the Russian throne, married the Princess Dagmar of Denmark, the sister of the Princess of Wales. A curious feature of the marriage of the Grand Duke Alexander Alexandrovitch was that the Princess Dagmar (Marya Fedorovna) had been previously betrothed to Alexander's eldest brother Nicholas and bequeathed to him on his deathbed. The Prince of Wales, successful in overcoming his mother's prejudice, came to St. Petersburg for the wedding, and thus made his first personal acquaintance with the Russian court. He was then twenty-four years of age, very handsome, and his social gifts made him easily popular among the Russians. "Every *moujik* in the streets seemed anxious to show some signs of good will," he wrote. The Prince attended parades, went wolf hunting, feasted and danced. On November 17 at a ball in St. Petersburg he appeared in Highland costume. The marriage of Alexandra's sister to the heir to the Russian throne, though it had not dispersed his suspicion of Russian designs on India, had gone far to make him a peacemaker.

Dynastic connections are no sure guide to tendency in foreign policy, but we may note as of interest a remove from the German courts in two royal houses, also alliances of the English and Russian heirs with the family of Christian IX of Denmark with whom Prussia was at variance. It did not imply isolation of Prussia in Europe, but it may have tended ultimately to that Anglo-Russian understanding in support of France against Germany which was the basis of the allied operations in the war of 1914–18.

The approach of England towards Russia was marked again by the marriage of the younger brother of the Prince of Wales to the Tsar's only daughter, the Grand Duchess Marya Alexandrovna. After all the Romanofs could not be considered pariahs if a son of Queen Victoria was allowed to marry one of them.

The Duke of Edinburgh was married in St. Petersburg on January 23, 1874. By that time the ill feeling against Russia had died down somewhat and awaited some new sensation in Central Asia or complication in Balkan politics to burst out afresh. Several English towns returned Crimean guns to Russia as a token that all enmity had disappeared. It may be remarked that Edinburgh itself did not do that. The Duke of Edinburgh might marry a Russian but Edinburgh would not relinquish its war trophies, and the captured Crimean guns remain on the Calton Hill to this day. Still it is possible that the Scots would have sent them back if the Russians had been willing to pay carriage.

Queen Victoria sent the Russian bride a sprig of myrtle and a prayer-book with illuminated hymns. She also gave Alfred a prayer-book, "a plain one," saying "My dear mother gave my beloved husband and me Prayer-books, which I now have, and often use, especially the dear Prince's."

To attend this marriage of the Duke of Edinburgh with the Tsar's daughter came the Prince and Princess of Wales and with them came Prince Arthur (of Connaught); and they stopped for a boar hunt on the way. The Crown Prince and Princess of Germany arrived at St. Petersburg on January 19, as also the Crown Prince of Denmark and the Duke of Saxe-Coburg and Gotha, and were received by the Tsar and members of the imperial family. Each party of royal visitors had a special train from the frontier provided by the Tsar. Dean Stanley described the arrival at St. Petersburg: "Never had we such a disembarkation before. There was red cloth laid down into the station, servants dressed like the doges of Venice in red embroidered cloaks and white ruffs."

At a reception at the Winter Palace the diplomatic corps was presented to the Prince of Wales.

The British Ambassador, Lord Loftus, then had audience of the Tsar. He said he trusted that the happy event of the union of the royal and imperial families would establish an intimate and cordial feeling of amity between the two nations. He expressed his satisfaction at seeing the flags of the two nations flying together in St. Petersburg and hoped that they would ever continue to do so. The Tsar reciprocated the solicitations and good wishes; he expressed his anxious desire to cultivate the most friendly relations with England, in the interest of peace, of civilization and humanity. The interview did not pass without some comment on those developments of Russian imperialism which were disturbing the British Foreign Office. The Tsar defended his expedition against Khiva. Loftus replied tactfully that the abolition of slavery in Khiva and the neighboring Khanates was the brightest page in the history of the Tsar's reign. He even assured Alexander

II that he considered as groundless all those fears of the English press regarding the advance of Russia towards India. In his memoir of the interview Lord Loftus wrote: "Nothing could exceed the gracious kindness of His Majesty, nor the heartiness of his expression of good will and friendship towards England."

The marriage of the Duke of Edinburgh and the Grand Duchess was solemnized in the chapel of the Winter Palace.

The Greek service was performed with due impressiveness. The deep tone of the choir, the thrilling force of the chants mingled with the grand voices of the clergy, the magnificent dress and jewelled ornaments of the priesthood, and the impressive forms of the Greek service gave an imposing and solemn effect to the ceremony.

The Emperor, who took his usual place on the right of the altar, looked pale and appeared deeply moved, no doubt feeling acutely his separation from his only daughter, to whom he was devotedly attached—who had been his daily companion—his idol of love and affection. The Empress, who had been in delicate health and showed symptoms of suffering, both physical and mental, stood on the right of the Emperor and next Her Majesty the Crown Princess of Germany, as sister of the bridegroom. Then came the Tsarevna [the wife of the Grand Duke Alexander Alexandrovitch] and the Princess of Wales, the two sisters, beaming with beauty and delight at being together, and on whom the eyes of all rested with admiration and pride.

On the left of the altar were the Prince of Wales, the Crown Prince of Germany, the Duke of Coburg, the Crown Prince of Denmark, and other foreign Princes and members of the Imperial family.

Immediately behind the bride and bridegroom stood the three brothers of the bride, . . . and Prince Arthur, who relieved each other in turn in holding . . . the golden crowns over the heads of the bride and bridegroom.*

* Loftus, Lord Augustus, *Diplomatic Reminiscences.*

And Dean Stanley says:

They were closed round by four groomsmen. There are no
bridesmaids. The crowns are held over their heads so long as
to give the impression of a more than fugitive interest. The
walking round and round the altar, with these four youths with
them, had quite the effect of what originally it must have been,
a wedding dance.

At the conclusion of the Orthodox service the procession moved to the Alexander Hall where Dean Stanley, having changed his robes from red to white, performed the ceremony according to the rites of the
Church of England. He wrote afterwards:

The hall was full from end to end. The Russian choir was
on my right; the English residents on my left; the two English clergy on each side. Then came up the Hall and stood before me the bride and bridegroom, with the Emperor and Empress on their right. The music of the choir broke out as they
advanced. It was a thrilling moment when for the first and last
time in my life, I addressed each by their Christian name—
"Alfred" and "Marie"—and looked each full in the face, as
they looked into mine.

After the marriage ceremonies, Lord Loftus says:

At half-past four, the grand banquet took place at the Winter Palace when 700 guests were seated at table. On this occasion I was seated immediately opposite the Emperor, having
on my right Prince Gorchakof and on my left Prince Reuss,
the German Ambassador. Nothing could exceed the grandeur
of this banquet. The display of magnificent jewels, the bril-
liancy of the uniforms, the mass of ornamental gold and silver
plate, the priceless value of the rarest Sèvres china, added to
the vocal talents of Patti, Albani, and Nicolini, who sang the
most lovely airs during dinner, gave a charm and perfection
to a scene, which, for its unrivalled beauty, is quite indescribable.

After the banquet a Bal Polonaise was given at the palace, at which I was told 3,000 persons were present. No one but the Imperial family and the foreign ambassadors took part in the Polonaise.

The ball terminated at ten o'clock, and at twelve o'clock the Duke and Duchess of Edinburgh, accompanied by the Emperor and the whole Imperial family, left for the station to proceed by special train to Tsarskoe Selo.

The streets through which the Imperial party passed were brilliantly illuminated, and a dense throng had assembled along the whole line to give a parting cheer and blessing to the daughter of their beloved sovereign. Thus terminated the day which I trust will be one of blessing and happiness to the illustrious couple, and will bind in closer amity and friendship the two nations.

Although royal marriages have not the political importance of former times, yet they greatly tend to produce amity and a friendly feeling between nations, and to bring them into more direct communication with each other. But we may assuredly, in the present instance, count on it proving to be a powerful auxiliary in promoting pacific relations between England and Russia, and in assuring thereby the general peace.

Directly after the wedding the Tsar was visited by Franz Joseph, the Emperor of Austria. It was the first visit of any emperor of Austria to St. Petersburg and it had considerable significance. Bismarck, who detested the English royal family, had declined the invitation to the wedding of the Duke of Edinburgh. It did not suit his book that England and Russia be drawn together by dynastic ties. Bismarck comported himself as the controller of Europe and it was his will that his policy and no other should be effective. By himself he did not feel sufficiently strong; he must hold Alexander II to the old alliance and friendship with Prussia. At the same time he had chosen to conciliate his old enemy Austria so that on all important questions he could confront Europe by the Pact of Three Emperors, the *Drei-Kaiser-Bund*. The visit of the Emperor of Austria to St. Petersburg while the English wedding guests were still there was a reminder of the realities of the situation.

The Prince of Wales, quite won over by Russian hospitality, had written his mother adjuring her to abandon her anti-Russian prepossessions, but his feelings were dashed by the reception of the Austrian Emperor and the speech Alexander made in praise of the *Drei-Kaiser-Bund*. The name of Queen Victoria was included in the toast but suddenly all reference to friendship with England sounded hollow in the Prince's ears.

The Emperors drank to peace. Alexander II said:

Je bois à la santé de mon ami l'Empereur François Joseph, que nous sommes heureux de voir au milieu de nous. Dans l'amitié qui nous lie tous les deux avec l'Empereur Guillaume et la Reine Victoria, je reconnais la plus sure garantie de la paix en Europe, si désirée par tous, et si indispensable à tout le monde.

The Emperor Franz Joseph confirmed the sentiment of this toast and asked that a divine blessing might rest upon their efforts for peace. It is, however, possible that this reconciliation with the Emperor of Austria had been sought primarily by Gorchakof with a view to Austrian coöperation in supporting the insurgent Slav nations in the Balkans conspiring to throw off the Turkish yoke.

In May of this same year, 1874, Alexander II left St. Petersburg for Stuttgart to attend the marriage of his niece the Grand Duchess Vera to Prince William of Württemberg. After the wedding the Tsar proceeded to Flushing where he embarked for England. He had intended this visit to be a private and family affair; not a state visit. He came to call upon Queen Victoria and to embrace once more his daughter the Duchess of Edinburgh. But it was not possible for the Tsar of Russia to come to London without it being an event of national importance. Great crowds gathered to stare at him in his carriage wherever he went. The Press dropped its Russophobia, the population cheered, the good points of Alexander were discovered and acclaimed. It seemed that national friendship between England and Russia was being proclaimed.

The Queen greeted Alexander at the foot of the staircase at Windsor Castle. She drove with him to Virginia Water. The Tsar rode on horseback in Windsor Park. Returning to London he dined with the Prince of Wales. He drove in state to the Crystal Palace and heard a choral society sing "Home, Sweet Home," which must have been one of the more trying experiences of his visit. It is said that the audience of 30,000 was "too much absorbed in gazing at the pale, weary, sad-looking gentleman, who took his seat in the Imperial box, to hear or applaud the performance."

The Tsar made his private devotions at the little Russian chapel in Welbeck Street. On the other hand he was welcomed hospitably by the English Church and was presented with an address voted by both Houses of Convocation. He was entertained at a banquet at the Guildhall by the Lord Mayor of London and Corporation. All the speeches on that occasion were on behalf of peace and Anglo-Russian friendship. On the nineteenth of May a grand review was held at Aldershot and the Tsar on horseback saluted the troops just back from the Ashantee War. The following day he visited Woolwich Arsenal. What with a state ball at Buckingham Palace, concerts, reviews, banquets, presentations, the Tsar's time was fully occupied. He expressed himself aś well pleased with the visit. He was impressed by the vast crowds kept so effectually in order by unarmed police. There was no audible demonstration against him—although he had many mortal enemies in London and another attempt on his life was not improbable.

It seemed that the Tsar's visit to England had done much to improve the relationship of the two nations, and certainly it had advanced the prospect of friendship. But nevertheless appearances were deceptive. The suspicion of Russia remained; it was ready to break forth in clamorous expression at the slightest provocation. In February of this year Mr. Gladstone, who was nascently anti-Turk and already somewhat under the influence of Madame Novikof, resigned and gave place to Disraeli, who, being Semitic, was not likely to follow a policy of trusting Russia. All the year, the Russians continued their advance in Central Asia, the English Press in the autumn raised once more the bogey of the menace to India, and the India Office advised the cabinet to order a naval demonstration in the Baltic and to declare war on Russia unless the Central Asian advance was halted.

Actually the time of the Tsar's visit to England was the beginning of a very stormy relationship between the cabinets of London and St. Petersburg, complicated first by the Central Asian advance and the threat to India, and second by the Balkan insurrections of 1875–

76. In both these matters the two nations came near to war.

But there is always in history an undercurrent which has more significance than the surface of affairs. Statesmen and sovereigns are borne along by the stream, perhaps at a barely perceptible pace towards a future not imagined by the contemporary generation.

The new current in European history was coming out of the Franco-Prussian War, the defeat of France, the rise of imperial Germany. In that current England, France and Russia were gradually drawn to sink or swim together.

In this connection an event in the year 1875 is significant. Alexander II interposed to stop a new war between France and Germany. Russia for the first time in modern history taking the side of France against the Prussians. Bismarck was of opinion that France was recovering too rapidly from the effects of her defeat in 1870. She had dispersed her Communists. She was prosperous. She had paid off the £200,000,000 war indemnity. With the mentality of the boxing-ring Bismarck wished to floor France again as she was rising to her feet. There was a military eagerness in Berlin. France was alarmed and appealed to Russia. Queen Victoria wrote to Alexander II asking him to use his influence to avert war. Gorchakof advised restraint to Wilhelmstrasse. And then Alexander II took matters into his own hands by paying the Emperor William I a personal visit. He told the old Kaiser that in his opinion another war with France was impossible. He received the redoubtable Bismarck in a room in the Russian Embassy in Berlin. Paléologue gives verbatim the Tsar's description of this interview with Bismarck. Whether, as often happens in French biographical works, the Tsar's words are fictionalized is not clear. But no doubt the sense of them is right.

Bismarck repeated to me the clumsy explanation he gave yesterday to Gorchakof. I let him have his say, but I warned him in plain terms that never on any pretext would I allow him to attack France. "Without my neutrality," I said, "Germany would be impotent. Now, understand this; I should not remain neutral." Bismarck tried to show me that France is becoming a danger to the German people, as she is reviving too quickly, and no time must be lost in bringing her back to her senses before she has completely reëstablished her military power. He even went so far as to say: "To-day nothing would be easier than for us to enter Paris. Soon we shall not be able to do that." Upon this I stopped him and repeated as firmly as possible that I should never allow him to attack France. He at once swore to me that personally he had no war-like intentions.*

From that date some coldness crept into the relationship between Germany and Russia and also some perceptible warmth entered the relationship of France and Russia.

* Paléologue, Maurice, *Le roman tragique de l'Empereur Alexandre II.*

XII.

THE ADVANCE INTO ASIA

THE nomadic nature of the Slavs who have wandered from their original cradle in the Carpathians all the way to Kamchatka explains why the Russian Empire continually expanded. Through the centuries the Russians went on and went on into hollow Asia till they reached the Pacific, and, not content with that, crossed the northern ice to penetrate the American continent in Alaska. It was not due so much to imperialism as to restlessness. There was nothing Roman in their conquest of Siberia. On the other hand the conquest of the Volga steppes, the Don country and the Caucasus represented revenge for Tartar and Mahometan oppression under the hordes. The nomadic characteristics obtained leadership and direction in the wars of the Cross against the Crescent. The southeastern expansion of Russia was a carrying of the Cross into Mahometan territory. The Byzantine Cross became the symbol of political liberation from Mahometans. In the Russian victories over the heathen the Cross obtained a worldly glory which was never coveted by Christ. But of course churches are not identical with Christianity. They are mostly political organizations of people who call themselves Christians. They are human institutions, each with a glory of its own, and need not be criticized with reference to the Gospel which was addressed to the heart of man and not to a committee or society.

The Russian Orthodox Church, for several centuries identified with Russian nationalism, was a very glorious church. It embodied in a visible form the ideals and aspirations of a young nation. Its triumph was the triumph of Russia. It marched into the nineteenth century with tapestried banners, wonder-working pictures of the saints, censers smoking and swinging, long-haired priests and monks chanting marvellous songs derived almost entirely from the folk music of the Russian people.

The West when it became aware of this Church looked upon it askance. Foreigners could not understand a word of its liturgy or grasp anything much of its practice. It was at first regarded as something *obscure*. Then it was identified with the Greek Church. The Greeks were in hopeless decadence; therefore the Church of Russia must be decadent. That the Tsar was the head of the Church and that there was no patriarchate was overlooked. That there was a great amount of superstition and belief in the miraculous was obvious, and no Russian denied it.

Russian emigrants in London and Paris, those who were freethinkers and revolutionaries, explained the Church unsympathetically as "a survival from the Middle Ages," "a department of tsardom," "a hocus-pocus of legend and tradition," "an institution used by the Government to keep people in oppression," "an instrument for raising popular enthusiasm for wars on the Turks."

From what they heard of it, Protestants disliked the Church because they prefer a religion founded on good works to a religion founded on faith and praise. The Roman Catholics could not approve of it because theirs is a religion of law and authority, whereas Orthodoxy is to them barbaric, uncontrolled, uncultured. The Jews hated it because it was intolerant of Judaism and never rebuked the persecutors of the Jews. It is not difficult to see why the Holy Orthodox Church obtained an evil or at least doubtful repute abroad. It was not until the late nineteenth century that it began to be undersood that the Orthodox Church, whatever its imperfections, represented the Russian people and was not merely part of the will of tsardom.

It would be idle to deny that the Orthodox Church was in part responsible for the Crimean War. That was not an unpopular war in Russia. The masses believed they were fighting for Christ, they were fighting to free the Christian Slavs of the Balkans and the Holy places of Constantinople and Jerusalem from the unclean hands of the Mahometan. Nicholas I had not the task of enkindling enthusiasm for that war; it was there in advance and ready to be used. There was a national and ecclesiastical ferment against the Mahometans. And when the war was over and lost, there was no ill feeling against the throne on that account. The revolutionary danger within Russia rose not from the loss of the war but from the restiveness of the nation under serfdom.

The war ceased but the movement against Mahometanism continued in the minds and wills of Russians, in the mountains of the Caucasus and on the plains of Central Asia. It was allied to the nomadic spirit. Russia conquered but she also colonized. She made all the territories she occupied into an extension of Russia.

The Russians moved south from Orenburg and Semipalatinsk, and east from the Caspian to take over the land of tribes wandering with tents and flocks over thousands of miles, to take over Seven Rivers Land, to take over Turkestan with the resplendent walled cities of Bokhara and Samarkand, ancient conquests of Darius and Alexander the Great. The new Empire was in frontier contact with Persia and extended to the borders of Mongolia and Kashmir.

The English asked the Russians: "What is your objective?" Quite frankly the Russians answered that they did not know. Asked why they had proceeded so far on the way to India they replied that they could have gone farther but preferred to stay to assimilate the territory they had annexed. England demanded that at least the Russians should not infringe the neutrality of Afghanistan. England demanded that Russia admit that Afghanistan was entirely outside her sphere of influence. The Russians were willing to admit it if it could be agreed where Afghanistan territory was supposed to begin. Lord Clarendon at the Foreign Office in Mr. Gladstone's ministry of 1868 conceived of Afghanistan as a "buffer state." Lord Augustus Loftus, British Minister at St. Petersburg, was constantly engaged in thrashing out the problem of the delimitations of British and Russian interests in Central Asia. The diplomatic wrangle continued when Disraeli became Prime Minister and Lord Granville Secretary for Foreign Affairs.

At first it was desired to have the Oxus River considered the frontier of Afghanistan. Then Gorchakof, who was rather vague in his knowledge of Central Asian geography, discovered that the domain of Bokhara extended a long way beyond the Oxus River. He instructed General Kaufman to make an investigation of the supposed frontiers of "these distant and imperfectly known countries." When he had obtained Kaufman's report he submitted an alternative plan to London. Negotiations in England were somewhat hampered by the fact that the Russian Ambassador, Count Brunnof, was aged and infirm and was in no fit state to attend to business. The Tsar became aware of his Ambassador's incapacity when he visited England. In 1874 Brunnof was retired and Count Shuvalof, at that time head of the Russian police, was given his place.

A neutral zone between Afghanistan and Asiatic Russia had been agreed upon in 1871 and ratified in 1872, but this had not prevented Russia from invading the neutral zone in 1873 and taking possession of Khiva. Lord Granville was a complacent foreign minister and made little protest against the infringement of the neutral zone. But Granville's passivity was not popular in England and did much to weaken Gladstone's administration. When Disraeli came into power in 1874 there was a much more spirited opposition to the imperial policy of Russia. It amounted almost at once to the danger of war.

English newspapers said that the next *étape* in the Russian march to India would be the capture of the city of Merv. Eventually someone wittily coined the word "mervousness" to express the fear of an invasion of India. It was said that in the last testament of Peter the Great the conquest of Constantinople was laid down as a sacred duty, and to Constantinople some people added India.

The British Ambassador took this question up with Alexander II personally. The Tsar said that the testament of Peter the Great was apocryphal and had been invented in Paris. The comment of Lord Loftus on this was interesting:

The misfortune has been that its ambitious designs have been in some measure acted upon and realised. This result has not originated with the Sovereign, although he is an absolute monarch, but rather from the dominant part played by the military administration. Where an enormous standing army is maintained, it is absolutely necessary to find employment for it. Every officer is anxious to gain the St. George, or some such decoration, while both men and officers seek to enrich themselves. When a system of conquest sets in, as in Central Asia, one acquisition of territory leads to another, and the difficulty is where to stop. It was so with ourselves in India, and even now it still continues.

The Tsar is very powerless in this question. Fresh conquests of territory are laid at his feet, gained by the prowess and blood of his troops. He cannot refuse them without offending his army; and troops, so far distant as Central Asia is from the control of the central power, are difficult to restrain. . . . There was no more peaceful sovereign than the Emperor Alexander II, but he was unable to withstand the racial fanaticism —supported by the military influence . . .*

Gorchakof referred to the extension of empire in Central Asia as "an extension of weakness," but it was not an extension of weakness, although at first the administration of the new territories was very costly. Actually it was a great economic gain. Its political significance was not a threat to England in India but an outflanking of the Mahometan world centered at Constantinople. It strengthened the conviction of the rebellious Christians in the Balkans that the Turk, but for the backing of England, was not so formidable that he could not be deposed from overlordship by vigorous insurrection. In Russia it enkindled once more the Slavophile fervor for "brother Slavs."

* Loftus, Lord Augustus, *Diplomatic Reminiscences.*

Russia was again conscious of great military force and feared no enemy, not even a combination of enemies such as had oppposed her in 1854.

Alexander II could have been called a pacifist. He had enforced peace upon Germany. He had extended an olive branch to Austria. He had repeatedly smoothed down English anti-Russian agitation. But he was a pacifist of Cromwell's stamp who prayed to God but kept his powder dry. In 1872 conscription was introduced in Russia and the army was greatly increased in numbers.

The emancipation of the serfs had made necessary a change in the method of recruiting. Up to 1861 the army had consisted mainly of serfs or of political or petty offenders who had been drafted into it. After emancipation conditions of army service were greatly improved. There is a famous Russian folk tale of how the devil once met a private soldier standing on sentry and agreed to change places with him for a short while. At the end of the stipulated period the devil was greatly relieved to give the soldier back his uniform because actually a soldier's life was much worse than anything he had ever experienced in hell. Alexander II improved the pay and increased the privileges of the private soldier and as a result before conscription was enacted he obtained a great number of volunteers.

The reform of the army rendered urgent by the failure of Russian arms in the Crimean conflict was long delayed because Alexander was not a man of war and intended, if possible, to keep his country out of foreign strife. Moreover domestic reform seemed to him much more important and must have the first place. There was an additional difficulty: reform of the army might be costly and the finances were in no fit state to stand the expense. Prince Vasilly Dolgoruky, afterwards head of the Third Section (the secret police), was the first war minister of the new reign. But his hands were tied. He was obliged to occupy himself altering the regimental uniforms and was scoffed at as a "military tailor." It was only in 1862, the year after the emancipation, that a reorganization of the military forces was seriously taken in hand. Then General Dimitry Miliutin was made minister of war.

Dimitry Miliutin was a younger brother of that Nicholas Miliutin who had made himself prominent in the labor for the emancipation of the serfs and he shared his brother's views. High society in St. Petersburg was greatly shocked: a man who was no aristocrat, *un homme de rien du tout*, made war minister—such an appointment was unheard of. To make matters worse the young minister consulted experts and technicians and not "gold-laced young nobles or spur-clashing horse guards." He was an unimposing quiet little fellow who looked more like a grocer than a statesman. His appearance did not belie his character; he despised gifted amateurs, fops, drawing-room society, and he could not be disturbed by gossip or intrigue because he felt sure of the complete confidence of the Tsar. His zeal was only checked when he proposed to abolish all the fancy regiments of St. Petersburg, the picturesque Chevalier Garde, etc. Alexander himself favored the ornate Circassian Guard and when he wore a uniform was always to be seen in theirs. But Dimitry Miliutin interpreted Alexander's humanity to the army, made certain that corporal punishment was really abolished, punished fraudulent quartermasters who sold the rations, made sure that the troops did not starve. He rooted out corruption. He made merit the motive for promotion and did much to check the influence of merely noble birth in the profession of arms. He hated "playing soldiers," parades, military ceremonial. For the first time Russia had a war minister who was purely realist.

As the years passed and the character of Alexander II somewhat changed, the Tsar began to regard his army more as a possibly aggressive force and less as a guarantee of security from invasion. He decided, after the Franco-Prussian War, to make a great increase. In 1872 nearly a third of the Russian army was voluntary. But an imperial ukase of that year imposed a new system of conscription. It came into force in 1874 and multiplied the available military reserves several times. The Guard regiments were armed with a new rifle, the *berdanka*, which was considered to be one of the best in the world. Artillery on the Prussian model had been introduced. The new Russian army in its equipment was not unlike the army of Von Moltke which had crushed France in 1870.

In 1878, when Russia, having made war on Turkey, stood with her army at the gates of Constantinople, Macdermot sang in the London music halls:

> We don't want to fight,
> But by jingo if we do,
> We've got the arms, we've got the men,
> We've got the money too.

The origin of the word "jingoism"—but in fact Russia had more arms and more men than England for the conflict.

XIII.

RISE OF BULGARS AND SERBS

IT is true that in 1871 Alexander II broke the covenant of the Treaty of Paris, tore up the treaty like "a scrap of paper." On the other hand, one of the allied Powers signing that treaty had also failed in certain obligations. Turkey had agreed to take steps to place her Christian subjects on a legal equality with Mahometans. England, France and Austria, the "concert of Europe," bound themselves to resume war on Russia if she failed to carry out the provisions of the treaty, but naturally enough they refused to use force with Turkey if she continued her barbarous treatment of Bulgars and Serbs in her dominions. The Sultan had a privileged position, propped up in his sick bed by the Western Powers, with a bundle of blank checks in his hand. In cash alone he helped himself to over two hundred million pounds. But the *baksheesh* of the West did not suffice; the Sultan taxed his subjects mercilessly. And his tyrannical oppression of his Christian subjects caused Russia to make several representations to the Powers. England, the chief protector of the Sultan, was not moved by the outrages on the Christian communities until the massacre of the Bulgarians in 1876.

The Slavs were disappointed by the result of the Crimean War but did not lose hope. Though shut off from Russia's assistance they conspired to throw off the Turkish yoke themselves. The proud motto of the Serbs —*Serbia herself alone saved herself*—was a fitting one.

The Serbs were pioneers in the struggle for Balkan freedom, rising in 1804 under Kara George, the ancestor of the Karageorgevitch kings (Peter I, Alexander and Peter II). They cleared a considerable area of the country of Turks, defeated all opposing forces, and the Sultan offered to grant home rule under Kara George as ruling prince in 1807. Encouraged by the Russians, the Serbs went on to fight for complete independence. But in 1812, with Napoleon invading Russia, the Russians hastily abandoned their Serbian allies. The Turks used their opportunity and reconquered Serbia. Kara George fled. The Turks put a Serbian governor, Milosh Obrenovitch, in control of the province. Two years later Milosh revolted and overcame the Turks. Serbia gained a further measure of self-rule, but it was not until the year 1829 that Milosh Obrenovitch was recognized as hereditary Prince of Serbia. The Turks still retained the right to garrison all Serbian strongholds. The rivalry of the Obrenovitches and the Karageorgevitches need not concern us here. Apart from an internecine struggle in domestic politics the nation was united in opposition to the Turks, in a desire to drive out the Moslem garrisons and to set free of Turkish rule more territory which was historically Christian and Slav.

The grandson of Kara George, Peter Karageorgevitch, was in exile in Paris in 1870. He volunteered to serve in the French army against the Prussians. After the war the soldier prince returned to the Balkans under the incognito of Peter Mrkonitch. He entered Bosnia in 1875 and placed himself at the head of the Serbian conspirators there. Aided by the Montenegrin tribesmen he raised a rebellion against Turkish rule and was completely successful. Prince Peter, afterwards King of Serbia, freed Bosnia and Herzegovina.

The news of this triumph like a wind ruffled the hearts of all the Slavs in the Balkans. It stirred up excitement in Russia likewise, where Slavophilism became Panslavism and the new movement for a war with Turkey was born.

The first sequel to the successful revolt in Bosnia and Herzegovina was a rising for freedom in Bulgaria in 1876.

One of the chief grievances of the Bulgarian peasants was the continuous expropriation of their lands by the Turks who pursued a policy of settling Tartars and Circassians in Bulgaria at the expense of the Christian populations. Lawless tribesmen from Asia Minor wrought havoc in the land and there was no redress. But, apart from grievances, the Bulgars had a sense that after centuries of bondage the dawn of freedom had been announced by the rebellion in Bosnia. There was a Bulgar awakening, and awakening, they took to arms. But the Bulgarian revolt of May 1, 1876, was neither organized nor led—it was natural and spontaneous, the movement of a few villages rather than the whole of the Bulgarian people. The Turks crushed it at once. The rebellion was not only defeated; the Bulgars were visited by a punishment of unusual ferocity: thousands of men, women and children put to the sword, the cutting off of women's breasts, children dragged to death by galloping horses, the customary barbarities, natural enough in a brutal race, but hair-raising in bulletins to the civilized West.

Disraeli supported the Turks and indeed scoffed at the outrages, but the stories of the atrocities in Bulgaria as recounted by Edwin Pears in the *Daily News* and officially reported by Mr. Baring, roused the conscience of many who began to think that England could not remain any longer security for the behavior of the Turks in Europe.

The Treaty of Paris of 1856 had become a dead letter as far as the coöperation of the Great Powers was concerned. It was no longer possible for England, France and Austria to combine to regulate the Eastern Question. France had become friendly to Russia. Austria-Hungary had her own interest in the Near East and had to recover the prestige lost in conflict with Italy and then with Prussia by a future domination of the Balkans.

Count Julius Andrassy, Chancellor of Austro-Hungary since 1871, did much to raise the prestige of Austria which had languished since the liberation of Italy and the conflict with Bismarck. He cultivated a friendly though insincere relationship with Russia and a better feeling between Prussians and Austrians. The three empires of Russia, Germany and Austria were in some sort of diplomatic unison, an achievement of diplomatic suavity on a basis of insincerity. Instead of England, France and Austria regulating the Eastern situation, it was Germany, Austria and Russia who met to consult and frame measures. They thought to localize the revolt in Bosnia and Herzegovina and prevent the insurrectionary spirit spreading to the whole of the Balkan Peninsula.

The Andrassy note presented to the Sultan on January 31, 1876, advised the granting of such reforms and privileges to the Bosnian insurgents as would insure a peaceful settlement of the rebellion. Approval of the terms of the note had been obtained from France, England and Italy, and it was presented at the Sublime Porte by six ambassadors individually. Europe ranged against him, the Sultan promised reform and a general amnesty.

But as the Turkish promises were not fulfilled the Slav insurgents did not lay down their arms. On April 3 following the presentation of the Andrassy note it was announced from Constantinople that the April interest on the Ottoman debt would not be paid. That was in fact the Sultan's rejoinder to Europe. The Balkan conflagration was extended on the first of May by the Bulgarian rising. The Turks proceeded to deal with that in characteristic fashion, without regard to the advice of European states. Their indifference to European opinion was shown by the outrage of the sixth of May when the French and German consuls in Salonika were murdered.

Alexander II with Gorchakof went to Berlin to consult the German Emperor and Bismarck as to further measures, and as a result the more peremptory Berlin memorandum was despatched to the Sultan. The Grand Vizier produced a new code of laws which Gorchakof said was not a code of laws but a novel. Elaborated by the atrocities which occurred later in the month the novel might have been called a "shocker."

Lord Derby, Disraeli's Foreign Minister, disapproved the Berlin memorandum and no support was given to it. Instead the British fleet was ordered to the Bosphorus to demonstrate the protection of England granted to Turkey in the face of the Russo-German menace.

Two days later, May 30, there was a palace revolution in Constantinople and the Sultan Abdul Aziz was deposed and thrown into prison. A few days later he was found dead. He was supposed to have committed suicide with a pair of scissors with which he opened one of his arteries, but there is another story that he was murdered with the scissors.

The new Sultan, Murad IV, was feeble-minded, and more incapable than his predecessor of controlling his country or his people.

The Balkan conflagration extended. On June 29 Prince Milan of Serbia and Prince Nicholas of Montenegro both declared war against the Turks.

It is highly probable that if Bosnians, Serbs, Bulgars and Montenegrins had been left without interference to settle old scores with the Turks, and if the Turks had not been armed, officered and financed by England there would have been a complete purge of Turkish rule and oppression in the Balkan Peninsula.

But if the Turks were to be hustled out of Europe, bag and baggage, Austria was at least interested to have a share in the spoils. And Russia could not allow the good work to go on without throwing herself into the trouble. As far as Alexander II was concerned it was against his will and better judgment that he ultimately declared war on Turkey.

His intellect was somewhat sluggish and he gave way to what seemed the logic of events. Bismarck was more interested in Russia going to war with Turkey than in keeping the peace. But it was not his intention to help Russia. He played a double rôle, assuring Gorchakof as "man to man" that Germany would give Russia armed support, though he said he could not use the same words as Chancellor of the Reich: "He reserved to himself a certain elasticity in the expression of his intentions." In truth he had not the slightest intention of military intervention in the Balkans. He said the whole matter was not worth the life of one Pomeranian grenadier. Bismarck moreover certainly did not wish to become embroiled with England.

Alexander II had to resolve the question: "At what point will Russia make war?" but instead of answering steadfastly, "At no point," he found his conception of the limit of national patience.

Russia herself, led by the Slavophile writers, Katkof, Aksakof and others, was much ahead of the Tsar in eagerness for war against the Turks. The press criticized the dilatoriness of the Government and its supposed apathy and indifference towards the interests of the Christian population. The Church was standing and facing the Near East like a congregation saying the creed. The *bourgeois*, the manufacturers and townsfolk would not be outdone in extra-territorial patriotism. The Moscow zemstvo voted twenty thousand roubles out of taxes for the relief of sufferers. Funds were opened, collections made. Volunteers enrolled themselves for hospital work.

The British Ambassador at St. Petersburg reported that the Government was embarrassed by the excitement of the Russian nation. He noted "the commencement of a religious movement which finally drew within its compass the court, the government and the nation, and became the leading spirit of a national policy from which there was no means of receding."

The news from the Balkans throughout the year 1876 was such as to keep the Russians in a state of fever—the massacres of the Bulgars, the first defeat of the Serbs, and the heroism and death of the first volunteer, Nicholas Kireyef.

Nicholas Kireyef was a brother of Olga Novikof and as strong a Slavophile as she was. He had been sent to Belgrade by the Russian Slavonic committee in charge of an ambulance. But when he found the Serb army in such poor case, almost devoid of officers and direction, he quit hospital work and took a commission. He was a Russian Guard officer with due military training and capable of helping the Serbs, but he was killed leading his brigade in action at the Battle of Zaitchar on July 18, 1876.

Kinglake has described this event and its significance:

Nicholas Kireyef was a noble, and by nature a man of an enthusiastic disposition, accustomed to the idea of self-sacrifice. Upon the outbreak of Prince Milan's insurrection he went on to Serbia with the design of acting simply under the banner of the Red Cross, and had already entered upon his humane task when he found himself called upon by General Chernyaef to accept the command of what we may call a brigade—a force of some five thousand infantry, consisting of volunteers and militiamen, supported, it seems, by five guns; and before long he not only had to take his brigade into action but to use it as the means of assailing an entrenched position. Kireyef very well understood that the irregular force entrusted to him was far from being one that could be commanded in the hour of battle by taking a look with a field-glass at a thing and saying a few words to an aide-de-camp, so he determined to carry forward his men by the simple and primitive expedient of personally advancing in front of them. He was a man of great stature, with extraordinary beauty of feature and—whether owing to mid-summer heat, or from any wild, martyr-like, or dare-devil impulse—he chose, as he had done from the first, to be clothed all in white. Whilst advancing in front of his troops against the Turkish battery he was struck—first by a shot passing through his left arm, then presently by another one, which struck him in the neck; and then again by yet another one, which shattered his right hand and forced him to drop his sword. But despite all these wounds, he was still continuing his resolute advance when a fourth shot passed through his lungs, and brought him at length to the ground, yet did not prevent him from uttering—although with great effort—the cry of "forward! forward!"

According to Salisbury, an English volunteer who also held a commission in the Serbian army at the time, when Kireyef thus fell to the ground shouting "forward!" two Serb soldiers raised him and carried the wounded soldier in their arms at the head of the column. Then a fifth bullet struck Kireyef in the chest and he was dead.

Their leader's death threw the soldiers into hopeless confusion; they paused a moment, then turned and fled. But, to the credit of the two militiamen, who were carrying the lifeless clay of their commander, they did not relinquish their burden, but attempted to bear it away. This, however, the Turks were determined to prevent, and they poured a storm of bullets on these two poor men who were so bravely endeavouring to perform an act of mercy. Both fell, pierced by bullets. . . . The Turks seized Kireyef's body and sent it to Widdin, where they mutilated it and exhibited it; and to the application of the fallen hero's friends for leave to convey the remains to Russia, Osman Pasha, to his eternal disgrace, gave a flat refusal.

But to resume the words of Kinglake:

These are the bare facts upon which a huge superstructure was speedily raised. It may be that the grandeur of the young officer's form and stature, and the sight of the blood showing vividly on his white attire, added something extraneous and weird to the sentiment which might well be inspired by witnessing his personal heroism. But be that as it may, the actual result was that accounts of the incident—accounts every day

growing more and more marvellous—flew so swiftly from city
to city, from village to village, that before seven days had
passed the smouldering fire of Russian enthusiasm leapt up
into a dangerous flame. Under countless green domes, big and
small, priests chanting the *"Requiem"* for a young hero's soul,
and setting forth the glory of dying in defence of "synortho-
dox" brethren, drew war-like responses from men who, while
still in cathedral or church, cried aloud that they too would go
where Kireyef had gone; and so many of them hastened to
keep their word that before long a flood of volunteers from
many parts of Russia was pouring fast into Belgrade. To
sustain the once kindled enthusiasm apt means were taken.
The simple photograph representing the young Kireyef's noble
features soon expanded to large-sized portraits; and fable then
springing forward in the path of truth, but transcending it
with the swiftness of our modern appliances, there was consti-
tuted, in a strangely short time, one of those stirring legends
which used to be the growth of long years—a legend half war-
like, half-superstitious, which exalted a really tall hero to the
dimensions of a giant, and showed him piling up hecatombs
by a mighty slaughter of Turks!

The mine—the charged mine of enthusiasm upon which this
kindling spark fell—was the same in many respects that we
saw giving war-like impulsion to the Russia of 1853, but to
the enthusiasm of a sensitive Church for the cause of its orthodox brethren—to the passion of a northern and predatory
state for conquest in sunny climes—to that kind of religious
fervour which mainly yearned after masses under the dome of
St. Sophia—to that longing for a guardian-angelship which,
however fraternal ostensibly, might perhaps carry with it the
priceless key of the Straits, there was now added the wrath—
the just wrath at the thought of Bulgaria—which Russia
shared with our people; whilst, moreover, this time there
blazed up the fierce hatred of race against race, incited by Pan-
slavonic agitation, and withal the eager joyous desire of a
newly usurping democracy to use the monarch's prerogative of
determining between peace or war.*

* Kinglake, A. W., *The Invasion of the Crimea* (6th ed.), Preface.

Count Nicholas Ignatief, the Russian Ambassador at Constantinople, was not obviously working for war. He wrote Gorchakof that in his opinion the war movement was being engineered by Bismarck in order to extend the influence of Austria in the Balkan Peninsula, and in order to weaken Russia's position in Europe by embroiling her again with England. Austria's view was that the Slav nations could not exist in a state of complete independence, and it was her intention, supported by Germany, to enter upon a protectorate of the liberated territory of Bosnia and Herzegovina. It is even considered in some quarters that Austria had deliberately inspired and encouraged the revolt of the Serbs in Bosnia, having always in view her ultimate occupation of the country.

The Tsar wished peace, not on mere political grounds, but because in any case he preferred peace to war, the harvest of reform and trade to the glory and aggrandizement of victory on a battle field.

General Michael Chernyaef, in command of the Serbian forces, was a Russian commander in chief, and that alone must have made it appear to England that Russia was behind the insurrection of Milan Obrenovitch. He was a hero of the Central Asian conquest. In 1864 he made a famous march with a thousand men across the flying sand deserts of Turkestan to Chimkent. Acting against instructions he attacked and captured the great city of Tashkent. So great was the popular enthusiasm for his success that his insubordination was at first overlooked by Alexander II and he was presented with a sword of honor. But he had not been allowed to return to Central Asia and he had retired from the service in July, 1874. Chernyaef was a Slavophile. As a civilian he devoted himself to Panslavism. He bought the *Russky Mir* and edited it on Slavophile lines. Prince Milan Obrenovitch of Serbia offered him the post of commander in chief of his army and he accepted. But although in a sense he was an independent person, he could easily have been forbidden to take a command which was so compromising for Russia.

Chernyaef declared that he had under his command 125,000 well-armed troops, 200 guns, 24,000 cavalry and a reserve of 100,000 men. This should have been a formidable force with which to oppose the Turks. Nevertheless the Serbian army suffered a series of defeats. Some hundreds of Russian officers had resigned their commissions in the Russian army, it being promised that they should be reinstated upon their return to Russia, and had hastened to place themselves under Chernyaef. But they did not know the Serbian language and they found the soldiers under their command to be wild and undisciplined. Chernyaef also discovered that the Turks were stouter enemies than the tribesmen of Central Asia. He was a failure as a commander: a Serb had been a better choice.

In September Chernyaef prematurely proclaimed Prince Milan Obrenovitch King of Serbia, but before the autumn was over the victorious Turks were within striking distance of Belgrade. The Serbian insurrection had proved a complete failure. Then Great Britain began to press the Turks to grant an armistice. It was impossible even for a pro-Turk government to stand by and see Serbia destroyed. Mr. Gladstone's agitation had borne some good fruit. Encouraged by the seeming change in the policy of England, the Tsar and Gorchakof went a stage further. On November 1 Ignatief

was instructed to inform the Porte that if within ten
days it did not agree to an unconditional armistice of
six weeks or two months, and if it did not give immediate orders to arrest military operations in Serbia,
the Ambassador would leave Constantinople with all
the members of the Embassy, and that diplomatic relations would be broken off.

Thus, it looked like war in November, 1876, but the
Turks gave way and promised the armistice which had
been demanded.

As a result of the stories of atrocities, public opinion
in England had become much more divided. The
friends of the Turks, led by Lord Beaconsfield and
Lord Derby, were placed in two minds by the clamor
of the Liberals. There were now some Englishmen
eager that England should make alliance with Russia
and coöperate to drive the Turks out of Europe. The
leader of popular sentiment against Turkey was of
course Gladstone, who besides being sincerely horrified
by the atrocities had his own personal object of dis-
crediting and dethroning Beaconsfield. He said:

> I entreat my countrymen, upon whom far more than per-
> haps any other people in Europe it depends, to require and in-
> sist that our Government, which has been working in one di-
> rection, shall work in the other, and shall apply all its vigour
> to concur with all the other states of Europe in obtaining the
> extinction of the Turkish executive power in Bulgaria. Let the
> Turks now carry away their abuses in the only possible man-
> ner, namely, by carrying off themselves . . . bag and bag-
> gage . . . clear out from the province they have desolated and
> profaned. This thorough riddance, this most blessed deliver-
> ance is the only reparation we can make to the memory of those
> heaps upon heaps of dead; to the violated purity alike of
> matron, of maiden and of child; to the civilisation which has

been affronted and ashamed; to the laws of God, or if you like of Allah; to the moral sense of mankind at large. There is not a criminal in a European gaol, there is not a cannibal in the South Sea Islands, whose indignation would not arise and overboil at the recital of that which has been done, which has too late been examined, but which remains unavenged: which has left behind all the foul and fierce passions that produced it, and which may again spring up in another murderous harvest, from the soil soaked and reeking with blood, and in the air tainted with every imaginable deed of crime and shame.

Lord Salisbury, at that time Secretary of State for India, was one of the first Conservatives to realize the effect of the atrocity stories upon the popular mind and he exerted a moderating influence upon the pro-Turkish sympathies of Lord Beaconsfield. "There is no doubt the British lion, whose nerves are not so good as they were, has been driven half-mad by the Bulgarian stories which indeed are horrible enough in all conscience," he wrote in September, 1876. And in the same month he informed Beaconsfield, "It is clear enough that the traditional Palmerston policy is at an end. We have not the power, even if we have the wish, to give back any of the revolted districts to the *discretionary* government of the Porte." To Sir Louis Mallet he wrote, "I deplored the Crimean War and I heartily wish the Turks were out of Europe."

Alexander II must have been aware of the change in public opinion in England. He told the British Ambassador how anxious he still was for a friendly understanding with England.

His Majesty spoke with feelings of deep emotion. He referred to his daughter, expressing the pleasure it had given him lately to see the Duke of Edinburgh, and the comfort it had been to him to witness the happiness of the Duke and Duchess, and with great warmth of feeling he said: "Is it likely that I should entertain views hostile to my daughter's adopted country, which might produce a rupture between the two countries?"*

Upon the acceptance by the Porte of the Russians' demand for an armistice, the British Government invited the Powers to a conference at Constantinople, and Lord Salisbury was sent as British Plenipotentiary. Later in November the Tsar received an address from the nobility and zemstvos, to which he replied:

I thank you for the sentiments you have been good enough to express to me in reference to the present state of political affairs. It is already known to you that Turkey has yielded to my demands for the immediate conclusion of an armistice, in order to put an end to the needless effusion of blood in Serbia and Montenegro. . . . I know that all Russia most warmly sympathizes with me in the sufferings of our brethren and coreligionists. The true interests of Russia are dearer to me than all, and I wish to spare Russian blood from being shed. I have, therefore, endeavored, and shall continue to endeavor, to obtain an amelioration of the position of the Christians in the East by pacific means.

Negotiations will commence shortly at Constantinople between the Great Powers to bring about a peaceful arrangement. My heart's wish is for a peaceful agreement. Should we not obtain from the Porte such guarantees for carrying out the reforms we have a right to demand, I am firmly determined to act independently; and I am convinced that the whole of Russia will support me, should the honor of Russia require it, and that Moscow will give the example. May God help us to carry out our sacred mission.

* Loftus, Lord Augustus, *Diplomatic Reminiscences.*

XIV.

COUNT PETER SHUVALOF

THE Tsar was represented at London at this critical time, when the jingoes wanted war, by Count Peter Shuvalof. He had passed from the Secret Police, the Third Division, to Chesham House, and it was not considered a promotion. Maurice Paléologue in his book about Alexander's love affair with Catherine says that the counter-espionage of the Tsar discovered that Shuvalof, in his cups, had said that he would break the influence of the Tsar's mistress somehow, and his words were reported to Alexander.

A little later, in the beginning of June, 1874, when the Tsar was taking the waters at Ems, the Chief of the Third Section came to him to make his usual report. The Emperor received him cordially with these words:

"I congratulate you, Peter Andreyevitch."

"May I ask, Sire, in what way I have deserved your Majesty's congratulations?"

"I've just appointed you my ambassador in London."

In a rather stifled voice Shuvalof stammered out his thanks.*

The transition from police service to Embassy seems at first glance astonishing but there is much to be said for placing the chief of spies in the domestic service at the head of the spies at a good look-out abroad. And Shuvalof was of good family: in London there was not the slightest objection to the appointment.

* Paléologue, Maurice, *Le roman tragique de l'Empereur Alexandre II*.

Shuvalof, who was responsible for the safety of the Tsar's person, had been a success at the head of the Third Division. Since he replaced the incompetent military dandy, Prince Vasilly Dolgoruky, in that function, there had been no further attempts on the Tsar's life.

Alexander had wavered between a lenient police system and a police terror. His personal inclinations were for leniency. He detested the blue uniforms and the officiousness of those who wore them. The spies would report an insolent expression used at the St. Petersburg Chess Club when someone's king was in jeopardy, and the Tsar would throw the report in the wastepaper basket and give the spy twenty-five roubles, telling him, "You are dismissed the service."

The most feared spy was a certain General Dubbelt who had been a pet of Nicholas I. Dubbelt over a whist table one evening said that the "sledge which he had drawn uphill for thirty years was now going downhill and was slipping over a precipice." He was obliged to retire.

But it is an unfortunate fact that severity has always paid rulers in Russia. The slave mentality does not understand moderation and leniency. It is the same in private as in public affairs; servants must be controlled with a severity intolerable in England or America, or servants will control masters. Dostoievsky's story *Foma Fomitch* is an amusing illustration of this truth. In severe regimes such as those of Peter the Great, Nicholas I, Alexander III, the life of the sovereign was safe from the assassin; in the more liberal periods of the reign of Alexander II and Nicholas II there was much more danger.

Prince Alexander Gorchakof

Count Peter Shuvalof

When Karakozof made his attempt on Alexander's life in 1866 it seemed to the Tsar that after all his father had been right and that leniency was a mistake. Prince Vasilly Dolgoruky humbled himself before Alexander II and said, "I am guilty; punish me." Alexander forgave him for his technical offence but removed him from his post and made him Lord High Chamberlain. The Tsar looked around for a more capable man and his choice fell on Shuvalof, the Governor-General of the Baltic regions of Courland and Livonia, another handsome and elegant courtier, but of proved capacity in administration.

Shuvalof raised the Third Division to its former position of prestige and dreaded power. He removed men with gloved hands and let brutal men like Muravief do the brutal work which a reduction of revolutionary activity demanded. He kept a rigorous straight course directed to security and would not be diverted by faction of any kind, either reactionary or liberal. He incurred the odium of the Slavophiles by the deaf ear he turned to the cause of the Slavs. But he earned such a reputation as a man of power almost greater than that of the Tsar that he was nicknamed "Peter the Fourth." Julius Eckardt, writing prematurely, thus summed up his position in St. Petersburg:

When it is rumored abroad, as has been recently frequently the case, that a brilliant career—possibly the post of Ambassador in London—is to be assigned to Count Shuvalof, it betrays a complete ignorance of our affairs. The chief of the Third Division can in fact be advanced no further; for, without ministerial title, he is the highest and most influential in the Russian Empire. If Count Peter Shuvalof ever exchanges his present office for a diplomatic post, it can only be because he is weary of the responsibility of the immense labor, and of the constant intrigues which make the chief of the Third Division the most harassed of all high Russian functionaries.

It is fair to say that Shuvalof enjoyed the complete confidence of the Tsar even if the story of Paléologue is true. And apropos of that story, the French author gives no authority for it. Shuvalof had been sent on a private mission to London in 1873, and was received by the Queen and by Lord Granville. He was not ignorant of British affairs and the appointment to London seems to have been judicious.

For Shuvalof was not a Slavophile. He was not a war-monger. Experience had taught him that the tsardom under Alexander was not strong enough to withstand the stress even of a victorious war with the Turks. He regarded the notions abroad that Russia would go to the assistance of the Slavs in the Balkans as exaggerated and absurd! He said that incorrect and absurd importance was attached to a supposed will of Peter the Great. For his part he was convinced, and every rational man in Russia shared in the conviction, that the acquisition by Russia of Constantinople would be immediately followed by the disruption of the empire. Here he was at one with the revolutionary Herzen who said:

When the Imperial Eagle of Byzantium returns to its Fatherland it will disappear from Russia. When Constantinople is won, then the iron sceptre of Peter the Great must break, for it cannot be lengthened to reach to the Dardanelles. St. Petersburg is colder, but also safer than Constantinople; and the Emperor Nicholas I did well in 1829 not to go to Constantinople.

Shuvalof had at first great personal success in England. He was a fine looking man in middle years. His hair had gone grey under the anxiety of the Third Division administration but he was only forty-eight years of age and a pleasant contrast to the infirm old man whom he displaced. He was unusually moderate and sensible in opinion for a Russian diplomat, and he set himself to be the mouthpiece of Alexander II who desired above all things at that time a cordial and friendly understanding with England. Shuvalof said that he considered that the two countries had a common interest in furthering civilization and the promotion of order and progress, and that their mutual interests would be better served by a frank understanding than by the prevalent jealousy and suspicious rivalry. He was opposed to the restless activity of the military party in Central Asia and of all those who wished to stampede the Tsar and Government into military adventures. He was sincerely annoyed when General Kaufman in Turkestan overrode the decisions of the Russian Foreign Office and made a treaty with Khiva on his own account. It should have been clear to British politicians that the Tsar of Russia was not the complete autocrat he was supposed to be and that other wills, or a collective will, could act in Russia in opposition to the will of Tsar and Government.

Shuvalof was not excited by the Bulgarian atrocity campaign in London, or by the hot words of Mr. Gladstone. He was relieved to see the suspicion of Russia's designs on Constantinople relax, but embarrassed by his new friends, the letter writers and journalists who encouraged Russia to go on and fight the Turks and to rescue their Christian brethren in the Balkans. There began to be almost as many Slavophiles in England as in Russia.

Madame Novikof was a pivotal figure. The grand, eloquent Gladstone, "intoxicated by the exuberance of his own verbosity," led out the English Slavophiles to battle. But there were more substantial persons than Gladstone in the movement against the Turks—such a man as Thomas Carlyle—on the platform of the St. James' Conference. And so great was the authority of Carlyle at the time that as one journalist said, "The appearance of Thomas Carlyle as a guide in eastern politics is almost as great and as pleasurable a surprise as if the Apostle Paul were suddenly to rise from the dead and advise our countrymen as to the county franchise."

The Russian Ambassador was well aware that atrocity stories can be countered by other atrocity stories and that the record of Russia in Poland and in Central Asia was not so clear of brutality but that the friends of Turkey might find material for a counter-attack. That counter-attack was soon forthcoming in the columns of the Tory *Pall Mall Gazette*. It was alleged that the troops of General Kaufman in Central Asia had put women and children to the sword and that there was very little to choose between Russians and Turks if it came to a question of brutality. Shuvalof refused to give the slightest help to Madame Novikof and Mr. Gladstone in their attempt to refute the accusation of Russian inhumanity in Central Asia.

There were in Russia at the time four clearly divided political trends. To the first belonged the court and government; to the second belonged Prince Cherkassky, the Grand Duke Nicholas, Ivan Aksakof and all the Slavophiles, including Madame Novikof and her Russian editor, Katkof; to the third belonged the radicals; to the fourth belonged the representatives of the minority, Poles, Finns, Balts, etc. Of these only the second was for military intervention in the Balkans, the nationalist party led by Cherkassky. Shuvalof belonged to the court and government group which held aloof, interpreting the Tsar's will as for peace, and being always ready to reprimand the Serbs for fighting Turkey and for enrolling so many Russian officers in their army. It was not until the Serb army under Chernyaef was completely defeated by the Turks that sympathy for the Serbs overcame Alexander's persistent pacifism.

There was a change of view at St. Petersburg, not at once communicated to Shuvalof in England. When the defeated Chernyaef came to London in December, 1876, to recruit English sympathy for the Serbs, he was treated by Count Shuvalof as a Russian in disgrace. Shuvalof was no doubt correct in interpreting the court view of Chernyaef's behavior in Serbia. But he was not completely representative of Russia in his dislike of Slavophilism. Slavophilism was becoming daily more victorious in Russia. It had overcome the strictly European outlook of Prince Gorchakof and it was convincing Alexander II that he must not merely be true to his private conscience as a pacifist and a hater of war: he must lead his people.

XV.

GENERAL IGNATIEF

THE Tsar through Gorchakof and Ignatief, the Ambassador at Constantinople, addressed to Turkey the ultimatum of November, 1876, demanding armistice for the Serbs and autonomy for Bulgaria, Bosnia and Herzegovina. The Turks agreed to grant armistice and the danger of war was averted temporarily by a conference at Constantinople. The British Government sent out Lord Salisbury. Nicholas Ignatief became a central figure on whom seemed to depend the issues of peace and war.

Ignatief was by origin a petty noble, which means little as that was merely a passport status which might be enjoyed by a cabman. He did not belong to the great families. At the time of the Crimean War he was a captain in the army. After the war he obtained an administrative post in eastern Siberia, showed ability and was sent as an Ambassador-Extraordinary to China. He did a number of odd jobs in the East and suddenly in 1865 was made Russian Ambassador to Constantinople. His only obvious qualification for the post was a certain facility in dealing with orientals. That meant he could say one thing and mean another, place all his cards on the table and still have some up his sleeve, therefore that he was not a man of conviction and force of character, that he was a time-server or tsar-server, which was probably all that was asked of him.

He had almost plebeian manners, that is, he was talkative, a born chafferer; he had not the calculated coldness of the typical aristocratic diplomat. But he protected himself by marrying an aristocrat. With the Princess Galitzin as wife he always had friends at court.

It was characteristic of the man that without necessity he committed himself to a double rôle in politics; on the one hand acting under the influence of Katkof, Aksakof and the Moscow Slavophiles, and on the other hand under the orders of Gorchakof who was European in politics and not particularly susceptible to Slavophilism.

What astonished other diplomats at Constantinople was Ignatief's unbounded self-confidence. He never showed himself in the slightest doubt as to course of action.

With unalterably cheerful expression and with a triumphant smile on his lips, he showed Turks and Christians alike the same somewhat insolently familiar friendliness, as he provoked the one against the other by fabricated untruths, and then submitted to the reproaches of both with the same jesting composure as if they could affect neither his political nor his social positions.*

There was a conflict between the Bulgars and the Greek Church. The Bulgars wished a national church with the liturgy in their own language. In this matter Ignatief sided with the Bulgars and offended the Greeks, but he won over the Greeks by the Russian support of the Greek revolutionaries in Crete. There was clever management and Ignatief was held to be making a great success of his mission to the Bosphorus. Some

* Eckardt, Julius, *Aus der Peterburger Gesellschaft.*

Russians began to clamor for the dismissal of Gorchakof in favor of Ignatief.

But Ignatief's success with the Greeks was shattered
when St. Petersburg refused to support Athens under
threat of war by the Sultan. That success of winning
over the Greeks then seemed illusory and worthless.
Ignatief's star waned somewhat in 1868.

But in 1871 when the defeat of France by Prussia
enabled Russia to denounce the Black Sea clauses of
the Treaty of Paris, Ignatief was again in high honor,
as if he had been responsible for Russia's "honorable
breach of faith." The strength of his position as Russian representative was enhanced. He shared the praise
with Gorchakof who had nevertheless done much more
than Ignatief to make the denunciation of the treaty
possible. What the talkative Ignatief did was to convince the Turks that the defeat of France would be
good for them. "Now," said the Ambassador, "Russia
will be your friend. Why not agree to work together?"

The destruction of the Empire of Napoleon III was
almost equivalent to revolution in diplomatic influence
at Constantinople. The French had lorded it there since
the Crimean War.

A contemporary says:

France, which, on August 1, 1870, had found herself in full
possession of almost boundless influence was reckoned four
weeks later in the eyes of the East among the powers of the
third rank; and the republic of September 4 claimed from
them no more respect than those of Holland or Spain. Nor
could it be asserted that the overthrow of the imperial power
called forth the same regret in Stamboul as the withdrawal of
the English interest had once done. While the English diplo-
matists ever knew how to use their power as gentlemen the
uncouth representatives of modern Bonapartism delighted,

after the fashion of upstarts, to treat the Turks as servants.
Even oriental placidity had grown weary of this helot relation; the Turks hailed the German victories as an act of deliverance from the French.

But it would be a mistake to imagine that the Turks
were sincerely friendly to any European power. They
did not imitate the West, or any nation of the West;
they were enough unto themselves. When they respected power it was one animal respecting a stronger
animal. There was no feeling of regard, sympathy or
interest. Any nation of the West, even England, could
have gone down like France in 1870, and for Turkey
it would have been one enemy less, another dog dead
in the street. Even potential allies were enemies. That
seems adequately demonstrated when the chief powers
of Europe, in 1876, ranged themselves with Russia demanding that Turkey put her house in order.

To what extent Ignatief knew in advance of the rising of Bosnia and Herzegovina, or encouraged or discouraged it is unknown. The same may be said of the
Bulgarian rising which followed it. But the Slavs were
encouraged to revolt by the increased influence of the
Russian Embassy at Constantinople. They were subsequently disappointed that the Russian military support
was delayed. They were unaware, as the Russian Ambassador himself was unaware, of the bargain being
made with Austria by Prince Gorchakof, and it would
have shocked the Serbs of Bosnia and Herzegovina to
learn that Russia was willing that they should pass
under Austrian protection after they had won their independence by their own unaided efforts.

The principality of Serbia was encouraged to believe that Russia would support her. The arrival of

Chernyaef and the other Russian volunteers seemed an augury of official military alliance with Russia. But Serbia's object was not so much to free the Balkan Peninsula from the Turks as to unite her territory with Bosnia and Herzegovina, to take Macedonia and southern Serbia and constitute a large independent Slav state. This was definitely frowned upon by Gorchakof. Gorchakof had in theory parcelled out the Balkan Peninsula into spheres of European interest. Russia striking a bargain with Austria on those lines, Gorchakof was not predisposed to help Serbia, and it seems that in this respect he was at one with Tsar and court. The Russian people were eager to help the Serbs but the Tsar and Government were almost indifferent to their fate. It is difficult to understand the lukewarmness of Alexander II and the lack of prescience of Gorchakof. The assignment of Bosnia and Herzegovina to Austria led to the *Drang nach Osten*, to the 1914 murder at Sarajevo and the fatal war of 1914–18. The Russian Government was far more willing to help Bulgaria than to consummate the Serbian insurrection. Bulgaria was considered a more immediate zone of Russian interest, being nearer to Constantinople and the Straits, and it was thought better to have an Austro-Russian partnership in the Balkans, shutting out England and France—the east of the Peninsula to be a Russian sphere of influence; the west to be an Austrian sphere.

It was the clamor of the Slavophiles that caused Alexander II to interpose to save Belgrade from occupation and the Serbs from virtual annihilation. The Russian nation, made aware of itself through the new force of journalism and enjoying for the first time in history comparatively free institutions, wished to announce its will, even in opposition to the policy of the Tsar and Government. That in part explains the mood of the Russian people in 1876. Alexander II thought his people were wrong: Let the Serbs fight their own battles! We support Bulgaria whose future can be assured by common consent. War meant the ruin of Reitern's financial structure and an undoing of the work of reform. But the Tsar was overborne by the great clamor for military action and gloomily gave way.

Ignatief had been imperfectly informed as to the policy of his Government; he was unaware of the Austro-Russian convention. That was a complete secret at the time and perhaps Gorchakof did not trust the talkative Ambassador with it. Ignatief pursued a pro-Bulgarian policy, regarding the policy of Bismarck as a temptation to a gambit in which Russia, being forced into an attack, would be weakened. For the rest he hoped to catch larks if the heavens should fall. After all, catastrophe for the Turks might result in the Russians obtaining control of Constantinople almost by accident—and that would make Ignatief great in history, whatever might be the calculations of Gorchakof.

Lord Salisbury went to Constantinople with many prepossessions regarding Ignatief. The Russian Ambassador had been represented in the pro-Turk press in England as an extremely cynical and wily individual, as no doubt he was. But otherwise there was a painful ignorance in England regarding the character of foreign statesmen. At the suggestion of the Prince of Wales, Salisbury, instead of going direct to Constantinople, made a circuitous trip by way of Paris, Berlin, Vienna and Rome, allowing a day or two at each capital for interviews with leading statesmen. Disraeli asked him "to lift our communications with the Powers out of the slough of despond they have so long grovelled in."

Salisbury at the time had very little experience of foreign politics but he was an unusually shrewd judge of character and motive. Bismarck at once tried to browbeat him, but he penetrated the Iron Chancellor's intentions, which is more than Prince Gorchakof had done with all his experience of affairs.

"Bismarck insisted on seeing me last night on my arrival from Paris," he wrote to Lord Derby. "I would gladly have had a night's rest first. . . . He lectured me for more than an hour."

Bismarck told him that the Turkish Empire was doomed and hinted that Great Britain should make up her mind to take a share of the spoil, take Egypt for instance. He indicated Bosnia and Herzegovina as Austria's portion. He made many jokes about Gorchakof whom he evidently regarded as the clown of the piece. "Let Russia go to war, it will weaken her and make her more reasonable when it comes to partitioning Turkey!" As a precaution and as a good security for future bargaining he advised Great Britain to occupy Constantinople. Salisbury came to the conclusion that Bismarck wished Russia to be weakened as a precaution in case of a French *revanche*. He dreaded a war between England and Russia because strict neutrality was a difficult part to play and he would not like there to be "any grudge against him, either on the part of England or of Russia, on the great day of the *revanche*, which is constantly in his thoughts."

Salisbury proceeded to Vienna. Count Andrassy

proved to be a very different character, talkative, incoherent, secretive. "He began our interview by making me promise to put nothing into a Blue-Book." He pretended that he was opposed to an Austrian occupation of Bosnia and Herzegovina. But Salisbury at once gave it as his opinion that Andrassy and Bismarck were much more likely to act in concert than Bismarck and Gorchakof, a shrewd and valuable judgment.

Andrassy also wished England to occupy Constantinople and it was clear that he reckoned upon the helpful antagonism of England to Russia when it came to a final settlement. He assumed that Salisbury was as anti-Russian as the British pro-Turk press. He never spoke of Gorchakof without a phrase or gesture of contempt. Bismarck had told Salisbury that Gorchakof was a vain old man, *"un vieux farceur," "un vieillard vaniteux"*; Andrassy said that Gorchakof did not want to die like a fading lamp but like a glittering star. This was Andrassy's nearest approach to a joke, for he was utterly humorless.

It is impossible to resist a feeling of admiration for Lord Salisbury's acumen in judging Bismarck and Andrassy. His immediate conclusions were correct. As a result of two wars Germany had two revengeful enemies, Austria and France. Bismarck, to secure the German position in case of war with France had decided to conciliate Austria by aiding and abetting that power in her pretension to take over Bosnia and Herzegovina. For the same reason he wished a weakening of Russia by war. Salisbury assumed that Bismarck and Andrassy had become partners, wishing the Constantinople conference to fail, wishing Russia to fight, but not wishing England to intervene at an early stage in the hostilities.

Constantinople should only be occupied after Russia was definitely committed to a war. The Russian crossing of the Danube should not be a signal for England to rush to arms.

It was the assumption of Bismarck and Andrassy that Ignatief's demands would be extravagant and that Great Britain would be forced to break off negotiations. But Lord Salisbury was agreeably surprised by the friendly and conciliatory reception which he had from the Russian Ambassador.

"I am told you are a very terrible man," said Lord Salisbury.

Ignatief smiled. "Everyone who fights for his country, who fights for his faith, who struggles for freedom in all these lands is my friend," said he. "I have thousands of these, twenty thousand, and they are *my* strength. But you are the support of the savagery and tyranny of the Turks."

Ignatief presented Salisbury with a memorandum on the Turkish constitution and he offered to place at the English Envoy's disposal all the documents in the possession of the Russian Embassy. "But," said he, "you must make up your mind whether you are a good Christian or a good Turk. If you have decided to be a good Christian then I will take your program as my own and support you loyally throughout; but if you are for Turkish tyranny, then I will take the Russian program, and will press it with all my force. That will certainly make it much worse for the Turks."

Ignatief told W. T. Stead in an interview:

"Lord Salisbury was a good Christian; so was Lady Salisbury. That was where I met them. I knew very well both his qualities and his defects. He is impulsive and vehement. I made play to have these qualities on my side rather than to have them against me, and I succeeded. But I did so only by doing exactly as I said, by supporting him faithfully and loyally. I did not 'mix 'em,' " said he, using a curious phrase. "I spoke the truth and acted straightly. If you look in the protocols of the conference at Constantinople you will see that I always supported him. No one could be more moderate, more pacific than I. It was Sir Henry Elliott, and Lord Beaconsfield, and Prince Bismarck who made that conference to fail, not either Lord Salisbury or myself."

Ignatief exaggerated. He was not always straight with Salisbury. He tried to cheat him once or twice but the Englishman called his bluff and both laughed very heartily over the matter. When caught Ignatief gave a beaming smile and shrugged his shoulders. *"Monsieur le Marquis est si fin, on ne peut rien lui cacher!"* Salisbury threw himself back in an uncontrollable burst of laughter. Bismarck was annoyed by the friendly relationship which had sprung up between Salisbury and Ignatief.

Six Powers were represented at the Porte and they agreed on terms of peace to be submitted to Turkey, Prince Gorchakof's "irreducible minimum." From these it will be seen how successful Ignatief had been in his conversations with Lord Salisbury. The following were the terms:

(1) The establishment of administrative home rule for Bulgaria, and for Bosnia and Herzegovina.

(2) The nomination of Christian governors for the three provinces for five years, subject to the approval of the Powers.

(3) Prohibition of the employment of irregular troops, likewise prohibition of colonisation by Circassians.

(4) Rectification of the frontier of Montenegro.

(5) No Serbian territory to be annexed by Turkey.

(6) The administration of the Christian provinces to be reformed.

(7) The use of the local Slav languages to be permitted in tribunals of law and by the administration.

(8) General amnesty to Christians condemned for political reasons.

(9) Commissions of control to be appointed by the representatives of the Powers, to superintend the execution of the reforms and assist the local authorities in the different measures affecting order and public safety.

(10) Formation of a militia and a *gendarmerie* of Christians and Mahometans in proportion to the religious population. Turkish troops to be concentrated within fortresses and towns.

(11) Execution of the reforms within three months, under an international commissioner, at whose service would be placed a force of six thousand gendarmes, to be enlisted in Belgium and Switzerland, for the maintenance of order and the security of the Christian population.

Quite naturally the Turks, who had been having some success in the field and had suppressed the Bulgar revolt and defeated the Serbs, were unwilling to accept the terms. They could not assess the danger of slighting the Powers of Europe and still imagined that if Russia intervened England would at least make war in their support. They did not see that Ignatief had in great part won Lord Salisbury over to his side and that public opinion in England, stirred by Gladstone and the atrocity campaign, had made armed intervention almost impossible. The terms were rejected and the conference failed. Lord Loftus wrote of it:

Lord Salisbury, with great tact and consummate skill, did everything that was humanly possible with the Sultan and Grand Vizier to warn the Turkish Government of the dangers which would result from a refusal on their part to listen to the voice of united Europe; but his beneficent purposes were frustrated by the obstinate determination of the Porte to admit of no foreign interference in the internal administration of the Empire.

But, in extenuation of their blindness, it must be admitted that the position of the Sultan and his Government was extremely difficult as well as perilous. They had to reckon with the enthusiasm and excitement of a restless and fanatic people, whose passions had been roused to a religious frenzy, and were under no control.

The Sultan had to choose between the alternatives of looking to foreign protection against his own subjects, or of acting with the public opinion of his fanatic people and, in reliance on its support, to appeal to arms. He was young and inexperienced in affairs, having only lately succeeded to the throne; he had no counsellors in whom he could confide, for they were all new to him. He hesitated as to assenting to the proposals of the Conference, and appeared to fear the effect of his acceptance of them on Turkish public opinion. He was impressed with a conviction that his empire would be exposed to less risk by a foreign war than by internal insurrection. He was more influenced by fear of the fanaticism of his own subjects than by the pressure of the foreign powers. He was surrounded by rival and ambitious intriguers for place and power, inexperienced in affairs, and guided by the influences of fatalism. He was, further, in fear of his life if he yielded to the demands of the Powers and was consequently unable to exercise his free judgment and decision in the grave crisis affecting his person and his throne.

The proposals of the Conference were almost unanimously rejected; consequently there was no course left for the foreign representatives but to break up the Conference and leave Constantinople.

The result of the Conference was graphically expressed by Lord Salisbury at the last sitting, when he said "that the Porte had only given promises and had refused guarantees." Lord Salisbury and his staff left Constantinople on January 22nd, 1877. Sir Henry Elliott likewise left Constantinople. The Ambassadors of Austria, France, Russia, Germany, and Italy were also withdrawn, leaving Chargés d'Affaires with instructions to conduct the current business, but not to treat any political question. In short, the Porte was put in quarantine, or, to use a modern expression, was "boycotted."*

Ignatief had accepted a friendly invitation of Lord Salisbury to visit him at Hatfield. On his way across Europe Ignatief visited Berlin, Vienna, Paris, in order to glean information as to the future reactions of Europe to peace or war.

* Loftus, Lord Augustus, *Diplomatic Reminiscences.*

XVI.

RUSSIA DECLARES WAR ON TURKEY

IN November, 1876, Alexander II had said that even if Europe were willing to receive rebuffs from the Porte he could no longer consider neutrality as consistent with the honor and dignity of Russia. Lord Salisbury gave it as his opinion that Berlin was the centre of a great European intrigue and that Turkey was a mere accident—a spark that might start a fire, but not in itself of much moment. He also reported that the Tsar was "tormentingly anxious to preserve peace." There is no doubt about that. Alexander moved towards war with a very heavy heart. He did his utmost to reduce the temperature of that section of society which was stricken by war fever. When Chernyaef and the survivors of the Russian volunteers to Serbia returned to Russia, they were not received with honor; and they were not allowed to retain the uniforms and exalted ranks obtained in the Serbian army. Officially they were not heroes. But the coldness with which they were received was held by the Slavophiles to be due to the hostility of a court camarilla rather than to the personal feelings of the Tsar. The Tsar was openly condemnatory of Serbia and of Serbia's program, but that was overlooked. Each cautious and unwilling utterance which Alexander made about the possibility of war was interpreted as earnest intention to play a heroic part in the Balkans.

Prince Meschersky spoke of the triumph of the union

of the Tsar and his people. Ivan Aksakof hailed Alexander as a tsar cut in the heroic line of Peter the Great and Catherine II. He heaped scorn on foreign interference in Slav affairs. He wrote:

Our great and powerful Russia, leaving the straight path of truth, is wandering in the forests and mazes of diplomacy, to the astonishment and satisfaction of all Europe. She has never ceased to labor for the arrangement of a benevolent European concert in favor of the Slavs, and each time, when at her instigation the concert has been arranged, the proceeds of the performance go somehow into the pockets of the Turks. We have witnessed a whole series of consultations, conferences, and diplomatic tours, in which all who took part, without deceiving each other, deceived Russia grossly and openly, without even having recourse to ruse. But no amount of deceit, no injuries or insults could shake the stubborn meekness and pacific spirit of Russian diplomacy, though the insults made the cheeks of Russia blush for shame. Meanwhile the Turks kill, impale, and violate Bulgarians, Bosnians, and Serbs, and hundreds and thousands of Slav families have been starving as fugitives in a foreign land. If the martyred people of Bulgaria, after the promises held forth to them by the popular movement in Russia of 1876, lose their faith in Russia, they will sink in such an abyss of despair that they will be morally ruined, and give themselves up to the power of the foreigner. The precious Russian blood, poured out in Serbian battlefields for the Slav cause, has not only remained unavenged but has been as little thought of as if it had been the blood of savages. . . . It has come to this, that our volunteers, to whom the Emperor himself was pleased to refer, were on their return regarded by many people, especially in the higher classes of St. Petersburg, almost as pariahs. The police, adapting themselves to the influence from above, eagerly stripped them of their Serbian uniforms and Montenegrin costumes, so that nothing should recall the "shameful enthusiasm" of last year. . . . Let us not lose courage or grow lax in our exertion. Let us rather redouble our efforts to alleviate the bodily and spiritual sufferings of the

Orthodox Slavs, to strengthen our mutual religious and moral solidarity, to confirm their faith in Russia, to uphold the dignity and honor of the Russian name in the unequal struggle with enemies abroad and at home—a struggle with ignorance and prejudice, and with voluntary and involuntary treason to Russian nationality among Russians themselves. May the historic mission of Russia be fulfilled! Behind us is the people, before us the Tsar's words spoken at the Kremlin!

He referred to moderate and guarded expressions of the Tsar which he dared to interpret as an expressed intention to pursue a forward policy.

The publication of this speech was prohibited but it appeared nevertheless in the *Moskovsky Vedomosti* and everybody read it. That was in March, 1877, a month before the declaration of war. Aksakof's words were hailed with great enthusiasm because they voiced the opinion of the greater part of the Russian people at the time. Meanwhile, half the Russian army had been mobilized and was in readiness in Bessarabia and not very distant, on the other side of the Danube, a Turkish army appeared. Von Moltke believed that the passage of the Danube alone would cost the Russians 10,-000 men. It was the German opinion that the Turks would prove a much stouter adversary than the Moscow firebrands imagined.

Turkey on second thoughts made peace with Serbia but not with Montenegro. Gorchakof clung to the opinion that the Eastern Question was a European one to be answered by the combined action of the Great Powers rather than by Russia single-handed. The fact that Austria-Hungary was in advance guaranteed a protectorate over Bosnia and Herzegovina seemed to him to be sufficient incentive to that Power to work with Russia for a peaceful settlement. Salisbury informed Beaconsfield that in his opinion Austria had been "squared." Count Shuvalof in London was instructed to propose a protocol for signature by the Powers. This protocol formulated afresh the common interest which the Powers took in the improvement of the conditions of the Christian population of Turkey, and in the reforms which must be introduced into Bosnia, Herzegovina and Bulgaria. It took cognizance of the peace with Serbia. As regards Montenegro it considered the rectification of the frontiers to be desirable in the interest of a solid peace. It invited Turkey to place its army on a peace footing and to put in hand with the least delay the reforms which had been discussed at the Conference at Constantinople. The Ambassadors of the Powers met at the British Foreign Office on March 31, 1877, and signed the protocol. But Lord Derby warned both Turkey and Russia that if they did not demobilize their forces the protocol would be considered as null and void. Turkey was given another chance to open negotiations with the European Powers but she refused to take it. The protocol was rejected.

The British Ambassador at St. Petersburg was instructed to ask Prince Gorchakof whether he had any objection to the publication of his memoranda in a Bluebook to be presented to parliament and he replied in two words, *"Fiat Lux!"* The Russian Government had very little to hide from British public opinion because it had worked steadfastly for peace. When the Tsar received the telegram announcing the failure of peace negotiations, he said:

If there is war the responsibility for it must fall on the government which has so greatly encouraged the Turks . . .

no one can imagine what I feel in this plunge into a war which I so greatly wish to avoid. I shall pass my birthday with my brave army, before it takes the field for the holy cause which we alone are willing to defend.

He was at the time at Kishinef reviewing the troops.

On April 19 Gorchakof, forced to admit failure, circularized the courts of Europe to the effect that all efforts for conciliation having failed there remained no alternative except military coercion. "Our august master has resolved to undertake this work which he had invited the Great Powers to pursue in common with him. He has given his army the order to cross the frontiers of Turkey." This intelligence caused a further excitement in the British cabinet, Lord Salisbury with difficulty restraining Beaconsfield from ordering a military occupation of Gallipoli; Disraeli was almost rude to Salisbury on this occasion. But England must remain neutral.

On April 23 the declaration of war was read to the troops in the presence of the Tsar. Chroniclers relate that while the army received the intelligence with cheers the Tsar himself had a distracted appearance as if he were weeping.

Although the declaration of war was hailed with unbounded enthusiasm in Russia there were many influential persons besides the Tsar himself who were apprehensive of its effect. Shuvalof had earnestly tried to prevent war. Reitern, still Minister of Finance, was opposed to it because he saw his budget surplus would be lost and the stable financial position of Russia which he had built up was liable to be wrecked. General Dimitry Miliutin, the Minister of War, was disinclined to put the ability of the new conscripted army to the test. But Gorchakof at the last moment threw in his lot with the nationalists and showed himself whole-heartedly in favor of the war. On the other hand the ardent Slavophiles were disappointed with the re-strained and rather colorless phraseology of the decla-ration of war. There was no word about the sacred cause of Orthodoxy, no mention of the heroic Serbs.

The worst fear of the Tsar was obviated at the be-ginning: Great Britain notified her neutrality. Bis-marck had said, "Let the Russians fight: do not inter-fere!" And as if recalling his conversation at Berlin Salisbury wrote to Lord Lytton four days after the declaration of war:

I cannot go very far with those who dread the Russians. Except the size of the patch they occupy on the map, there is nothing about their history or their actual condition to explain the abject terror which deprives so many Anglo-Indians and so many of the military party of their natural sleep. Except in conflict with barbarous orientals, or the Poles, who were little better, their military history has been one long record of de-feat. . . . Their naval history simply does not exist. . . . Their social condition is a prolonged crisis threatening, at any moment of weakness, socialist revolution. Their people are un-warlike; their officials corrupt; their rulers only competent when borrowed from Germany. Maritime population they have practically none. And yet we are asked to believe that their presence in the Black Sea or the Bosphorus would be a serious menace to England in the Mediterranean. . . . We shall prob-ably have to defend Constantinople, if attacked, for reasons of prestige which those who govern oriental nations cannot afford to overlook. But the grounds which are usually assigned for such a policy appear to me wholly untenable. To make a mari-time power, something more is wanted than a good port. . . .

In the face of such strong opinion it is not surprising that Great Britain agreed to observe neutrality in the

Russo-Turkish War, but she did so on conditions. It was important that the war should not spread. If it spread, interests might be imperilled which Great Britain might be compelled to defend; the most important of those interests being:

(1) The necessity of keeping open, uninjured and uninterrupted, the Suez Canal. An attempt to blockade or otherwise interfere with the canal would be regarded as a menace to India and as a grave injury to the commerce of the world.

(2) Constantinople—Great Britain would not be prepared to witness with indifference the passing into other hands than those of Turkey of a city holding so peculiar and commanding a position.

(3) The existing arrangements, made under European sanction, which regulated the navigation of the Bosphorus and Dardanelles were wise and salutary, and there would be in the judgment of the British Government serious objection to their alteration in any material particular.

In notifying the terms on which Great Britain would remain neutral, Lord Derby said that the Government felt confident that the Emperor of Russia would appreciate Great Britain's desire to make its policy understood at the outset of the war and he recalled the assurances previously given by the Tsar when he pledged his word of honor that he had no intention of acquiring Constantinople, and that if necessity should oblige him to occupy a portion of Bulgaria, it would only be provisionally and until the peace and safety of the Christian population were assured.

Gorchakof replied that the Suez Canal would not be affected by the hostilities; that there was no intention to take Constantinople unless possibly for temporary occupation; that the question of the Russian mercantile traffic in the Straits might, he thought, be reconsidered after the conflict. All was clear for a war between Russia and Turkey without military interference on the part of any other power. The lists were set, the heralds had sounded, the engagement began.

XVII.

CHARACTER OF ALEXANDER II

IN 1877, the year when he made war on Turkey, Alexander was fifty-nine years of age; his Chancellor Gorchakof was in his eightieth year. Young Russia was fighting the war but it was an older Russia at the head of affairs. And Alexander, though capable of enduring the hardships of a campaign, was no longer hale and energetic. He was afflicted by an internal complaint which made him nervous and restless and he suffered seriously from asthma. And in any case, Alexander had never been possessed of the energy of his father Nicholas I, who could work sixteen hours a day; in the evenings he grew tired of affairs and at night he could not sleep. His insomnia was written in his lined face and sunken eyes.

The Tsar had become more indolent. He was guided by others and went with the tide of public opinion. He had delegated his authority. He was not weighed down by responsibilities as Nicholas I had been. He had more leisure than any other tsar, but freedom and leisure had not made him a stronger personality.

It is possible that he was made to read too many serious books in childhood and doubtful if he ever read another after he became Tsar. He was made to live too active and Spartan an existence as heir to the throne. As Tsar the habit of disciplined activity remained but he gradually relaxed. Small details are characteristic;

Nicholas had strongly opposed his son's smoking, but Alexander must have the sedative of tobacco. He let his capable ministers work and he smoked his cigar. Nicholas had had little time for cards but Alexander must have his rubber of whist every afternoon. Nicholas did not idle away the hours in the company of a fair lady but Alexander in his later years was happy only in the presence of Catherine Dolgoruky—and with her he could relax and be indolent and sentimental.

High St. Petersburg society looked askance upon his illicit union with Catherine. Not that a tsar might not have a mistress; almost every aristocrat had one. The typical St. Petersburg society man was not regarded as smart if he had not a second establishment of some kind. But the Tsar's reputation was built on virtue rather than on strength of character, and the union with Catherine greatly discounted his moral grandeur. Had he been a brainless soldier like his brother the Grand Duke Nicholas, who could prove the magnificence of his nature at table, a mistress would only have been a natural adornment. But as the man whose exploits were the liberation of the serfs, the abolition of corporal punishment, the reduction of graft, the granting of justice and local government, a *mésalliance* was almost as weakening as it would have been for Mr. Gladstone.

And it was a real weakness because it caused the house of Romanof to be divided against itself. A tsar must be tsar in his own family first.

The Empress, it has been stated, counted for little. She was passive under the humiliation of alienated affection. She was absorbed by the pettinesses of religiosity, a mother-superior with seven children. But without intending it she became a bulwark of resistance to the Tsar's will.

The Tsar, no doubt as compensation, was willing to allow her to have her own way, and her father-confessor, Bashanof, had the freedom of the palaces. Bashanof was far from being a merely private and spiritual guide. He was an enthusiastic Russian nationalist and Slavophile intent on furthering a certain policy, and using his privileged position to that end.

The Empress indeed held herself aloof but she was not isolated. She became the source or seed of a court party secretly hostile to the Tsar. Ivan Aksakof who held such a privileged position that he dared try to stampede the Tsar into war in 1876 and arranged to have his speeches published in defiance of the censor, had married a Miss Tiutcheva, a lady-in-waiting of the Empress.

Tiutcheva was an intimate friend of the Countess Bludof, a rather ugly old maid who was a crony of the confessor, Bashanof, and shared his rapturous views of the future glory of the Orthodox Church. Through Tiutcheva and Bludof, Katkof, Pogodin and the rest of the Moscow Slavophiles had a voice in palace opinion. The Countess Bludof was also a confidante of the Empress who came to believe that Russia could only be saved by the Orthodox Church and that Poles, Protestants and heathens must be hated by all true Russians.

This clique was happy in the bloody revenge which Muravief took on the Polish people after the rebellion of 1863. The humane Tsar was troubled in mind and soul by the chastisement, but already his will was becoming enfeebled and he took no steps to check Count Muravief when the insurrection had been quelled. He merely prepared to ignore his servant's work. It is probable that he would have turned a cold shoulder on Muravief but for the efforts of the Countess Bludof. The Countess, backed by Bashanof and the Empress, insisted on regarding Muravief as a national hero and they prepared a great reception for him when in the spring of 1865 he returned from Poland to St. Petersburg.

The Countess Bludof was at the head of the committee which was preparing a festive reception for Muravief. She had collected the money for the costly image representing St. Michael, Muravief's patron saint, which was to be presented at the railway station to "the restorer of orthodoxy in our western frontier land"; she had arranged the garland with which the chair was to be decorated on which the half-paralyzed old man was to be borne to the carriage; she delivered the speech of welcome in the name of the ladies of St. Petersburg; by her the verses were suggested in which the "great missionary" was greeted by Tiutchef; to her instigation the pathetic articles were due in which Lamansky launched forth in eulogium of the event, and challenged all the world to imitation. The whole of the fashionable world was at that time divided into two hostile forces; in the foremost rank of Muravief's disciples stood the Countess Bludof, unweariedly engaged in inspiring the court with enthusiasm for her fearful *protégé*, "the national hero." At the head of the opposition party stood Prince Shuvalof. That the Countess was victorious, and that she achieved a brilliant reception at court for her friend, was soon enough to be learned by his adversaries to their cost.

When in the spring of 1865 the eldest son of the Empress, the Grand Duke Nicholas, died, Wilhelmina, who had always been peculiarly attached to this son, sank deeper and deeper in despondency and devotion—the number of hours she spent before her sacred ikons increased to a more and more serious extent. Bashanof and the Countess Bludof scarcely left her side, endeavoring to direct the thoughts of the sorrow-stricken woman more exclusively than ever to the interests of the

Church and to the task which it had to accomplish in the western Catholic provinces for the honor of God and the welfare of Russia. Just because the Emperor recovered himself quickly and resumed his usual habits, he could not forbear listening to the Empress, when he saw her, and entering into her plans. The Countess Bludof took good care that the articles framed against the European party by Katkof and his colleagues should meet the Tsar's eye in his languid hours; to their influence it was due that the *Moskovsky Vedomosti* ventured with impunity to challenge the minister Valuyef and to refuse to print in its pages the warning given by him; due to her that the Emperor graciously cancelled the sentence proclaimed in the summer of 1865 against the Slavophile journalist; due to her that Aksakof's anathemas upon Poles and Germans were allowed to pass without censorship.*

The Countess Bludof also contrived that Muravief should be President of the Investigation Committee appointed after the attempt on the Tsar's life by Karakosof in April, 1866.

It cannot be supposed that the Tsar regarded his wife's weakness of health with much anxiety since he had promised to marry Catherine Dolgoruky as soon as the Tsaritsa died. His overt act of July, 1874, granting to his children by Catherine the status of prince and princess and the enjoyment of his own patronymic Alexandrovitch, was an announcement of the importance he attached to his illicit union. It came to be within the bounds of supposition that if the Empress died he would indeed marry Catherine and that if he did so the heir to the throne by his first marriage might ultimately be set aside in favor of the illegitimate George Alexandrovitch. The ukase to the Senate regarding the position of Catherine's children came di-

* Eckardt, *Aus der Peterburger Gesellschaft.*

rectly upon the birth of a son and heir to the legitimate Grand Duke Alexander Alexandrovitch. In May, 1874, Nicholas, destined to be Nicholas II, had been born.

The heir, the Grand Duke Alexander Alexandrovitch, was as loyal in action towards his father as Alexander II had been before him to Nicholas I. But in his thoughts and sometimes in conversation he must have been found taking his mother's view of affairs. Russians said that he was Slavophile, that he had sent money to help Serbia, that he approved the program of intervention in the Balkans. Pobiedonostsef implored him to be discreet and not compromise himself by making a premature public statement of any kind. But at the same time Pobiedonostsef wished that the Grand Duke could throw in his weight for war. It is clear from the long letters which Pobiedonostsef, member of the Council of Empire in 1872, rising to be Procurator of the Holy Synod in 1880, wrote to the Tsarevitch, how strongly this great personality in Russian politics felt that the liberal regime of Alexander II was inept. "Russia must have a strong leader, must have authority, must be aware of strong Government" is the plea of many of the letters.

Pobiedonostsef wrote to the Grand Duke Alexander in 1876:

Perhaps there will come a time when the flatterers who like to lull the monarch to sleep, saying to him only pleasant words, will try to convince you that you have only to grant a constitution on Western lines to Russia and all will go smoothly and sensibly, and the Government would have peace. That is a lie, and God grant that a true Russian may never live to see the day when that lie is realized.*

* Pobiedonostsef, K. P., *Pisma k Aleksandru III.*

It is curious that after the first defeat of the Turkish War the Grand Duke Alexander was approached not by radicals, but by the nationalists and Slavophiles. People asked him to lead a movement to set aside the Tsar Alexander II and to form a constitutional government under Alexander III. Factions at court had reached to such a point that a palace revolution for a constitutional regime seemed to some hotheads not impossible.

The apathy of Alexander II had communicated itself to the whole of the Government and its effect was felt by the financiers and trading community. Even while the Tsar seemed steadfast in his peace policy there was a severe commercial and financial depression, and the paper rouble lost value rapidly. But the Tsar's apathy continued after he had declared war. The Slavophiles were delirious with pleasure. Yet the Tsar himself was not elated by his own action. On the contrary, he became more depressed, more passive to fate. All his reign he had pursued a domestic policy diametrically opposed to that of his father, but it seemed he was destined to resume his father's life and reign at the point of suicidal despair at which Nicholas I had died.

It was in Alexander's power to have scored a resounding success by this "war for civilization," had he only appointed the right general and given scope to soldiers of talent. Had he even been commander in chief himself he might have done better, for he was shrewd enough, knew he was no soldier, and could listen to competent advice and take it. But he suppressed his own judgment and gave the command to the incompetent Grand Duke Nicholas Nikolaevitch, preferring to remain himself a looker-on.

Chernyaef, who at least had experience of the Balkan War, was not used. The Tsar's young brother, the Grand Duke Nicholas, took for himself the post of commander in chief and appointed his own staff without reference to the War Minister Dimitry Miliutin. In fact, Miliutin's policy of encouraging merit and frustrating mere influence went for nought. The Grand Dukes decided to run the war themselves. Ignatief had told them that the Turks would be easily beaten, that the campaign would be a "promenade to Constantinople." So the incompetents, believing that it would be easy, were zealous to keep the glory for themselves. Thus, Todleben, the heroic defender of Sebastopol, was at the outset kept in obscurity. He was told to revise and organize the defences of the Baltic ports. But the heir to the throne, the Grand Duke Alexander, was of course given a command. Each division of the army was commanded by a Grand Duke. Cocksure of success, a civil administration had been organized, on paper, for the conduct of the Turkish provinces intended to be occupied.

Catherine was at Kishinef in Bessarabia with the Tsar in May, but at the end of the month Tsar and mistress were parted by the needs of war. Catherine went back to St. Petersburg, the Tsar in company with his sons, Alexander, Vladimir and Serge, with the aged Gorchakof, the anxious Dimitry Miliutin, and the optimistic Ignatief, crossed into Rumania and arrived at Bukarest on the sixth of June.

Gorchakof amused himself gossiping in erudite and inscrutable phrases about foreign policy, deigning even to show off in the presence of pretty girls offering their services to the Red Cross. The Tsar and the others passed to the Danube shore. It had been a rainy spring and the army's passage across the river in flood presented difficulties which had not been foreseen. This flooding was providential for the Russians who were deterred from crossing the river at those obvious points which were as well known to the Turkish leaders as to the Russians. The army was delayed and foreign correspondents who were mostly unsympathetic to the Russian cause gloated over the first setback. But the delay saved many lives. In considering the necessary change of plan Alexander took a part, his object being to save as many lives as possible. It was he who discovered the point at which the transit of the great river could most safely be made. The army, with its boats, pontoons, transport, horses, took to the water on the twenty-seventh of June. Michael Skobelef, a commander of Cossacks, disgruntled by having been recalled from his exploits in Central Asia, signalized the opening of his Balkan glory by swimming his white horse across the Danube.

There were many casualties; the Turkish shells fell thick and fast; showers of bullets whistled through the air and zipped into the water or found the solid obstruction of flesh. But there was no panic or confusion. The army and its generals and its cannon and the Tsar crossed on to Bulgarian soil. The Russian soldiers carrying little bags of Russian earth with them compared it with Bulgarian earth and found it kindred. They were on Slav ground. There was a great parade and the Tsar congratulated his army on being on this holy and Orthodox Bulgarian soil.

And after that, as frequently has happened in Russian wars, the Russians were flattered by great initial successes and later dashed by serious defeats. The Turks fell back. There was a remarkably rapid advance of Gurko's army across Bulgaria. The news hailed by the ardent Slavophiles in Moscow flattered Russia; it seemed indeed that the war would prove to be a mere promenade.

The war, however, had two fronts: one was in Bulgaria, the other south of the Caucasus in Armenia. While there were heartening victories in Bulgaria there were disconcerting defeats in Armenia. There the Grand Duke Michael, who was even more incompetent than the Grand Duke Nicholas, was in command of an army corps. He pushed forward to the investment of Kars, but was successively defeated at Zevin, Zicharisi, Karakilissa, by Turkish troops, officered in some cases by Englishmen—so it was said in Russia. There was naturally much unofficial aid in the shape of munitions and guns given by England to Turkey, and the threat of war by England was in the air from the beginning of the campaign.

The initial successes in Bulgaria were obtained without regard to strategy. A capable little Turkish army under Osman Pasha was allowed to take and fortify Plevna, a position which menaced the Russian base. This was at first disregarded, while the Russians pushed on southeast to take Tirnovo, Kazanlik and the Shipka Pass. General Gurko was prematurely ordered to take Adrianople and the Russian advance began to have all the appearance of a raid upon Constantinople. It is not surprising that in July there was excitement in London and that something like war fever seized Disraeli's cabinet.

The Tsar, in a shabby old uniform, tried to share

a soldier's life, without fighting. Until the battle for
Plevna commenced he was far behind the lines. He
imagined that the Turks might be made to acknowledge defeat and agree to any terms after a month's
fighting. Let General Gurko take Adrianople and
threaten Stamboul itself and the Moslem would see
reason! He made no alteration in the dispositions of
the Grand Duke Nicholas, though upon occasion he
gave advice. He followed all the operations on large
scale maps and was kept informed of every intended
action. He refused pomp and ceremony, lived in a cottage with a table, a few hard chairs and a cubicle military camp bed. When the nights were chilly he had a
hot brick put in his bed, as he suffered from rheuma-
tism. There was but little drinking and feasting at
headquarters. He discouraged that. When he was told
of victories he was calm and said that they were no
cause for undue merrymaking. It was thought he was
still lukewarm about the war. He was shown bodies of
Bulgarians, mutilated horribly by the Turks, in order
that he might be convinced of the righteousness of the
Russian cause. He did not doubt the cause but he was
apprehensive of foreign intervention, for the dispatches
he received from London filled him with dismay.

Still the real danger for Russia lay not so much in
England's bellicose mood as in the neglect by the
Grand Duke Nicholas of the first rules of war. A rein-
forced and well organized and equipped Turkish army
under Osman Pasha threatened the Russian base, and
if it proved successful in attack must cause the hurried
retreat of Gurko to avoid envelopment. The Russian
forces before Plevna in July, 1877, numbering only a
few thousand, were not adequate to defeat Osman

Pasha. The main strength of the army was pushing forward to Adrianople and the Bosphorus. The Grand Duke Nicholas, however, regarded the Turkish concentration as a slight matter and ordered Krüdener to attack it and take Plevna. Krüdener, on his knees, besought the Commander in Chief to postpone battle till he should have adequate forces, but the Grand Duke was obdurate. Krüdener advanced against Osman Pasha at Plevna on July 20, 1877 and suffered a severe defeat. The Tsar, field-glasses in hand, watched the engagement from a little hill. This was the first Turkish victory and came as a great surprise to friend and foe. The news was hailed with glee in London; it was suppressed in Russia.

The Tsar's heart was lacerated when he saw his troops mown down. And he was not indignant when he saw the survivors of Krüdener's army in flight. To the humanitarian Alexander it seemed better that his soldiers save themselves in flight rather than die facing odds. It dawned on him that his brother Nicholas was incapable and, in the evening after the fight, he wrote to Catherine:

> The great mistake has been that General Krüdener, knowing the numerical superiority of the Turks, decided to attack them as he had been ordered to do. But, by taking upon himself the responsibility of not carrying out that order he would have saved more than a thousand lives, and a complete rout, for it must be confessed that such it was. Happily the Turks did not pursue the remnants of our brave troops, otherwise few would have escaped.

The Grand Duke Nicholas, still underestimating the enemy, decided to attack again, this time with a division instead of merely a brigade. The army of Osman

Tsar Alexander II

Pasha was also increased and numbered forty-five thousand, still not a very large force, but the position he held was a strong one. On the first of August Krüdener and Shakhovskoy were ordered to advance against him. Plevna, a dirty, low-built, provincial town, in a deep valley, had become the objective of the Russian army. Take Plevna first, then perhaps Constantinople!

The painter Vasilly Verestchagin accompanied the army. He had been wounded at the passage of the Danube on the twenty-seventh of June, but returned from a Bucharest hospital to the front in time to witness the second battle of Plevna. He was a privileged person well received at court. The Grand Duke Nicholas threw his arms round the artist's neck and kissed him. The fat Ignatief, also watching the battle, almost suffocated him with embraces. The Tsar contented himself with saying, "How d'you do?" and giving him the most gracious smile. There would have been a conversation but Verestchagin, who had a cold, put his hat back on his head, without imperial permission, and the Tsar turned to speak to someone else.

The Grand Duke Nicholas was still optimistic. A success on the first of August would cover up the defeat of the twentieth of July, and impatient Russia could be informed of the two events together. But the rout of the Russians at the second attempt was greater than before.

The defeat was so great that it would be difficult for anyone who did not see it to imagine it. It was not a retreat; it was a disorderly flight, a complete dispersal. Had it not been for the covering action of Skobelef, with a battalion of infantry and some Cossacks, the defeat might have become complete annihilation. Without exaggeration it can be said that had the Turks been more venturesome and disregarded the brave stand made by Skobelef, they might have driven our troops back to the Danube.*

The Turk, like a bulldog which has driven off another dog, returned to kennel, ready to show teeth and be as fierce again at a third attack. The Russians were wholly swallowed up in panic. The Grand Duke collapsed and cried like a hysterical woman. Of the other commanders, everyone was blaming him or one another.

Panic indescribable. It was enough for someone to cry "The Turks are coming" for transport to stampede, and the wounded, with doctors and nurses to be abandoned. At Sistof the cry "Turks, Turks, Turks!" caused not only the local Bulgarian population but the whole mass of Russian officials, clerks, quartermasters, cavalry, infantry, wounded, and sick to flee in mobs to the Danube bridge. The bridge became choked with traffic—and many, taking to the water, were drowned. Those who reached the Rumanian side of the river still continued northwards in disorderly flight, in a whirlwind of dust, with vast commotion and shouting.†

In vain Skobelef rushed after the deserters, rounding them up, driving them back to the defence of the battle line.

Some sort of order was restored but in the middle of the night a telegram came through that the Turks were observed to be moving forward to another attack. The Tsar was wakened. He alone might be able to give confidence. He got out of bed, mounted his horse and went the round of the army, even to Sistof and the scene of

* Verestchagin, Vasilly, *Na Voine.*
† *Ibid.*

the disorderly flight. There were no signs of a Turkish advance. It was a false alarm.

Next day serious measures were taken. Gurko was recalled from his advanced position. The main Russian army began its retreat through Bulgaria, allowing the Turks to wreak their vengeance afresh upon the Bulgars in village after village, another wave of dreadful cruelty and barbarity! The Guard regiments in Russia were ordered to leave for the front. They had all the best weapons and equipment, and had been left in reserve in case Austria, despite agreements, should seize the opportunity to invade Russia.

A short official bulletin was issued to the Russian people at home: "In an engagement near Plevna Russian arms were not victorious."

Although it was harvest time the reserves in Russia were called out and that caused considerable murmur and complaint in the villages. It became impossible to hide the extent of the reverses in Bulgaria. There was at once a great revulsion of feeling in Russia, and the nation, supposed to have been so eager for war, seemed to become revolutionary in tendency overnight.

The army in front of Plevna was doubled; preparations were made to increase its strength threefold or fourfold. The aid of the national army of Rumania, some forty thousand men, was accepted on terms. Todleben, whom otherwise the Grand Duke Nicholas could not tolerate, was ordered to quit supervising fortifications on the Baltic, and come to Plevna to give advice. Preparations were made for a third attack on the town which had now grown to be a fortified position extending twelve miles. Some Russians still re-

garded the Turkish redoubts as "big earthenware pots"
and were still optimistic. The third attack would shiver
all the earthenware pots. The Russian guns shelled the
forts, but, by Alexander's order, were not allowed to
shell the town, for its population was Bulgar and
Christian. The Turkish artillery did not reply. The
Turks saved their shells and in doing so deceived the
Russians into imagining that they were ill supplied. At
other times the Turkish artillery replied briefly, as in
a conversation where one person is doing all the talking and the other interposes a word now and then. It
was deceptive. When the Russian attack commenced,
in mass formation, it was met by a murderous concentration of artillery fire.

The day chosen for the third attempt on Plevna was
that of St. Alexander Nevsky, the patron saint of the
Tsar. It began with prayer. The guns were sounding,
the rifle fire sounded like tom-toms; the armies were
already engaged, when the chanting of the religious
service began—on a little hill at the Commander in
Chief's headquarters.

The Sovereign stood in front, the Grand Duke Nicholas a
little behind him, and then the imperial suite and the officers
of the general staff. Soon all were on their knees and I remem-
ber how the voice of the priest trembled when he prayed God
"to preserve His army." The picture of the immense general
staff praying with bowed heads, against a background of dark
clouds flecked with the white smokes of battle was very interesting to me and I commenced a painting of it later. During
the service there was suddenly a dreadful chorus of rifle fire
from the centre of our position and we could hear the shouts
"Hurrah! Hurrah!" and it was evident that an advance to
take the Turkish position at the point of the bayonet had been
commenced. As the time for the grand attack had been fixed

for three o'clock in the afternoon this premature movement could not be understood. The Commander in Chief interrupted the service to send a messenger to inquire what had happened. The service was concluded in a mood of anxious excitement.*

Forty bottles of champagne were waiting to blow out their corks in honor of the Emperor and his patron saint.

The Tsar lifted a glass brimming with champagne. "To the health of those who are now fighting—hurrah!" exclaimed Alexander II in a loud agitated voice.

On the one hand the little hill with tables and tents and Russian officers and dignitaries sprawling on the grass; on the other the hullabaloo of general battle; an unceasing deafening roar of artillery, a crackle of rifle fire as of dry forests burning; shouts, screams. The answering "Hurrah!" of the General Staff drinking with the Tsar could nevertheless have been heard in the Turkish lines, but owing to the smoke it could not be seen which way the battle was going. Only Skobelef's left wing was visible to the Tsar's company.

From each of the Turkish mud forts, those great earthenware pots, were visible the puffing smokes of cannons. There was no doubt then that the Turks were well supplied with shells. The main redoubt, "Grivitsa," seemed to be the objective of the Russian army whose centre was a wide double file constantly fed from the wings as men fell under rifle and artillery fire. Much progress was delayed by soldiers carrying back the wounded, a way of escape for the living from almost certain death in advance. The common soldier was soon convinced that Plevna would not that day be

* Verestchagin, Vasilly, *Na Voine.*

taken. The hurrahs grew less, died away altogether, the shrieks of "Allah! Allah!" rent the air as the Turks advanced and Russians and Rumanians fled.

"Beaten!" exclaimed Prince Charles of Rumania, trembling. "A horse, quickly, a horse!" and he jumped to the saddle and galloped away to the rear.

But, unseen under the cover of the smoke, the Russians rallied. In each of these battles for Plevna, when things were going wrong, there appeared one heroic commander of Cossacks in the thick of the fray, Michael Skobelef, dressed as for a parade before a palace, in white uniform, on a white horse, the famous "White General," affecting thousands by his personal courage and wild determination to save the day. The Tsar remained staring through his field-glasses at the smoke of a seemingly lost battle. The Grand Duke Nicholas and General Staff were in consternation. It seems strange that there was not a service of runners from the field of battle to headquarters or that intelligence officers did not report hourly from every section. The Commander in Chief seemed to have simply started the battle and then waited the result in a spirit of resignation. Up galloped a certain Mr. Green, an American correspondent, and the Tsar and the rest eagerly took the story of the battle from him. He painted the picture in very dark colors and probably was ignorant of much that he pretended to know. He had left the field at the moment when the Russians and Rumanians seemed to be beaten at all points. No one came to contradict his story and it was not until late at night that it was known that two of the principal forts had been taken by the Russians. Skobelef had obtained a resounding success, capturing a fort which absolutely commanded the town of Plevna. Grivitsa had also been taken. But the Tsar in despair wrote to Catherine, "Would to God this odious war were over!" The commander in chief was informed of the success but sent no reinforcements and did not make the necessary arrangements to advance in strength on the following morning and consolidate the position. He might have been in possession of Plevna in the month of September. Instead the Turks counterattacked, drove Skobelef out, and the Russians had to stand three more weary months in front of Osman Pasha.

The Tsar gave no orders, he was a looker-on. He interfered in no way in the military plan. But he suffered greatly. When asked whether it was not his intention to return to Russia he replied that he would stay with his army until Plevna was taken.

All September, October and November, the reserves kept arriving from Russia, till the forces of Osman Pasha were outnumbered many times. Suleiman Pasha, with another Turkish army, should have come to the aid of Osman Pasha, but he made a mistake in giving battle to Radetsky, who repulsed him and held the Shipka Pass. Todleben arrived and under his direction the town of Plevna was completely invested. No foreign Power came to the assistance of the Turks, and Russian victory was ultimately certain. At the fourth attack on December 9, 1877, in the snow, Osman Pasha surrendered and Plevna fell into Russian hands. The Tsar then decided to leave his cottage at Gorny-Studen and to return to St. Petersburg.

The good news preceded him and in Russia there was a tremendous reaction from gloom. The popular mood in St. Petersburg was akin to that experienced in London during the South African War when Mafeking was relieved.

But there was one cloud amidst the general joy. The changed appearance of His Majesty attracted universal notice and regret. His pale and mournful face, his hair now turned completely grey, and the painful efforts he betrayed to maintain his wonted soldierly bearing and upright carriage, troubled as he was with asthma—all this showed only too plainly that the anxious months of the summer and autumn spent in the peasant's cottage at Gorny-Studen had seriously shaken his health. His asthmatic attacks, not dangerous, but still extremely troublesome, often came upon him so suddenly as to unfit him for all activity or even movement; and he was compelled, much against his former custom, to sit down in an armchair on festive occasions, and when giving audience. His state of mind was described as one of settled melancholy and gloom; he seemed only momentarily touched by the joyous excitement of the court and capital at the news of victory.

No one knew better than Alexander II that the terrible time of trial he had just passed through had been more than a mere bad dream, and now no bridge of retreat was left open for returning to the state of things which had been abandoned when war was declared.*

The Tsar was ready to open negotiations with the Porte for an early peace. Curiously enough the British Government advised the Turks not to treat for peace at this point. It was probably thought better in England to wait for some Turkish successes. And now few in Russia wished to have peace. The popular enthusiasm for the war had been born again and the Russians must march on Constantinople. It was now no secret that the Grand Duke Alexander Alexandrovitch differed entirely from his father on war policy.

* Eckardt, Julius, *Russia Before and After the War.*

The Emperor desired a speedy termination of the war, and the conclusion of a peace, not only compatible with the maintenance of friendly relations with the courts of Berlin and Vienna, but with the reëstablishment of the former system of government in Turkey. The heir to the throne on the contrary would not listen to any consideration being paid to Germany, or to any limitation of the object of the war. In his opinion the internal administration of Russia required searching reform, supported by the coöperation of Russian society; her foreign policy needed bold and resolute action, bold enough to satisfy the wishes of the nationalists and disarm all possible elements of opposition.*

The war was continued in a series of brilliant successes of the Russian army and the utter discomfiture of the Turk.

* Eckardt, Julius, *Russia Before and After the War.*

XVIII.

THE LIBERATION OF BULGARIA

THERE was a similar change of fortune on the Armenian front and Russia completed her conquest of the Caucasus by taking the valuable port of Batum. In Transcaucasia Erzerum was taken and Loris Melikof captured the great Turkish stronghold of Kars.

In the Balkans, Radetsky held the important Shipka Pass which was a key position defending northern Bulgaria, but of no particular advantage to offensive operations. Beyond Shipka extended the forested mountainous region of the Balkans proper, deep in snow and swept intermittently by blizzards. A day's ride from Shipka on the heights there was a strong Turkish army well provided with artillery and excellently armed, for the most part with British rifles. Suleiman Pasha, who had previously failed to support Osman Pasha, was moving forward from Philippopolis, endeavoring to stop the advance of General Gurko, and unite his force with the Turkish army which was facing Skobelef at the entrance to the Balkans.

General Radetsky was opposed to an advance against the Turks as sheer madness. Skobelef, however, undertook to disperse the enemy and advance through the forests on the mountains in extended lines offering no easy target for the enemy when he emerged facing their position. His chief of staff was the more cautious Colonel Kuropatkin who at a later time was Commander in

Chief in the Russo-Japanese War. Kuropatkin shared with Radetsky the opinion that the Balkans could not be crossed in the depth of winter, and he was absolutely opposed to the adventure. On the other hand Skobelef scented a great exploit. "Onward!" he exclaimed, "and if we do not take the heights at least we die in glory!"

"To die is quite an easy proposition," rejoined Kuropatkin. "The question is: is it worth while?"

The question seemed to have become more urgent half an hour later when in a rain of bullets the Colonel's shoulder-blade was shattered. Kuropatkin on a stretcher was carried back through the forest to a field-hospital out of range of fire. Skobelef, with another chief of staff, went on to win a brilliant victory.

Some thirty-five thousand Turks surrendered; ninety guns were captured. The Russian losses were heavy, but the victory shortened the war by at least six months. It enabled the Russian army to cross the Balkans and join forces with Gurko in the advance on Adrianople. That city was occupied by the victorious Russians on January 20, 1878. The army of Gurko and Skobelef was only halted by imperial ukase, when it was within thirty miles of Constantinople.

The alarm among the holders of Turkish bonds was great. With the utmost ease the triumphant Russian soldiers could have swept Turkish power out of Europe. They were with difficulty held in leash by the Tsar. Alexander chose to play a most unpopular rôle. But he had given his word to England that he would not enter Constantinople, and as far as he was concerned he was determined to keep it. That was the first reason for halting the army. The second was that the object of the war had been achieved. Bulgaria had been liberated. Russia was in a position to exact guarantees for Bulgaria's freedom and independence. The immediate danger of reprisals on the other Slav populations was eliminated. The Montenegrin frontier question was a small matter easily adjusted. The Serbs were not likely to be challenged by the Turks for some time. But to take Constantinople was not an honor which Alexander as Tsar coveted.

The position at the seat of war caused great alarm in England, for it was felt that a Russian occupation of Constantinople by a victorious army—which it might be difficult to restrain, notwithstanding the assurances of the Emperor—would lead to serious consequences. Under these circumstances Her Majesty's Government ordered the British fleet under Sir Phipps Hornby, to Constantinople for the protection of British subjects, and Parliament voted by a large majority six millions sterling for armaments.

The anti-English feeling at St. Petersburg became intense, and my position was not one of "velvet"; but I was careful not to allow a word of menace, which could give offence or cause irritation, to drop. I was left to the exercise of my own judgment in regard to any opinion I might express. I cautiously said to my intimate friends—in the way of friendship, and not of menace (knowing that it would be repeated at headquarters)—"N'allez pas à Constantinople—c'est la guerre." I was told afterwards that the Grand Duke Nicholas was greatly disappointed at receiving stringent orders from the Emperor not to enter Constantinople, so that my warning was not without effect; but I believe that the Emperor and Prince Gorchakof were fully convinced that had the Russians entered Constantinople there would have been a frightful carnage, the result of which would have led to the ruin and dissolution of the Turkish Empire in Europe, which, Prince Gorchakof often told me, was not desired by the Imperial Government and, should it occur, would be a serious embarrassment to them.*

* Loftus, Lord Augustus, *Diplomatic Reminiscences.*

The Sultan himself had begun negotiations for a peace with Russia and on January 31, 1878, an armistice was concluded, signed at Adrianople. The terms were basically the same as those incorporated later in the Treaty of San Stefano. They were as follows:

1. Bulgaria, within the limits of Bulgarian nationality to be an autonomous tributary state, with a national Christian Government, a native militia, and no Turkish troops to be within the principality except at some points to be determined.

2. The independence of Montenegro, with increase of territory, equivalent to the military *status quo*, the frontier to be decided afterwards.

3. Independence of Rumania, with sufficient territorial indemnity.

4. Independence of Serbia.

5. Autonomous administration, sufficiently guaranteed, to Bosnia and Herzegovina.

6. Similar reforms for the other Christian provinces of Turkey in Europe. Provision was made for the retrocession of Bessarabia to Russia; Rumania to receive the Dobrudja in exchange.

7. Indemnity to Russia for the expenses of the war; in a pecuniary, territorial, or other form to be decided afterwards.

8. The rights and interests of Russia in the Bosphorus and the Dardanelles to be regulated upon a new agreement.

The Russian troops were at Tchataldja on the eve of the signing of the peace of San Stefano. What excited England was the proximity of the Russian army to Constantinople, what irritated the rest of Europe was that the Powers had not been consulted as to the terms of the peace treaty. Even the previously agreed protectorate of Austria over Bosnia and Herzegovina was ignored.

It must be said that throughout the whole of the winter of 1877–78 there was great danger of a war between England and Russia. To the Russians the danger may have seemed more real than it actually was. The jingoes were clamorous; the English gentry, the sporting type, was very pro-Turk, holding that the "Turk was a gentleman"; financial interests were also for Turkey because more money had been sunk in that barbarous country than was justifiable or safe; the imperialists kept their turnip-lantern of the menace to India alight at night; music-hall audiences crooned

> We'll show the Russian Tsar
> The kind of lads we are
> And the Russians shall not have Constantinople!

The fleet had been ordered to Besika Bay. By an irony of fate the Turks forbade it to enter Turkish waters. The admiral was instructed to return the Turkish fire if the Turks tried to prevent his approach to the imperial city. War credits had been voted in the House of Commons. The only force that prevented a war between Russia and Great Britain at this juncture was the pacifism of Alexander II. Salisbury said that if the Russians had taken Constantinople they could most easily have been shelled out of it. But the Tsar did not intend that the city should be occupied and strangely enough the army on the spot did not disobey as it had been in the habit of doing in the Central Asian campaigns.

Beaconsfield, though there was much difference between him and Salisbury on the Eastern Question, gradually submitted to the views of the younger statesman. And when war between England and Russia seemed to have been averted the two leaders began to think as one. Salisbury vehemently defended Disraeli from the onslaughts of Gladstone. At the same time he began to be less friendly towards Russia. In effect he began to do the will of Bismarck and Andrassy, which was to rob Russia of the spoils of victory.

Prince Gorchakof proposed that the representatives of the Powers should meet at Berlin, ostensibly to confirm the Treaty of San Stefano, though he knew that of necessity the terms must be altered. That was Great Britain's opportunity. She agreed to be represented at the Congress at Berlin, but stipulated as a condition of participation that the Treaty of San Stefano be placed on the table for revision or annulment as the Powers should decide.

England's consent to take part in the Congress was not, however, easily obtained; there was much exchange of views between Lord Derby and Count Shuvalof, much shuffling of papers and changing of phrases. Lord Derby resigned, and in April Lord Salisbury became Foreign Minister. Meanwhile the British fleet in Turkish waters and the Russian army in Thrace had kept the world expecting war for several months. Queen Victoria said, "I don't believe that *without fighting* and giving those detestable Russians a good beating any arrangement will be lasting."

The nationalists in Russia were still in favor of the Tsar defying England, but Alexander was more prudent than his people. The real war was over; he had no wish to embark on an unreasonable war. The problem of making a durable peace by consent of jealous parties did not seem to him insoluble. He was supported by the opinions of Gorchakof, Shuvalof, and the new capable Giers who was assisting the Chancellor.

The opening of the Berlin Congress was on June 13,

1878. Beaconsfield left London for Berlin on the eighth of June; Salisbury on the tenth. Gorchakof was ailing and proceeded in an "invalid carriage." The Tsaritsa was very ill, thought to be dying, and it is said that for that reason Alexander II did not go to Berlin. The Emperor of Germany, seriously wounded by an assassin, was unable to take part in the Congress. He had followed the Russian victories with great enthusiasm and he was still a sincere friend of Alexander. His absence from the Congress was a blow to Russia. Bismarck dominated the proceedings. It is said that he took revenge on Russia for the interference of the Tsar and Prince Gorchakof when he had been warned, in 1875, not to make a second war on France. Bismarck explained to Salisbury:

> When Gorchakof chose in 1875 to invent that French scare, climbing on my shoulders in order to pose as a peacemaker before Europe, I told him that though I should continue to value the alliance of Russia, all confidence was at an end between us.

There is no doubt Bismarck was personally resentful, and that Gorchakof was ill fitted to be the Russian representative at the Congress. The old man, thwarted at every point, even made absurd scenes and upon occasion flung out of the conference chamber as if intending never to return. He was obliged to stand by and see Shuvalof make concession after concession to European opinion massed against the Russians. And he had a bad press in Russia.

The Moscow Slavophiles were enraged. Ivan Aksakof said that if there were even a figment of truth in the many letters and telegrams going in all languages to the ends of the earth from Berlin, bearing the fatal news of Russian capitulation to the demands of the West and not once contradicted by the Russian Government, then the Russian people must die of shame.

The Russian nation is murmuring, indignant, agitated, confused by the daily communications from Berlin and waits, as for blessed tidings, a decision from above. It waits and hopes. The hopes will not prove false because the Tsar's promise will not be broken. "*The sacred task will be carried to accomplishment.*" The duty of all loyal subjects commands us to hope and believe; the duty of all loyal subjects commands us to give utterance in these days of unrighteousness and falsity, telling of a rising barrier between Tsar and country, between the Tsar's purpose and the popular mind.

The Tsar was exceedingly angry with these words and spurred to action by Prince Dolgoruky, the Governor of Moscow, who reported that Aksakof had told him he had already received in his lifetime seven reprimands from the Tsar. Despite his advanced years and his position in society Aksakof was arrested and banished from Moscow under "administrative order."

At the Congress Russia had no friends. She expected the support at least of Germany; Bismarck in a speech to the Reichstag had declared his intention of acting merely as an "honest broker." Austria, in the person of Count Andrassy, was antagonistic. She declared she would not tolerate the presence of a large Slav state in the Balkans. Because of Austria, the big Bulgaria of which Russia had cut the pattern at San Stefano was reduced to a little Bulgaria. We can see now in the light of history that Russia was right, because the limitation of Bulgarian territory resulted in a further war with Turkey. But she had been unwise in the bargain

she had made for Austrian neutrality. Austria insisted
on practical annexation of Bosnia and Herzegovina,
robbing the Serbs of these regions of the freedom they
had won for themselves in 1875. That resulted eventually in a Slav revolutionary movement in Bosnia and
Herzegovina, directed against the power of the Emperor Franz Joseph, the murder of Franz Ferdinand at
Sarajevo in June, 1914, and the subsequent Great
War. The losers at the Congress of Berlin were very
definitely the Slavs, and the ultimate losers the European Powers. Germany and Austria-Hungary were
drawn together in interests and in the year following
the Congress, Bismarck concluded with Andrassy a for-
mal defensive alliance, avowedly directed against Russia. This developed in course of time into the Triple
Alliance and was answered by the Franco-Russian Alliance and ultimately by the Triple Entente. In the Congress of Berlin one may see the origin of the causes of
the great destructive European catastrophe of 1914–18.

Despite the popular Russian outcry of betrayal and
disgrace Russia did not come out of the Congress without certain substantial gains in territory. Salisbury and
Shuvalof had come to a preliminary understanding that
they would not oppose the annexation by Russia of
Batum and Transcaucasia. This secret deal was given
away in advance by a Foreign Office worker to the
Globe newspaper, and its publication made it difficult
for Great Britain to oppose the annexation or use it as
a bargaining point at the Congress. Russia obtained
Batum.

She also had returned to her that strip of Bessarabia
which had been given to the principality of Rumania

by the Treaty of Paris in 1856. It is curious that Russia's ally Rumania had to suffer this loss. The Rumanians were most indignant and said they did not wish the territorial compensation of the Dobrudja which was offered them. Great Britain found it difficult to understand why Russia should require Rumanian territory, and liberal supporters of the Russian cause became somewhat disaffected. Mr. Gladstone hotly defended the rights of "gallant Rumania." But the claim to Bessarabia was the one point on which the Russians were completely determined. Alexander would not give in. He was sentimental about it. His father Nicholas I had lost that strip of territory; he, the son, must make good that loss. What seemed almost dishonor to Mr. Gladstone was a point of honor with the Tsar.

The Treaty of Berlin was signed on July 13, 1878. By it, Serbia, Montenegro and Rumania became independent states. Bulgaria was created as a tributary state under the sovereignty of the Sultan but with a Christian Government and national militia. By the original Treaty of San Stefano Bulgaria had been given a large amount of seaboard on the Black and the Ægean Sea, leaving to the Sultan of Turkey only a small strip of territory round Constantinople. She was to have had a port on the Ægean. But by the Treaty of Berlin she was confined to the river frontier of the Danube. This petty state was to have a prince of its own, freely elected by the population but confirmed by the Sultan. No member of the reigning dynasties of the Great Powers was supposed to be eligible as a candidate. The portion of Bulgaria, east of the Balkans was parcelled out in another petty state called Eastern

Roumelia, subject to the military rule of Turkey but having administrative home rule and a Christian governor.

The occupation and administration of Bosnia and Herzegovina by Austria was agreed, though, as Lord Salisbury said, Count Andrassy had been very "coy" about it. He would not take the provinces; he must be asked by Turkey to take them. "I have heard," said Bismarck "of people refusing to eat their pigeon unless it was shot and roasted for them; but I have never heard of anyone refusing to eat it unless their jaws were forced open and it was pushed down their throats."

Montenegro was given the port of Antivari. Serbia also received a small increase of territory. Rumania restored to Russia the Bessarabian territory lost in 1856, and as compensation received the Dobrudja. Turkey ceded Kars and Batum to Russia.

This was the celebrated "Peace with Honor" which Lord Salisbury brought back to London in July, 1878. The Order of the Garter was conferred on both Beaconsfield and Salisbury in recognition of the services they had rendered at the Congress.

The conclusion of the deliberations was marked by no such honor and acclamation in Russia. Gorchakof sneaked off and left Shuvalof to sign the unpopular treaty on behalf of Russia. Shuvalof was greatly depressed but he was convinced that the treaty was the best that could be obtained under the circumstances. Gorchakof had been loquacious and pompous, full of old saws and modern instances embellished by French elegancies of language. Bismarck, listening to him, scrawled jokes on his blotting pad. Shuvalof was the brains of the Russian delegation, but he was hampered by the vanity of Gorchakof who first quarrelled and blustered and made scenes and then allowed himself to be fooled and flattered by the British Prime Minister.

Gorchakof said:

Personally I cannot complain of Beaconsfield. He called on me no end of times and was most complimentary. He called also on my son. He told me among other things that whenever he hears a *bon mot* he always says; "Oh, it is not so good as what used to be said by Prince Gorchakof."

He was told that Disraeli's power lay in his shameless habit of flattering everybody. Gorchakof replied, "Oh, but I am not easily taken in by flattery!"

The terms of the treaty cost Alexander II the greater part of his popularity in Russia. He had no one who could interpret the treaty for him to the Russian people and place the whole transaction in a better light. He was sadly in need of an efficient press bureau. Much could have been made of the terms. It could even have been claimed that for Russia also it was "Peace with Honor." But all the malcontents and fanatics raised their voices against Alexander, and the house of Romanof became visibly unsteady.

XIX.

REVOLUTIONARY FERMENT

EVERY modern war in Russia resulted in a manifestation of a revolutionary movement. After the Crimea it was feared that the serfs would move and liberate themselves; there was widespread incendiarism and rumor of revolt. After the Russo-Japanese War came the violent revolutionary outburst of 1905. In the course of the war of 1914–18, which extended longer than any other war in which Russia had been engaged, came the great Revolution of 1917. And after the Turkish War of 1877–78 followed the terror of 1879–81.

This post-war revolutionary ferment has been due to three circumstances: (1) the sufferings entailed by war; (2) the scandals of corruption and incapacity; (3) the fact that the working class and peasants, rifle in hand, had been inflamed by war to violence and were in a mood to take a short way with their masters. It may be remarked that in time of war the Russians lack the sense for national solidarity and discipline under misfortune which characterizes the English and Germans. And this weakness in national character is rendered the more dangerous by inordinate vanity. Dostoievsky wrote that if you gave a Russian schoolboy a plan of the heavens and the solar system, though he might never have seen such a chart before he would in all probability hand it back to you *corrected*. The words of Shakespeare apply aptly to Russians:

Could great men thunder, Jove himself would ne'er be
    quiet;
For every pelting petty officer would use his heaven for
    thunder,
Nothing but thunder.

That is true of the Russians of both camps. The Slavophile thunder of Aksakof and the rest was followed by
the dynamite explosions of the revolutionaries.

Ivan Aksakof declared that the peace of Berlin was
a worse blow to the dynasty of Romanof than any act
of Nihilist. Therein spoke injured vanity. Aksakof and
the other Slavophiles believed that Russia could and
ought to defy western Europe, seize the whole of the
Balkan Peninsula and impose the terms as they wished.
That also was the opinion of the brave and intrepid
Skobelef. These people with their indignation against
the Treaty of Berlin swept away from tsardom almost
the whole of its national support, but the people who
took advantage of this alienation of support were much
more hateful to the Slavophiles than the court, more
hateful than the Grand Duke Nicholas, Count Shuvalof, Prince Gorchakof, the Tsar.

Much the same things were said in 1878 as were
said later in 1917, that the court was pro-German, that
the army had been sacrificed to speculators, that there
was corruption and incapacity in high places, that the
Tsar ought to delegate his authority to a union of
zemstvos, that the time had come when Russia had no
need of a "little father" and could very well govern
itself. But while the nationalists were fulminating in
the name of God over the whole of the Balkan Peninsula and also over benighted Russia, the revolutionaries
saw their opportunity to make a thunder of their own.

After the attempt on Alexander's life in 1866 by Karakozof and the severe resultant repression, there had been an extended period of domestic peace in Russia. In 1873 the Tsar ordered all the Russian students at Zurich to return home under pain of having their passports rendered invalid. Zurich had been a university of revolution. It was said it was imprudent to bring the short-haired girls and fanatic lads back to Russia, but it was also argued that it was better to have the young revolutionaries in Russia where at least they would be in daily touch with the institutions they condemned. At a distance they were generally ready to see Russia blacker than she really was. On the other hand, most of the students did come back to Russia as propagandists for revolution. Tchaikovsky's Circle soon had affiliated petty groups in every town in Russia. They kept the police busy tracking down distributors of leaflets to the peasants and factory workers. But they contented themselves with the work of peaceful penetration. There was no "terror" until after the Armistice of San Stefano in January, 1878. But in the year 1877, in the midst of the war, a great trial of Nihilists was staged in St. Petersburg. On October 30 some 183 of these were arraigned on the charge of sedition.

The most remarkable event and the one most significant of the state of Russian society was unquestionably the public prosecution of the 183 Nihilist conspirators. Over no less than thirty-seven provinces of the Empire the net had been spread from St. Petersburg, by means of which the proletariat in the towns and the peasants in the villages were to be drawn into the circle of those young enthusiasts who professed the doctrines of Bakunin. The Government had laid plans and at length a swoop was made. On one and the same day in May, 1875, these revolutionary fanatics were seized according to a

pre-arranged scheme of the Third Division, throughout the
limits of the Empire. Every class in society and all the provinces of Russia, with the exception of the Baltic regions and
Finland, had furnished its contingent. The main body of the
accused, excepting those at St. Petersburg itself, came from
certain provinces of the Volga, from Lithuania and the south.
Most of them were the sons and daughters of small officials
and village priests, and had been at the higher institutes of
education. There were not wanting a few, however, who belonged to the high nobility, as well as some of the laboring
classes. It was remarked in particular that numerous young
Jews from Lithuania had taken part in the conspiracy. The
preliminary proceedings conducted in secret had lasted for a
whole year and a half, owing to the vast mass of materials
collected, and the obstinacy with which those chiefly accused
refused to give any sort of information. The public trial, however, could no longer be delayed; and it took place at a moment
most opportune for those young revolutionaries who wished to
create as much noise and display as the occasion permitted.
Notwithstanding the strict supervision of the reports in the
newspapers, the limited dimensions of the court itself, and the
similarity of the various indictments, the interest of the public
in this trial was as passionate as the wishes of many people to
give the most palliative aspect to the offences were transparent.
Not indeed that this sympathy was of a very practical kind.
To interfere directly on behalf of the enthusiasts who, dis-
guised as working men, had gone about among the people distributing revolutionary tracts imported from Geneva to the
peasants and artisans—such a notion occurred to very few, if
any, of their admirers. The enterprise in question had too little
prospect of success, and had been too childish and too badly
prepared, to be of any real service to the cause of progress. On
the other hand, the number of those was extraordinary who
sympathized with the position, and part acquiesced in the object of the accused. They declared the charges made by the
Nihilist fanatics against the ruling system to be "not without
cause or justification." They noted the wide extension of socialist ideas with a certain pleasure, as a remarkable symptom
of the increase of the social movement. They were as much

edified by the energy and resolution of the accused as by the embarrassment the whole affair caused to the Government. And this embarrassment was not a small one. It was bad enough that some of the most guilty of the prisoners, such as Myshkin and Rabinovitch, wrought upon the breathless audience by the passionateness of their demeanor and their wild declamatory eloquence, and aroused ideas and aspirations which, from the very charm of novelty, produced their effect upon the listeners. It was worse that even the counsel for the defence did all they possibly could to give importance to the cause, to awaken the sympathies of the numerous young men and girls who were among the audience, and to perplex the judges, unaccustomed to scenes of that kind. The demeanor of French advocates under similar circumstances was imitated. The gestures, the very tricks of that forensic oratory were copied, which had been the fashion in France some thirty or forty years before, whenever a political issue was involved in a trial. The accused were surrounded with a halo of martyrdom on account of their independent views, erroneous perhaps, but from their consistency very remarkable. When Myshkin claimed the right of expatiating on topics wholly unconnected with the case, and of unfolding the program of the social revolutionary party in detail, his claim was treated as a sacred right of man, and its rejection as a menace of despotism. It was attempted to intimidate the witnesses, and excite the public against the officials of the police whose duty bound them to report what they had discovered or observed. And in many cases the disgraceful attempts succeeded beyond the expectations of their orders. Myshkin's counsel was able to remove from the court an officer of gendarmes by the remark loudly made that "the sight of his uniform might excite the public." He attacked the judges with such warmth and vigor, that they were forced to allow his client to hold forth in a long speech, bristling with the most insane invectives against the Government. The noise of the audience—men and women shrieking and screaming—became so intolerable that the proceedings had virtually been suspended when at length the president mustered up sufficient energy to order the court to be cleared and the prisoners to be removed. But just as if it had been intended by the Government to diffuse as widely as possible the excitement caused by these scandalous scenes, and to give the public the most imposing ideas of the extent and danger of the conspiracy, the utmost importance was attached to the treatment of each particular circle, such as the "Orenburgers" and others, grouped around one mysterious centre, and the proceedings were spun out over weeks. The brevity and meagreness of the reports issued to the public served to intensify the greed for news and to awaken curiosity about these strange phenomena of national life. When at last the verdict was given, by which ninety-nine of the accused were condemned, there was scarcely any doubt that the injury caused by the trial had far outweighed all the mischief which was alleged to have caused it. Enough food had been given for scandal to glut the public appetite for months. Authority had received a heavy blow by the public manner in which the system had been attacked and by the equally public manner in which it had been defended. Nor was the mischief over with this prosecution, it was known quite well that another must follow shortly, bringing fresh excitement and fresh scandal.*

The trial of the rioters in Odessa in December, 1876, was about to be held, and news was daily arriving of new revolutionary demonstrations in consequence of it.

The Communist historian Pokrovsky is agreed

that the Government had only to start baiting the socialists for the socialists to win the sympathies of that very *bourgeoisie* whom they had abused as a matter of course. This was entirely unexpected, and opened up unlooked for vistas but it also demanded a complete reorganization of the whole revolutionary front. . . . It became desirable to diminish the number of reactionary individuals and to exterminate as many of them as possible.

The new policy was then to start a campaign in favor of political terror against individual members of the

* Eckardt, Julius, *Russia Before and After the War.*

Government, and in the first place against the head of the Government, Alexander II.

Bourgeois writers, torn between sympathy for the revolutionaries and a mortal terror of everything that smacked of revolution, had actually made it appear that if the revolutionaries turned to terrorism it was only under the influence of police persecution; they were goaded by the police, as it were, into shooting at governors and laying mines under the Tsar's trains and palaces. This view is very characteristic of the *bourgeois* mind, which considers revolutionary action as a kind of disease or epidemic madness, and tries to understand the reason why so many people should have gone mad. We, who regard revolutionary methods as quite normal, have no need to ask this question. The only thing we want to know is why people should have chosen this particular revolutionary method rather than another. The answer was given by the revolutionaries themselves at the conference where they decided to adopt terrorist politics, at Lipetsk in the summer of 1879. "The duty of the party," said Zhelyabof, the spokesman of the new policy, "is to do as much as it can. If it has sufficient strength to overthrow the despot by means of an insurrection, it must do so; if it has sufficient strength to punish him personally, it must do that; if its strength is not even sufficient for that, it must at least loudly protest. But our strength," he continued, "is unquestionably sufficient and the more decidedly we act the more it will grow."

As early as April, 1879, an attempt on the life of Alexander II became the subject of discussion in the Land and Freedom Party, and those who were in favor openly announced that the attempt would take place whether the majority approved of it or not. This made some so indignant that there were exclamations of: "We shall have to inform." Of course, nobody turned informer. The attempt was carried out by Solovyof and was a failure.*

Russia sided with the terrorists until it was too late. Very remarkable was the acquittal of Vera Zasulitch

* Pokrovsky, *Brief History of Russia.*

after she emptied her revolver into the body of the St. Petersburg Chief of Police, Trepof. She enjoyed trial by jury, and the verdict of "not guilty" according to one writer was met "by a hurricane of applause" from the court. That was still in 1878. On the fourteenth of August Stepniak murdered Mesentsef as reprisal for the execution of the revolutionary Kovalsky. That resulted in trial by jury for revolutionaries being abrogated, and the terrorists came under the rigors of martial law. General Drenteln was appointed chief of the Third Section, and inaugurated his regime by the arrest of hundreds of suspected persons. But he failed to lay hands on Stepniak, who escaped to freedom in London. Then on March 26, 1879, a certain Leon Mirsky rode up to the carriage of Drenteln in broad daylight in St. Petersburg and fired two shots, wounding the police chief. He was sentenced to penal servitude for life.

After this attempt on Drenteln most of the ministers in St. Petersburg took the precaution of having a Cossack escort when they drove in the streets. Few ventured out-of-doors for exercise. But the Tsar took no particular precautions for safety. No matter how bad the weather he always went for his "constitutional" at eight every morning, leaving the Winter Palace and walking along the palace quay at a good pace. Any ordinary civilian might see him on these daily walks. In the afternoon he generally went for a drive. It is true that plain clothes men were on the watch for suspected persons. But they were somewhat lax in defending the person of the Tsar.

The police did not even know that the revolutionary Solovyof had set forth to kill the Tsar and that every morning in April he was practising with a revolver so as not to make a mistake when he came face to face with Alexander II.

The Emperor, with saggy cheeks and blear eyes, wrapped up in himself—for his inward sufferings were great at this time of depression, was walking along the quay on the morning of April 14, 1879, and was passing a guardhouse where the pavement was narrow. A young man coming in an opposite direction met him there and saluted, as it were giving a Judas kiss. The Tsar returned the salute and at the same moment the man who called himself Solovyof fired at him. Alexander was alert enough to see the rapid movement of the revolver, and dodged the shot. He retreated zigzagging, but facing the terrorist, and dodged the second shot. Solovyof then lost his nerve and taking to his heels fired another shot which went completely wide of the mark. He was seized by a passing milk woman, whose thumb he almost bit to the bone. Others overpowered him. The Tsar returned to the Winter Palace and a large crowd came to demonstrate its sympathy outside.

Alexander came out to show the people that he was entirely unhurt and he said: "I heartily thank you for the feelings of devotion displayed and I regret they should be called forth by such a sad event. It has been God's will to save me once more from the danger of death and my heart is full of gratitude to Him. May God help me to serve Russia and to see her happy and peaceful. Again I thank you."

Alexander was a brave tsar; soon after the attempt he drove to church without an escort.

XX.

THE RUSSIAN NATION

WARS and murders often place the common view of history out of perspective. That Dostoievsky's novel *The Brothers Karamazof* first began to appear in the *Russky Vestnik* in 1879, is of more significance in history than the attempts on the life of Alexander II the same year.

But in this statement there is no desire to underestimate the significance of the pistol shot of the revolutionary. A revolutionary group had condemned Alexander to death. It failed at the first attempt. It instructed others to carry out the sentence, and two years later it was successful: Alexander II was killed. The significance of this, if we look ahead thirty-six years, was the destruction of the Romanof dynasty and the setting-up of a proletarian dictatorship.

Alexander II, as monarchs go, was above the average in kindness, goodness, wisdom. It is difficult to see how any tsar could have done more for Russia in the nineteenth century than he did. But the Executive Committee of the *Narodnaya Volya* condemned him to death, and the official Bolshevik historian remarks in a work for use in schools: "Alexander, it must be admitted, had done everything to justify such a sentence in the eyes of every sensible person."*

But the sentence of death on Alexander II made it clear to his successors that they could never satisfy the

* Pokrovsky, *Brief History of Russia.*

revolutionaries by wise government or a liberal conduct of affairs. It was the beginning of a life or death conflict in which any means on either side were justifiable. Therefore the attempt by the Nihilists in 1879 had great significance.

But the novel *The Brothers Karamazof* has a greater significance. It has survived the Romanofs and it will survive the Communists. The Bible has survived all wars, traditions, ferments, upsets in history, and Dostoievsky's novel is part of that extra Bible of modern man which supplements, without enlarging, Holy Writ.

In considering the life of Alexander II, the development of the Russian nation must figure much more prominently than in the biographies of his predecessors. He was the first partially representative monarch in Russia. It is doubtful whether even the initiative for reform started with him. He was borne along by a current of the popular will and when he attempted to stem that current he failed. At several moments the tail was seen to be wagging the dog.

The life of Alexander II is not so much his personal actions, the actions of his nearest servants, Gorchakof, Reitern, Shuvalof, etc.—it is the impulse communicated upwards from the inarticulate to the articulate, it is a resultant of national temperament and character. The seventy or eighty million people of Russia, talking, working, procreating, loving and quarrelling, getting educated or remaining illiterate, praying, fumbling for reality—must never for a moment be lost sight of.

In the first place it is a humdrum picture, as of bees going from clover to clover in a drowsy noontide. Rural

Russia was not dramatic. Serfs had become free men and yet lived more or less as they had lived before, cultivating the soil by primitive methods, cutting the wheat with the sickle. There was no ill feeling against ex-masters. Village life was founded on births, baptisms, marriages and again births, religious holidays, fasts, vodka drinking, rowdy singing in the houses and divine singing in the churches. There was no atheism, no free thinking, but instead a superfluity of belief. Tolstoy said that the Trinity was an absurdity, and that belief in the Trinity was like a granary with a hole in the floor. No matter how much good wheat you poured in—it would roll out again by the hole in the floor. But Tolstoy was an intellectual—one of those to whom Dostoievsky addressed the words: "Be humble, proud man, and first of all break thine own pride!" The Trinity was no hole in the floor for the Russian peasantry in the nineteenth century, or if so there were many bigger holes, for the peasants not only believed in the Trinity but had a superfluity of beliefs, an eagerness to believe in the supernatural, even in the absurd. And it is not clear that the peasantry lost anything by it.

All through the reign of Alexander more and more schools were opened in the villages. In these schools were taught reading and arithmetic, and the law of God. It was a rudimentary education where arithmetic seldom went beyond addition and subtraction. Very few ever learned to add or subtract without the aid of beads. The teaching of reading was largely a failure because there was so little to read. If a child learns to read, but there are no books or newspapers to practise on, it very quickly forgets what it has learned. The great Russian newspapers did penetrate to the village but they were written in a language which no one there could understand. The vanity of the journalist expressed itself in very long words and in involved sentences which in no way reflected common speech. As far as the newly educated peasant was concerned the newspapers might just as well have been written in Greek.

But the illiteracy of the masses was not the dark shame which it has been represented to be in the West. In the human scale the illiterate peasant was spiritually richer than the English or American farm laborer of the same period, even when the latter could read and write. His outlook might sometimes seem strange but it was not cheap. He had an education which is not recognized in universities—it may be called "folk" education, the development of character and mentality under the influence of folk music, folk legend, the lore of tradition and custom handed from one generation to another, and he had his church which was not intellectually his superior, not erudite, not dependent on sermons and expositions. This folk church of Russia, whose colorful character is abhorrent to the matter-of-fact thinker, expressed the peasant to himself. It was his university, his theatre, his concert hall—and more than all these. The church and peasantry were one and provided that grand chorus of the nation which made it possible for the tsardom to call itself Holy Russia.

It is certain that not one of the Romanofs had the slightest pretension to sainthood. There was a tincture of religiosity in the behavior of Nicholas II but he was not religious and had nothing in common with peasant Russia, though he came under the influence of that tremendous and very characteristic Russian peasant, Rasputin. Alexander II was temperamentally a Protestant whose religion expressed itself in good works. Protestantism could not quite cover his life because he must have his mistress and believe that God who sees all would forgive him that. But his leisure from administration was not spent in pilgrimage and prayer, but rather in shooting wild ducks and in playing whist. He was nevertheless a living centre of Holy Russia. The peasants did not know him as Alexander Romanof but as Tsar. His personal character did not matter much to them.

Alexander's Russia had this enormous peasant Russia, the thing which Dostoievsky indicated when he talked of *narod*, the people, when he said that the people were right, when he told the educated that they must return to the people, because the people alone understood brotherhood. Intellectualism makes a nation of warring egos, each refusing to acknowledge the other. But the peasantry only felt and believed, and therefore preserved that sense of unity which Christ died to give to all men.

Communicating with the peasants as a first link was the shop-keeping and merchant class which bought and sold the products of the land, which also bought manufactured goods and sold them to the peasantry, the numerically small class of petty *bourgeois*, partly peasant in outlook and tradition but becoming also cynical and vulgar under the demoralizing influence of chaffering and trading. This class lived between the samovar and the ikon and clacked the abacus all day. Its children took advantage of town education and grew up to laugh at the superstitions of fathers and mothers. They became the petty intelligentsia. These could read the papers. They were clearly the citizens to whom leading articles could be addressed. Newspapers fanned their vanity.

Next nearest to the peasants were the factory workers because the peasants themselves in great numbers began to work part time at factories. The proletariat was recruited largely from the peasantry. But the factories proved to be a disintegrating force in national life. The worker received his wages and there responsibility for his welfare ended. Society and the proletariat were connected by the cash nexus and not by much else. The long struggle for the protection of the worker from the evils of industrialism was in any case slow in making even a beginning in Russia.

In the village the church was the big building, the big institution which focussed attention. For the proletariat the big building, the symbol of existence, became the factory. The workers were often accommodated in barracks rather than in homes. The influence of families and tradition was less. Religious practice lost its sway. There was more "jolly companionship," more drinking, more prostitution. But also there was more ambition, more restlessness, more laughter. The proletariat divided into two classes, one roisterous, the other morbid.

Once this class began to question the validity of its traditions there was no point at which it could stop, short of complete negation. It was fruitful soil for revolutionary propaganda. There were innumerable grievances for sick minds to feed upon. It seemed easy to prove that the factory worker was born into a world in which there was no justice, in which one class in no way superior got wealth and comfort, and another class, the producers of that wealth, obtained only a pitiful wage, verminous houses, unhappiness and disease.

The revolutionary propagandists taught the disaffected workers that they must learn to read, learn to read in order to break the power of the masters, learn to read in order to understand the literature of revolution, the pamphlets, circulars, books which the police were so anxious to discover and destroy.

The Government, raising tariff barriers to foreign goods, developed the home industries. It captured the caravan routes for the export of their cotton into Asia. It built munition works and arsenals. It built railways and docks. It was pleased with the progress of manufacture—and yet at the same time it was weakening the political organism of the tsardom by the creation of a disturbed and a disturbing class.

And the part-time workers at the factories must return to the villages and bring their new sense of grievance with them. The revolutionary agrarian movement among the peasants was in some degree due to the murmur of the semi-proletarian; "Why should the masters have so much land and the peasantry have so little?"

Undoubtedly proletariat and peasantry possessed the vital force of the nation. The other classes lived somewhat separately. The clerks and petty civil servants were politically sluggish and conservative, but not of strong national impulses. The higher intelligentsia were so brilliant and talented that there was no bridge between them and other classes.

The manufacturers and financiers would have liked a system of ennoblement as in England, allowing them to identify themselves and their families with the aristocrats. But they were cold-shouldered by the ancient nobility. Revolution raised its head as much against them as against the throne. They were obliged to take a middle course in politics and for the most part profess themselves liberals.

There remained the great landowners, titled gentry, high functionaries, the executives of the military and the police. These were a separate Russia which assumed that all other classes were subordinate to them.

But Russia could be differentiated in another way. There were country folk, town folk and gentry. Over against the vast rural background, the great new cities were growing in ever sharper contrast to village and provincial factory centre. Stone pavings replaced the wooden footways. Large shop fronts with a magnificent display of Western goods dazzled the eye of the drab passer-by. Great railway stations vied in grandeur with the cathedrals. Universities teeming with student life were pointed to with pride, even by the illiterate. Newsboys rushed about with daily papers. Droshky drivers offered any man who had a fare the transitory grandeur of a carriage and pair. Cafés with all the newspapers of Europe on cane frames made corners of the Nevsky and Tverskoy one with Paris and Vienna. The high-class *restoran* appeared over the way from the old-fashioned popular eating house—the *trakteer*. At kiosks on street corners men sold tobacco and cigars. In rainy weather men and women were seen carrying umbrellas. Horse trams gallivanted gaily along the main thoroughfares.

There was much to flatter man into a belief that he was accomplishing something in the cities. St. Peters-

burg and Moscow, but especially Moscow, were growing in vanity. They assumed that their opinion was
identical with the opinion of Russia as a whole, that
indeed they were Russia. These cities proved an escape
from the melancholy featureless plains of the south and
the more melancholy endless forests of the north. Something of that poetic Russian sadness which is quite
genuine became dissolved in St. Petersburg and Moscow, and only showed itself as sentimentality. St.
Petersburg and Moscow became places where almost
every resident got out of touch with peasant Russia.
And it must be said of Dostoievsky that despite his belief in the people he was much more sure of himself
depicting townsfolk and that he seldom ventured on
anything more than a very sketchy presentation of a
peasant. His strength, however, derived from his roots
which were in the peasant soil.

Of course much was added to the sense of the dignity of the Russian people by artistic accomplishment.
During Alexander's reign Russia produced the two
greatest novels in world literature—*War and Peace*
published in 1865–69 and *The Brothers Karamazof*
published in 1879–80. In other glorious epochs of Russian history, in the reign of Peter the Great and Catherine II, the Russian people had nothing to read beyond
the lives of the saints. In the reign of Nicholas I there
were Pushkin, Gogol, Zhukovsky, Belinsky; but the
writers of the time of Alexander II presented Russia
with a brand new classical literature of the most remarkable merit. It received *Anna Karenina* as a serial.
It had the succession of all the brilliant short novels of
Turgenief. It had Goncharof's *Oblomof*. It had Dostoievsky. It had the poet Fet. It had the gifted Alexey

Tolstoy with his romances of the reign of Ivan the Terrible. At the same time it had a vigorous and flourishing journalism. In music it had Tchaikovsky. In fine art it had Verestchagin and the young Repin. It is not surprising that the nation was a little swollen-headed in the late seventies and ready to follow the lead of the Slavophiles and defy Europe. It is not surprising that the revolutionaries should say—"If we only had complete freedom as a nation, what would we not accomplish!" Russian revolution would only be the preface to world revolution. For even then leaders of the revolutionary movement such as Bakunin envisaged not merely revolution in Russia but the complete overthrow of the existing economic system throughout the world.

It was folly to look upon achievement as promise. Better to have looked upon it plainly as achievement. To have taken Constantinople would not have added one jot or tittle to what Dostoievsky, Turgenief and Tolstoy had accomplished. To have bewildered tsardom by terror and grasped power for the working class and the intellectuals would also have added nothing to real achievement. The defects of the national arguments were that politics, the politics of Slavophilism or of Socialism, were given precedence over religion and self-expression.

There was a further characteristic not without significance. The nation had many leaders but acknowledged no leadership other than that of the Tsar. Herzen was a leader until he took the part of the Poles in 1863 but then his following fell away. There was no magic in the names of the other revolutionaries in exile. In Russia herself there was the great personality of

Tolstoy, self-consecrated as a teacher of the Russian people, but he obtained no large following and remained unrepresentative in his views. As an example we may quote the appeal he made when at last Alexander II was murdered by the revolutionaries. He advised the Grand Duke Alexander, then become Alexander III, to forgive the murderers of his father, thus in the spirit of the Gospel returning good for evil.

Monarch! If you were to do this: were to call these people and give them money, and send them away somewhere to America, and write a manifesto headed with the words, "But I say, Love your enemies," I do not know how others would feel, but I, poor subject, would be your dog and your slave! I should weep with emotion every time I heard your name, as I am now weeping. But what do I say?—"I do not know how others"!—I know that at those words kindliness and love would pour forth like a flood over Russia. . . . All Revolutionary struggles will melt away before the man-Tsar who fulfils the law of Christ. . . .*

But the son of Alexander II could not have behaved in that way unless he had been to that extent imbued with the teaching of Christ, and in that case he must have renounced tsardom also. The Russian people would not have forgiven the murderers nor the Tsar for forgiving them. They required that laws for the protection of society be applied.

Tolstoy was a member of a powerful aristocratic family which had enjoyed powers and privileges and lived on the fat of the land for centuries. He belonged to the slave-owning class and he was near the peasants as a master is near his chattel. He had a greater understanding of individual peasants than any other writer,

* Maude, Aylmer, *The Life of Tolstoy.*

without particular understanding of the peasantry as a whole. He was involved in the contradiction of wishing to change the peasant, make him a modern educated individual, and of degrading himself from polished aristocrat to uncouth villager. The tragedy of his life lay in his inability to achieve humility and make himself one with the peasants. His strong intellect and violent egoism stood in his path like fiends which could never finally be overcome.

There occurred a great moment in Russian national life in June, 1880, when the Pushkin monument in Moscow was unveiled. Turgenief returned to Russia for this event, and his first action was to go to Yasnaya Polyana to persuade Tolstoy that it was a great national occasion and he must come also. But Tolstoy would not budge. He admired Pushkin's writings but he was not going to make himself one of many round about the Pushkin statue. Dostoievsky intended to be present and had prepared a long and remarkable address. The speech which he made moved the imagination of Russia and raised Dostoievsky on to a higher pedestal than he ever enjoyed from the success of his novels. Russia seemed at last to have a popular leader.

Dostoievsky's main theme was that the poet Pushkin, with his deeply penetrative genius, had first remarked the principal and most deadly phenomenon in Russian life—the educated class dominating society but uprooted from the peasant soil, the restless and unreconciled types unable to believe in Russia and in the strength of the Russian people. But Pushkin, said Dostoievsky, did believe that the disease could be cured by holding to the mirror of art a positive type of national beauty, exemplifying the authentic character of Russia, returning to the actual soil of the Russian people and seeking truth there.

Most strong convictions of thinkers and artists are obtained early and remain with them all their life. The message of Dostoievsky in 1880 was much the same as it was when he returned from Siberian exile thirty years before—"The people are always right. Had my case been taken to the people I should have been sent to Siberia just the same, and I accept the punishment."

"The Russian organism must develop on national lines and not slavishly copy Europe," said Dostoievsky. He told an anecdote: someone said that Russia must become Western. Another objected: "The people would not permit that." The first man then exclaimed, "In that case we should have to destroy the people."

Russia shall be destroyed—if only some new system of government be realized! A prefiguration of Bolshevism.

Humble thyself, proud man, but first of all break thy pride! Humble thyself first of all and get to work on natal soil! That is Pushkin's solution. Truth is not outside of yourself. It is within you. Finding yourself in yourself, submitting yourself to yourself, you gain possession of yourself and see the truth. That truth is not in material things, not outside yourself, and not somewhere beyond the sea, but first of all in your own personal work upon yourself. Conquer yourself, pacify yourself and you will become free as never before, as you never imagined yourself before, and you will begin a great work, and you will make others free and you will find happiness because the cup of your life will be full, and you will understand your people at last and its sacred truth.*

In short, Dostoievsky said that a tree could only

* Dostoevsky, F. M., *Dnevnik Pisatelya.*

grow from its roots, and it did not grow by hanging things on its branches.

This speech, the report of which swept Russia at the time, came at a critical moment in Russian development. Everyone was aware that in Alexander's reign there had been great progress. The speech called a momentary halt to ask the question: Where are we going? On a road that leads outwards from a Russian heart and soul, or on a road charted out for us by those who say that Russia is without intuition or vision of her own?

It was a very strong counter-cry to the revolutionary watchwords and it was repeated rapturously. It could not stop the activity of the Nihilists but it did much to stave off revolution and start youth thinking in a more positive way. At that time Dostoievsky was engaged in writing the unfinished *Brothers Karamazof*. That great novel was his last novel as this great speech was his last speech. In the February following Dostoievsky died. He died at the zenith of his power and fame. He had revealed Russia to Russia as a child astonishes and gratifies its mother. At his decease there was spontaneous national grief. Russia went into mourning. Fifty thousand people with bared heads followed his coffin through the snow to the cathedral of St. Isaac in St. Petersburg.

XXI.

THE BOMB EXPLODES

IT was far from Alexander's character to surrender to panic. A nervous or apathetic man would probably have been killed by the terrorist Solovyof on April 14, 1879. He had outlived his popularity with the Treaty of Berlin but he still had a strong instinct for self-preservation. And for him self-preservation meant also preservation of the tsardom and of the Romanof dynasty.

At once after the attempted assassination strong measures, strong but ineffectual and belated, were taken. Makof, a new Minister of the Interior, had been in office only since the beginning of the year. His authority was superseded by six military governor-generals, mostly men who, like Loris Melikof, had distinguished themselves in the Turkish War. Melikof had taken the supposedly impregnable fortress of Kars. He became Governor-General of Kharkof and later Dictator of Russia. These governor-generals had power to suspend civil law. The appointments were tantamount to placing the whole of Russia under martial law. The governor-generals took control of the censorship of the press and of the ministry of public instruction.

There were house-to-house searches for pistols; printers were forbidden to lend their type on pain of the revocation of their licenses; many books of a radical tendency were banned; public comment on the attempted assassination of April 14 was forbidden. Such a police inspection of student life ensued that many professors of the universities of St. Petersburg asked to be allowed to resign.

Indeed the measures taken against the revolutionaries to some extent obscured the sympathy which was felt for the Tsar. At the same time, when at the trial of the would-be assassin it was discovered he was merely attempting to carry out a sentence of death pronounced on the Tsar by a society of widespread affiliation, the need for stringent methods became apparent.

The shadow of the black hand was on Russia and there were panics in many places. The town of Kostroma, built almost entirely of wood, was warned by the revolutionaries that it was intended to burn it down, causing great terror among the inhabitants. Kostroma was not burnt, but there was a general outbreak of incendiarism in the Volga cities. The Nihilist Solovyof was tried and condemned to death. He bore himself with such self-complacency that it seemed as if he expected to be rescued before the sentence was carried out. He was hanged on June 10, 1879.

Pokrovsky said that between December, 1878, and December, 1879, seventeen men were hanged in Russia, but that is not a great number considering the excitement that had been aroused. The most severe of the new military governors were the heroic Todleben in Odessa and General Gurko in Moscow, both men who had brilliantly distinguished themselves in the service of Russia. Gurko had led the victorious Russian army to Adrianople, and his military prestige was great. If Todleben and Gurko considered that it was necessary to be severe they were probably justified. Doubtless some comparatively innocent persons suffered when revolutionary terror was met by governmental terror, but if so the responsibility was divided. By terrorizing Russia the revolutionaries placed the life and liberty of all manner of normal persons in jeopardy. They did not take that into consideration, for the destruction of tsardom seemed to be worth the price.

The Tsar who had been shot at on the fourteenth of April left for Livadia on the twenty-fourth of the month, accompanied by the Tsaritsa who was extremely ill. The villa overlooking the sea near Yalta was a favorite retreat of the Tsar in the spring, an escape from the snow and sleet of the change of season at the capital to the brilliant sunshine of the south. On this occasion, however, the journey was prompted more by the condition of the Tsaritsa than by consideration of weather. The Tsar's presence was urgently required at the seat of government; he soon returned. He remained in St. Petersburg throughout the trial of the terrorist, approved the sentence of death and certainly did not consider granting a reprieve. He neither forgave nor refused to forgive the would-be murderer. The man was an enemy of the state and must be removed. Likewise all other enemies of the state, as discovered, must either be executed or banished to Siberia.

The tremendous energy of repression seemed to have some immediate effect. There was a short lull in revolutionary activity after July, 1879. During the summer the Tsaritsa, who was now in the last stages of consumption, had been removed from Livadia and taken to Kissingen, whence she was taken to Cannes, still seeking softer airs. In September the Tsar returned to the Crimea. His mistress Catherine and his illegitimate children were waiting for him there, and there was

happiness. There were two months of happy domestic
life in which the Tsar escaped from the terror and from
all the anxieties and responsibilities of government. To
what extent he was afflicted by the fact that his wife
was wasting visibly towards death at Cannes it is difficult to say. The death of Wilhelmina (Maria Alexandrovna) would enable him to marry Catherine, but he
was too conscientious a man to wish his wife's death
without reproving himself for it at once. He was com-
passionate towards his sick wife, very sorry for her, but
he was not likely to be prostrated by grief when the
end came. When he returned to the north about the end
of November he telegraphed on his way, at Moscow, to
the Tsaritsa at Cannes:

> Just arrived safely in Moscow. Fourteen degrees of frost
> here. Deeply grieved you are no better. I am feeling well, not
> tired. My tenderest love.

But he did not tell her he had narrowly escaped being blown to bits on the journey. The terror had recom-
menced and two attempts had been made on the imperial train. The terrorist Zhelyabof had mined the rails
to destroy the train as it was passing Alexandrovsk in
the Ukraine; Sophia Perovsky fired a packet of nitroglycerine to destroy it as it was nearing Moscow.

Revolutionary activity in the latter part of 1879
was expressed by mining instead of shooting or bomb
throwing. The symbolism of undermining tsardom and
of communicating a current to an explosive force was
pleasing. And the leader of the terror, Zhelyabof, was
an enthusiast for the dynamite and electric current type
of outrage. One of his projects was to blow up the
Kamenny Bridge in St. Petersburg as the Tsar was

passing over it. He was the inspiration of a plan to undermine the anchorage of the imperial yacht at Nikolaef. This was foiled by the police who discovered the battery and the lines leading to the mine. On the Tsar's return journey from the Crimea he could travel by either of two lines. Zhelyabof organized explosions on both of them and a third near Moscow after the junction of the lines.

Zhelyabof is a hero of the Russian revolutionary movement.

> He was the biggest personality in the whole movement. The son of a serf, in whom the memory of serfdom was green, for he was eleven at the date of emancipation; afterwards a penniless peasant who married into a well-to-do *bourgeois* family, he united in his person all three elements of the movement; the peasant masses, the intelligentsia, and the *bourgeoisie*. At the time of the movement to the people his part was insignificant . . . but as the organizer of a conspiracy he at once became foremost. . . . The name of the great organizer became popular; he was the terrible Zhelyabof, the organizer of ever new attempts in the most varied and most unexpected places and conditions. He possessed an extraordinary energy of action, and was not one of those who tremble and remain silent.*

All the same, most of his electrical experiments in murder went wrong. The mine near Alexandrovsk was laid in an embankment where even a moderate explosion would have tumbled the whole imperial train over a precipice into a ravine. Zhelyabof pressed a button, something fizzled in the embankment, there was no explosion, the train went safely on.

Sophia Perovsky was in charge of the mine near Moscow. This did go off but it blew up the wrong train.

* Pokrovsky, *Brief History of Russia.*

Many people were killed; many injured. Sophia Perovsky and her assistant escaped. She was undeterred by the reflection that she had killed the wrong people and she went on to an even greater act of terror. For she had a leading part in the killing of the Tsar. Sophia Perovsky could have been tried on a prior charge of murdering Russian citizens in the Moscow train. It is interesting to speculate whether Tolstoy's advice to forgive her and give her money to go to America would hold good in dealing with the destruction of the Russian passengers.

The next attempt on the Tsar's life was the work of Stefan Khalturin. Khalturin was a carpenter who organized in 1878 the Union of the Workers of North Russia. According to one account he was a waiter who pretended to be a carpenter. He believed that revolution would start from a general strike and could not be obtained as a result of terrorist outrage. Nevertheless he was himself infected by terrorism and undertook one of the most audacious exploits in the history of revolution in Russia. Some repairs were being carried out in the Winter Palace. Khalturin, through some petty influence within the palace, obtained a job and the privilege of sleeping on the premises. He used his opportunity to prepare to blow the palace up. Each day he brought packets of dynamite into his room and concealed the explosive in his bedding. He then proceeded to lay a mine in the basement of the building. This mine was set to go off at half-past six on the evening of February 17, 1880. Alexander II had invited his nephew to dine with him, Prince Alexander of Battenberg, who had just been elected Prince of Bulgaria. There was a tremendous explosion and the dining-room of the palace was completely shattered. Dinner was to have been at half-past six; the table was laid; servants were in attendance and waiting; but otherwise the dining-room was empty. The train by which Prince Alexander of Battenberg had arrived had been late. That had caused a delay in serving dinner. The Tsar was in his study talking to his nephew who had just arrived and the trivial delay saved their lives. Again there were a great number of innocent victims. Sixty-seven men of the Finnish Regiment were buried under falling walls and masonry; many were killed and many injured.

Zhelyabof was also concerned in this outrage. Apparently it was he who provided the dynamite which Khalturin had carried daily into the palace. But this mine was not exploded by electricity but by the lighting of a time fuse. It was Khalturin who lit the fuse, and having done so he hastened out of the palace to meet Zhelyabof at an appointed rendezvous outside.

The two terrorists stood waiting together, watching with breathless suspense for the result of the explosion. They heard the detonation. They saw the palace windows go to shivers and heard the low roar of falling masonry; still suspense. Then there was a commotion of moving *gendarmerie* and guards, the fire brigade, ambulances. It was dangerous to ask who exactly had been killed. The conspirators drifted into the gathering crowds and hid themselves—escaped.

Khalturin had a nervous breakdown as a result of his disappointment at the failure to kill the Tsar, but he did not give up terrorism: two years later, in 1882, he murdered the public prosecutor of Kief, was arrested and duly executed.

A feature of the terrorism of the period was the ability of the revolutionary organizations to give the news of these outrages to the people. The censorship was frustrated by illicit sheets. The Government would have liked to minimize the general alarm caused by the attempts on the Tsar's life, but it was impotent. The Nihilists advertised their crimes with great success. The police could not find the printing presses. One of the revolutionaries, however, betrayed the address of an important press, the *Cherny Perediel* and it was stormed by armed police. The revolutionaries condemned the informant to death and he was killed on March 5, 1880.

That the Tsar seemed to bear a charmed life was not of much significance. His thanks to God for deliverance from his enemies began to have a tone of almost idle repetition. What was clear was that while he might be thankful to Almighty Providence he could not feel much gratitude to those who were supposed to guard his person, nor to the governor-generals whom he had appointed to protect society and the state. The explosion in the Winter Palace caused a political crisis.

On February 25, 1880, Alexander II summoned the governor-generals to St. Petersburg to confer with himself and the heir to the throne, the Grand Duke Alexander, and with the Tsar's brother, the Grand Duke Constantine, on devising new measures for public safety. Loris Melikof, Governor of Kharkof, was the only one who had a program. He advised the granting of a constitution to Russia. The Tsar grasped at a straw. Perhaps the granting of a constitution would stop the terror and bring peace and happiness to his people. But there must be an interim period during which the details of a constitutional regime might be considered and approved. For this period Alexander resolved to abrogate the powers of the other governors and to make Loris Melikof dictator. Thus an autocrat at his wit's end how to deal with Russia created another autocrat to do his work.

It is said that the terrorists had notified the Tsar that they would grant him an armistice on the condition of the granting of a constitution, but how much truth there is in that it is difficult to assess. The majority of revolutionaries were not working for a constitution. A constitution implied liberal institutions and not Communism or even Socialism. Such an offer could not have been made, for instance, by Bakunin. Nevertheless, upon the appointment of Loris Melikof, the release of a number of political prisoners and a new liberalism in the administration, the attempts on the Tsar's life were discontinued for the space of a whole year.

There was another lull in terrorism and during that lull several important events in the reign of Alexander II took place. Far from the political hubbub, away in Central Asia, the White General Skobelef continued the military adventures of Russian imperialism, slaughtering the Turkomans and advancing towards the historic gates for the conquest of India. He at least did not regard India as beyond the scope of Russian imperial ambition. The Tsar was preoccupied and received congratulations on the acquisition of new territory without much show of interest. Skobelef, largely on his own responsibility, was taking revenge on England for aiding and abetting the Turks in the Turkish War and there was no saying where his army would have halted had he not been disavowed and recalled.

In Alexander's domestic situation there was a change. On the sixth of June the Tsaritsa died. It had been expected that she would die at Cannes, but consumptives linger on for a long time between life and death. She had decided that she would not die in a foreign land and had returned to St. Petersburg to her apartments in the Winter Palace. The Tsaritsa was in bed in the palace at the time of the great explosion in February, but she was unconscious at the time and did not hear it. The Tsar's mistress Catherine, and the children, were also in the palace on that occasion, and they also were unhurt. Catherine heard the explosion and is supposed to have rushed at once to the Tsar and clasped him in her arms, thanking God for his preservation. It may well be imagined that but for Catherine the Tsar would have become tired of life. His chief cause for gratitude in being spared was that he was spared for the protection of Catherine and her children. For their sake he must survive.

The Tsar Alexander and his sons bore the coffin with the dead Tsaritsa from the cathedral to the tomb. Princess Catherine Dolgoruky was not present at the funeral. Her position was awkward because it must seem that for years she had been waiting for the Tsaritsa to die. It was not a moment of grief and mourning for her. And for the Tsar after the funeral there was not a moment to lose: he must marry Catherine before he was assassinated. He could never be sure on any day that that day would not be his last on earth. At the earliest possible moment, having regard to a limited period of mourning and to the fast of St. Peter, on the eighteenth of July he married Catherine.

The preparations for the marriage were kept secret

till the last moment. There was some objection on the part of court dignitaries such as Adlerburg, but that was overruled. Even the heir to the throne was not informed. Loris Melikof had nothing to say on the matter as he was not notified until after the event. There could be no protest by the Senate or the nobility because the proposed marriage was kept secret from them. The ceremony at Tsarskoe Selo was a private one; no guests or representatives of foreign powers were invited.

The Tsar wore a blue cavalry uniform. Catherine had no special bridal dress, but an ordinary habit which she commonly wore when out walking with Alexander. She arrived without her hat at the apartment, which had been converted into a chapel for the occasion. In this apartment of the palace of Tsarskoe Selo a priest, a deacon and a chorister were awaiting them. An altar had been set up and directly the royal pair arrived the service commenced. Two aides-de-camp held the wedding crowns over the heads of the kneeling Alexander and Catherine. Count Adlerburg, who had played so many rubbers of whist with the Tsar in the evenings, was also in attendance. An important feature in the ceremony was that Alexander was named each time as Tsar, so that it should not be assumed that he was marrying Catherine simply as a private person. In the Tsar's Deed of Marriage which he had had drawn up the legitimate character of the marriage was indicated.

In the year one thousand eight hundred and eighty, on the eighteenth of July at three in the afternoon in the military chapel of Tsarkoye Selo, His Majesty the Emperor of all the Russias, Alexander Nikolaievitch, has been graciously pleased to contract a second legitimate marriage with Princess Catherine Michailovna Dolgoruky, Maid of Honor.

At the same time the children of the union were legitimatized by imperial ukase.

It was only ten days later that the new dictator, Loris Melikof, was told of the marriage, and then under an oath of secrecy. The Tsar asked him to protect his new wife and children in the event of his being killed by the revolutionaries. On the thirty-first of July the Grand Duke Alexander, the heir to the throne, was informed by his father that he had a stepmother. If he felt indignant he nevertheless repressed his feelings and kept his counsel. There is no record of any protest having been made by him.

Catherine, as Princess Catherine Yurievsky, accompanied the Tsar in the imperial train to the Crimea and Loris Melikof went with them. Loris Melikof, who was of Armenian origin, possessed a Semitic subtleness of character and intellect, clever but showy, liberal but sentimental. The task of conciliating the revolutionaries was too great for him. It was much easier to execute them than to placate them with reform. The terrorists expected nothing of him and one of them attempted his assassination in March, 1880. Liberals have generally been more distasteful to the Russian revolutionaries than violent reactionaries. The terrorists persisted in their murderous attempts on the liberal Alexander II but left his heir, who was in the reactionary camp with Katkof and Pobiedonostsef, severely alone. The paradox remains: they insisted on murdering a liberal, intelligent tsar to make a stupid reactionary grand duke emperor. They attacked Melikof: they left Pobiedonostsef to fulfil his destiny. Loris Melikof had seemed to have abolished the Third Division, that G.P.U. of tsardom. In effect he placed it under the control of the Ministry of the Interior and thereby curtailed its secret power of intimidation. Having done that he had proposed to relinquish his dictatorial power and become himself Minister of the Interior. He seems to have indicated that the unchecked Third Division had been the root of the evil. Controlling it simply as Minister of the Interior he would have as much power to pacify Russia as he had in the more exalted position. But Alexander would not at first agree to this renunciation. He wished Loris Melikof to go a stage further in his plans for a new political system.

At Livadia the retainers and servants of the Tsar were surprised, and probably scandalized, to see Catherine in a Tsaritsa's place sharing the Tsar's apartments, inseparable from him day and night. They did not know that a marriage had taken place.

Catherine was not addressed as "Your Majesty" and she had not got the position of Tsaritsa. She was Alexander's wife, but to be Tsaritsa she must be crowned Tsaritsa. It is possible that Loris Melikof played with the idea of making a public announcement of the marriage, having Catherine proclaimed Empress. That would have been a dramatic accompaniment to the calling of a *Zemsky Sobor*, an executive assembly of delegates from all the zemstvos, called to place the tsardom upon a new constitutional and national basis.

The Tsar is married to a Russian princess. For the first time for centuries the imperial house is Russian. The court is national, and the hated Germans fade out!

There is no doubt that if that had been done there would have been an invincible movement to set aside the Grand Duke Alexander in favor of George Alexandrovitch, the eldest child of Catherine and Alexander

—a Russian. Loris Melikof was not on the best of terms with the Grand Duke Alexander nor with the Grand Duke's friend and adviser, Pobiedonostsef. The idea of setting the Grand Duke Alexander aside could not have been obnoxious to the dictator.

But it was not possible to persuade the Tsar to resolute and swift action of any kind. He had no intention of setting aside the Grand Duke Alexander whom he regarded as his legitimate heir. He even wrote to him in November, 1880, placing Catherine and the children under his protection should he, the Tsar, die unexpectedly. He could not have done that if he had had the slightest idea of setting the Grand Duke Alexander aside.

And as regards a constitution for Russia, he was of two minds. Filial and dynastic sentiment interfered with what in his judgment might be wise and prudent. As he had received the throne from his dying father, Nicholas I, he would bequeath it at his death, with all privileges and powers intact. To part with his power in his old age seemed to him dishonest; it would amount to robbing his heir. What he required of Loris Melikof was a scheme to grant a constitution and at the same time preserve the autocracy. That was the problem set the Armenian at Livadia, and, clever as he was, he was somewhat desperate about it.

When he returned to St. Petersburg as Minister of the Interior, but still possessed of dictatorial powers, he called a gathering of editors of newspapers and told them to moderate their expectations. He gave them freedom to express their opinion in the press but warned them not to go on deceiving the people with chimeras. In this he was warning himself not to deceive himself that any great reform of the constitution was possible.

The Tsar, on second thought, had allowed Loris Melikof to consider himself merely as Minister of the Interior, but he remained the man of greatest authority under the Emperor. In September Alexander awarded him the highest decoration possible in Russia, the Order of St. Andrew.

Before leaving Livadia to return to the explosive ground of his capital, Alexander made his last disposition in case of untimely decease and wrote a testament in favor of Catherine and her children. Both his letter to the Grand Duke Alexander and this testament show that prevision of death was uppermost in his mind. And as he departed from Livadia it must have occurred to him that he was looking on it for the last time.

He set out on the long drive over the Crimean ridge from Yalta to the railway station of Sebastopol on December 1, 1880. The Tsar and Catherine and the children dined at a table in the open at an inn at the gate of Baidari. At Baidari the whole wild mountainous Crimean shore sits before the sea and dreams. It is a place of majestic beauty and serenity, far from the world, from all trouble, exalted over the far and sparkling sea and nearer the sky than troubled humanity. It was just perfect that day—a picture of that eternity of peace and happiness into which a man may escape by death.

Thence they drove past the field of Balaclava and the cemeteries of the Crimean War, to stonebound Sebastopol and the waiting imperial train. Each railway journey since the blowing up of the Moscow train must have seemed fraught with danger. The Tsar and Catherine were ready to die together, and calm in a submission to God's will. They occupied the same coupé. They must have been tense under the apprehension, but they belonged to one another and to die together had been felicity. But there was no mischance. At a station on the way they were met by the Grand Duke Alexander, and as if to show his son that his marriage with Catherine in no way affected the position of the heir to the throne, the Tsar kissed his eldest son with some show of tenderness. The following day they arrived safely at the Winter Palace in St. Peterburg where the Tsar had had a luxurious suite prepared for his wife.

They went to the Kazan Cathedral to give thanks for the safe journey. The same day there was mass for the soul of the late Tsaritsa, it being six months after her decease. The Tsar did everything to show the world at large, and especially the scandalmongers of the capital, that there was no rift between him and the heir to the throne. The existence of a reactionary group centred about the person of the Grand Duke Alexander was a serious menace to Alexander II and Loris Melikof in their design of promulgating a constitutional reform. It was also important for the Tsar that the bond of sympathy between him and the heir to the throne should not be weakened by any assumption the Grand Duke might make with regard to the status of the Princess Catherine.

The Tsar in St. Petersburg in December, 1880, did not behave like a man who was panic stricken. It was with difficulty that he could be persuaded to have armed protection in the streets. He believed that it was his duty to keep in immediate touch with his subjects and not to keep a barrier of soldiers between him and the populace wherever he went. He had the simple faith, which almost amounted to fatalism, that if God were his protection, the precaution of military and police added little to his security. His personal life was very little altered by the circumstances of mortal danger in which he stood. In the conduct of affairs he was not preoccupied by fears of what the terrorists might do next. On the other hand to show his charitable outlook on his enemies he granted several pardons, even to men who were condemned for murder.

In January, 1881, Loris Melikof presented his plans for accommodating a representative system within the autocracy. More than that, he was able to boast that he had won the Grand Duke Alexander's assent to the proposed innovation. That the heir to the throne should approve was most important in the light of Alexander's determination not to take anything away from the power which he bequeathed at death to his successor. The plan did not amount to very much, a widening of the powers of the zemstvos. These municipal councils were provincial and local in authority, without power to combine and present a united representative front. It will be understood that as they were elected, a union of zemstvos would have amounted to something not unlike a national parliament. Loris Melikof's scheme was that each zemstvo should be empowered to send delegates to the Council of Empire, the *Gosudarstvenny Soviet*, which would thereby be greatly enlarged but would not be given executive power. It would remain a deliberative assembly, not unlike the Duma which came into being later in the reign of Nicholas II, though the Duma had also legislative power. Like the Duma it could have been regarded as the beginning of parliamentarism in Russia. This novelty was warmly supported by the Grand Duke Constantine. The Tsar appointed a committee under the presidency of the Tsarevitch to work out details of the reform.

There was much rumor of the granting of a constitution. It was confidently expected that on the anniversary of the emancipation of the serfs the imperial proclamation would be made. But it was too much to expect in Russia that a commission appointed in February would report in March. The opposition to constitutional reform was too great to be countered within the space of a month. It took several years for the committees to come to agreement about the emancipation of the serfs. And in 1881 the Tsar had not the personal driving power and initiative which he displayed in 1861.

On March 2, 1881, the anniversary of the emancipation of the serfs and also of the death of Nicholas I and of the Tsar's accession, Alexander attended a Requiem Mass for the soul of his father. That was the day of the expected public announcement of a constitution. It passed in silence. The public then postponed its expectations. Perhaps on Easter Day, April 24, a constitution would be proclaimed. Actually Loris Melikof and the commission had worked with uncommon celerity, and on the morning of March 2 the Minister of the Interior brought a draft of the new Act to submit to the Emperor. It advised the founding of two commissions, one financial and one economic and administrative, to take in hand a series of reforms which would be submitted to the Council of Empire; this Council, the *Gosudarstvenny Soviet*, to be enlarged by fifteen new members, representative of public opinion. The Tsar kept this document several days under his consideration. Then he asked Loris Melikof to prepare a manifesto which he would sign. On Sunday March 14, 1881, the Minister brought this manifesto and the Tsar gave orders for its publication in the press on the following morning. It was a copy of this which was the "draft of a constitution" said to have been in the Emperor's pocket when he was assassinated.

The winter of 1881 was one of unrelieved gloom. Although the Third Division had been abolished, the number of police agents had been greatly increased. In the cafés, in the taverns and in the streets, every stranger seemed to the ordinary citizen to be a spy. If a man stopped another to ask the time or the way, he was frequently met by silence. Ordinary citizens trudging through the snow were repeatedly under the impression that they were being followed. Sledge drivers did a good traffic with the timorous, whirling heavily cloaked figures from the business centres to their homes. In the churches the prayers for the Tsar were offered with exaggerated solemnity.

Loris Melikof, as Minister of the Interior and head of the police system, was probably more efficient than his predecessors had been. Given time he would have caught all the dangerous terrorists in the capital. Of these there were a limited number. If he could have laid his hands on Sophia Perovsky it is probable that he would have saved the Tsar's life. She was the strong personality behind the new conspiracy which was brewing. She made men do her will. Her chief confederate, Zhelyabof, would not have been so terrible but for her. She was his mistress, but that did not merely imply a sexual connection. She kept him to the mark, the goal of tsarecide. Her personality made the other terrorists in the group willing to risk their lives in order to kill.

Late in 1879 a very serious blow had been struck at the revolutionaries by the capture of Goldenberg, a prominent member of their executive committee. Goldenberg under arrest had made a full confession, and to save his life had furnished a list of important terrorists. The names of all the dangerous spirits became known to the police who had succeeded in arresting a number of them. Goldenberg's betrayal had caused a police terror among the terrorists. All the year 1880 the police agents were working with very substantial clues. They were not tracking down unknown enemies.

The terrorists had decided, under the circumstances, that it was not profitable to continue plotting smaller acts of terrorism. They had to concentrate on one grand act, the outcome of which could not be in doubt. They ceased causing explosions on the chance of killing the Tsar and planned an attack in which he must certainly be killed.

Very elaborate preparations were made. Several St. Petersburg streets were mined on the chance of the Tsar being upon them. The mine on Malaya Sadovaya would not only have made an immense hole in the roadway but must have wrecked the houses on both sides of the street, causing considerable loss of life and property. The terrorists had abandoned dynamite for a purer form of nitroglycerine. The new compound, much more dangerous to handle, could be made up in hand-bombs no bigger than a snowball but capable of doing great damage. If an explosion under the Tsar's feet failed there were to be bombers on the spot to finish off the work with bombs. Loris Melikof was on the track of the new conspiracy but there would seem to have been something lacking in the efficiency of a police system which could not discover the source of supply of such large quantities of explosives as were in use. It is said that the police discovered packets of the new compound, but as it was sweetish in taste, not bitter, they concluded it was not dynamite.

In February two terrorists were arrested, but they did not betray the others. On March 13, on the very eve of the great outrage, the famous Zhelyabof was seized by the police. He said confidently that nothing could save the life of the Tsar. The plans for the Tsar's destruction were so far advanced that they could be realized without his further coöperation.

Undoubtedly on the eve of the catastrophe Loris Melikof learned more than he dare admit. For a Minister of the Interior and head of police to have to confess that he had allowed St. Petersburg to be mined was enough to cause his disgrace. He needed some days to use the information he had obtained upon the arrest of Zhelyabof. Could he have persuaded the Tsar to remain indoors for three days he might have been able to make the arrest of Sophia Perovsky and the others and to have earned his country's gratitude for a great victory over the terror and for saving the menaced life of Alexander II.

On Sunday, March 14, when he presented the constitutional manifesto to be signed, Loris Melikof was most urgent in his plea that the Tsar make no public appearance that day. He asked him especially not to go to the parade of the Guards. It was part of the fixed routine of Sunday for the Tsar to be present at the mounting of the Guard.

The Tsar was in an uncommonly good humor, having made the decision to publish the manifesto. It seemed to him that his reign was about to pass out of the clouds and reënter that sunshine of peace and popularity which had lighted his earlier years. He was pleased by the capture of Zhelyabof, of whose name and ill fame he had long been aware. He underestimated the danger to his person, or did not realize that the representations by the Minister of the Interior were unusually serious and that there must be grounds for apprehension.

Catherine had also urged him warmly not to go out of the palace.

Nothing actually took place on the way out to the riding school or at the mounting of the Guard. There was snow in the St. Petersburg street but not fresh snow; it was possible to drive in a wheeled carriage. Alexander set off at a quarter to one in the afternoon accompanied by a guard of six Cossacks, a seventh Cossack standing, rifle in hand, upon the coachman's box and keeping a sharp look-out. Police officers followed in sledges.

After the parade, which was concluded within an hour, the equipage with the Tsar proceeded to the Michaelovsky Palace where the Tsar called upon the Grand Duchess Catherine. He did not stay. At a quarter past two the Cossacks and the closed carriage and the following sledges were hastening over the snowy streets back to the Winter Palace.

The terrorists had been signalling all the Tsar's movements and were waiting for him near the Catherine Canal. On Enginirnaya, as if having an intuition of danger, the coachman suddenly whipped up his horses and set a pace which for a few moments caused the Cossacks to lag behind. They galloped in a rush towards the rear of the carriage. There was a young man with long hair walking along. He carried a small parcel. At a street corner a short distance away stood Sophia Perovsky who waved a handkerchief. But for these and the Tsar's party there was no one in the wide street. Sophia Perovsky's signal was not seen and the Cossacks had not caught up in time to drive away the man with the parcel.

But the speed at which the imperial coach was travelling caused the man with the parcel to mistime his discharge. He threw his packet of nitroglycerine a moment too late. It fell between the carriage and the Cossacks, who had just caught up. There was a deafening explosion, glass flying, horses rearing, thrown and mutilated Cossacks lying shrieking in the snow, shouting. The Tsar calmly got out of his shattered carriage. He was unhurt. Once again for a moment it must have seemed to him that he had been miraculously saved from certain death. The police jumped from their sledges and seized the assassin. People hurried on to the scene from all sides and there was a great commotion, not to say confusion. Apparently the trembling coachman was the first person of sufficient sense to advise the Tsar not to wait in the roadway but to hasten to the Winter Palace with the utmost speed. But the Tsar characteristically refused to quit the scene until he had inquired into the condition of the wounded Cossacks.

One of them was dead; the others must be removed to a hospital and cared for at once. A police officer begged the Tsar to get into his sledge and drive away, but Alexander turned away from him. At that moment another of the gang of assassins hurried up and threw the "snowball" which blew the Tsar to bits. It was a terrific explosion. Even the Tsar's clothing was torn to rags and his orders and accoutrements scattered on the snow. One of his legs was blown away; the other shattered to the top of his thigh. Windows a hundred yards away were broken. The assassin himself was by the same explosion blown to bits. There was little life left in Alexander II. The shattered body was taken to the Winter Palace, the last sacrament was administered, and he was dead. Thus, in order to promote the welfare of mankind, the revolutionaries had killed one of the kindest and most humane of monarchs. The murder must be held to be one of the most monstrous crimes in modern political history.

March 14, 1881. History is nothing but anniversaries. Twenty-six years later, almost to a day, the great revolution broke out which destroyed the house of Romanof and the rule of the Tsars.

BIBLIOGRAPHY

THE bibliography of the reign and life of Alexander II is capable of considerable extension, because many works dealing with the history and social experience of the nineteenth century may be held to contain relevant opinion or detail. On the Russian side there is an immense quantity of material which is illustrative of social history but not yet edited in an impartial spirit. The official communist theory holds that there is no absolute truth in history and that history only becomes vital as it is interpreted to illustrate a political theory and advance a cause. This theory is capable of substantiation in argument. Although to me as a writer "fair play is a jewel," it could also be shown that this biography is a special interpretation of the drama of Alexander's life and is written with the presumption that self-expression and national development are the only justifiable aims of political movements. I have always considered the cause of revolution and also the cause of tsardom as subordinate and entirely secondary to the cause of national self-expression. The fact that most modern Russian historians have placed the cause of revolution first has rendered my task more difficult.

The following are the chief works to which I have had personal reference:

ALEXANDER II, Gody ucheniya (Sbornik Russkago Istoricheskago Obshchestva, Vols. XXX, XXXI). (Years of Education of His Imperial Highness.)

———— Vospominaniya o poseshchenii svatyn.

ARGYLL, DUKE OF, The Eastern Question.

BAPST, E., L'Empereur Nicolas et la deuxième République.

BOROZDIN, I. N., "Universitety v Epokhu 60-kh Godof," in Istoriia Rossii v XIX Veke, Vol. IV (A. & I. Granat & Co.).

CARR, E. H., The Romantic Exiles.

CHARNOLUSKY, V. I., "Narodnoe Obrazovanie v Pervoi Polovine," in Istoriia Rossii v XIX Veke, Vol. IV.

DAUDET, ERNEST, Soixante années du règne des Romanoffs.

DOSTOIEVSKY, F. M., Dnevnik Pisatelya.

DUBROVIN, N. T., Materialy k Biografii.

DZHANSHIEF, G., Iz Epokhi Velikikh Reform.

ECKARDT, JULIUS, Aus der Peterburger Gesellschaft, etc.

ENGEL, U. D., "Muzyka v XIX Veke" in Istoriia Rossii v XIX Veke, Vols. IV, VII.

HERZEN, A. I., Memoirs.

HEZEKIAL, J. E. L., Life of Bismarck.

IVANIUKOF, I., Padenie Krepostnogo Prava v Rossii.

JOURDIER, AUGUSTE, De l'émancipation des serfs en Russie.

KORNILOF, A., Kurs Istoriia Rossii v XIX Veke (Modern Russian History).

KOVALENSKY, M. N., "Sredniaya Shkola," in Istoriia Rossii v XIX Veke, Vol. VII.

LAVIGNE, ERNEST, Introduction à l'histoire du nihilisme.

LEE, SIR SIDNEY, Edward the Seventh.

LENSKY, Z., "Polskoe vozstanie 1863 Goda," in Istoriia Rossii v XIX Veke, Vol. III.

LEROY-BEAULIEU, A., Un homme d'état Russe.

LOFTUS, LORD AUGUSTUS, Diplomatic Reminiscences.

Materialy Dlya Istorii Uprazdnenia Krepostnogo Sostoiania.

MAUDE, AYLMER, The Life of Tolstoy.

Minutes relating to the years 1863–65 (British Museum).

MIRSKY, D. S., Russia.

MOERDER, K. K., Vospominaniya.

OGAREV, V. V., V. Zhukovsky, Ego Zhizn.

PALÉOLOGUE, MAURICE, Le roman tragique de l'Empereur Alexandre II.

POBIEDONOSTSEF, K., Pisma k Alexandru III.

POKROVSKY, I. I., V. Zhukovsky, Ego Zhizn i Sochinenia.

POKROVSKY, M. N., Istoriia Rossii.

——— "Krestianskaya Reforma," in Istoriia Rossii v XIX Veke, Vol. III.

PROTHERO, ROWLAND, The Life and Correspondence of Arthur Penrhyn Stanley.

ROSTORGUEF, E., Poseshchenie Sibiri v 1837.

RUSSELL, EARL, Dispatches.

SAKULIN, P. N., "Russkaya Literatura 60-kh Godof," in Istoriia Rossii v XIX Veke, Vol. IV.

SALISBURY, MARQUIS OF, Life and Letters.
SEMENOF, N. P., Osvobozhdenie Krestian.
SKREBITSKY, A., Krestianskoe Delo v Tsarstvovanie Aleksandra II.
STEAD, W. T., Life of Mme. Olga Novikof.
TATISHCHEF, S. S., Imp. Aleksander II, Zhizn i Tsarstvovanie.
VERESTCHAGIN, VASILLY, Na Voine.
VINOGRADOFF, PAUL, Self-Government in Russia.
ZEITLIN, S. Y., "Zemskaya Reforma," in Istoriia Rossii v XIX Veke, Vol. III.
ZILLIACUS, K., The Russian Revolutionary Movement.

INDEX